IN THE LION'S DEN

DANIEL MACDONALD, IRELAND AND EMPIRE

Niamh O'Sullivan

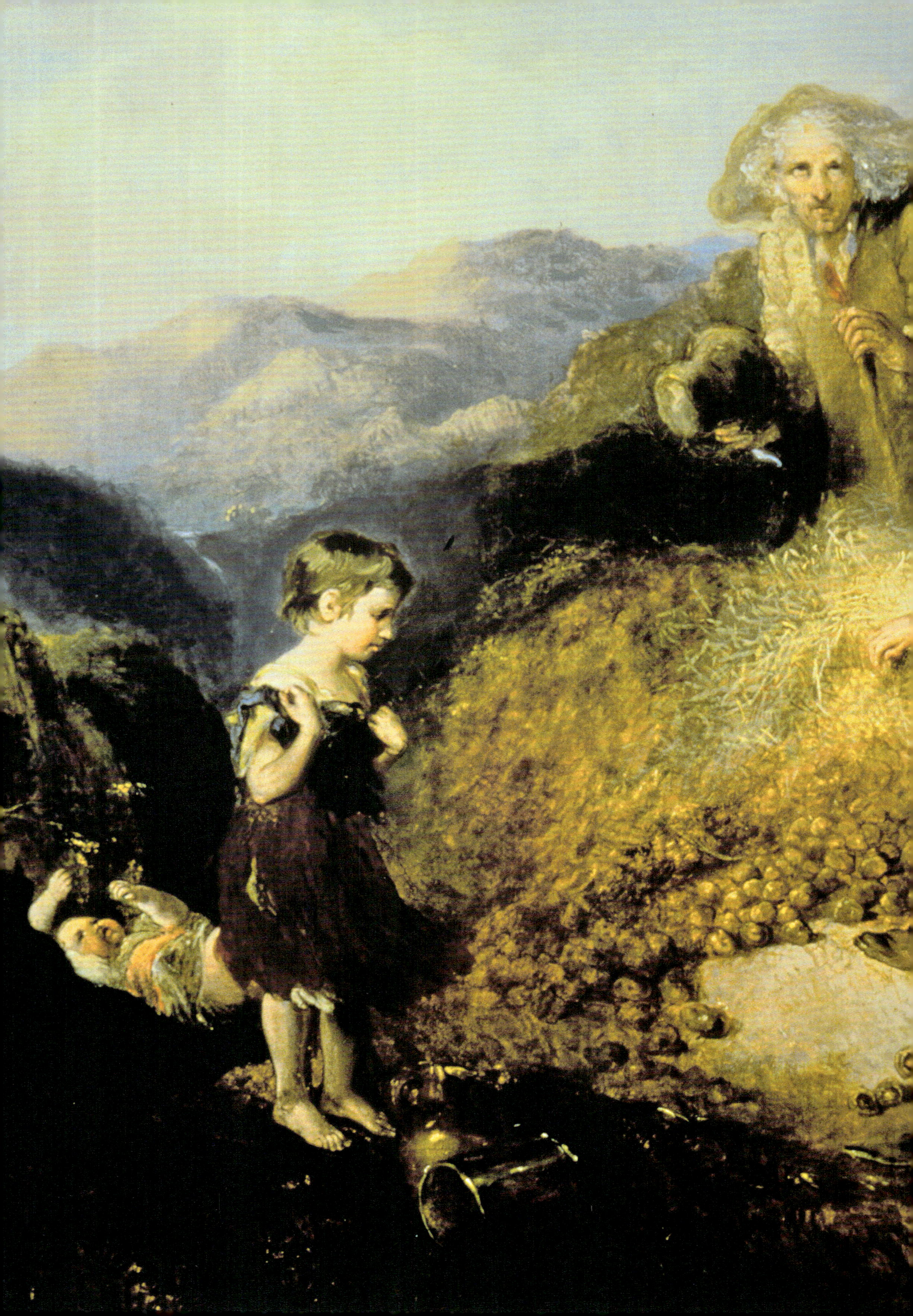

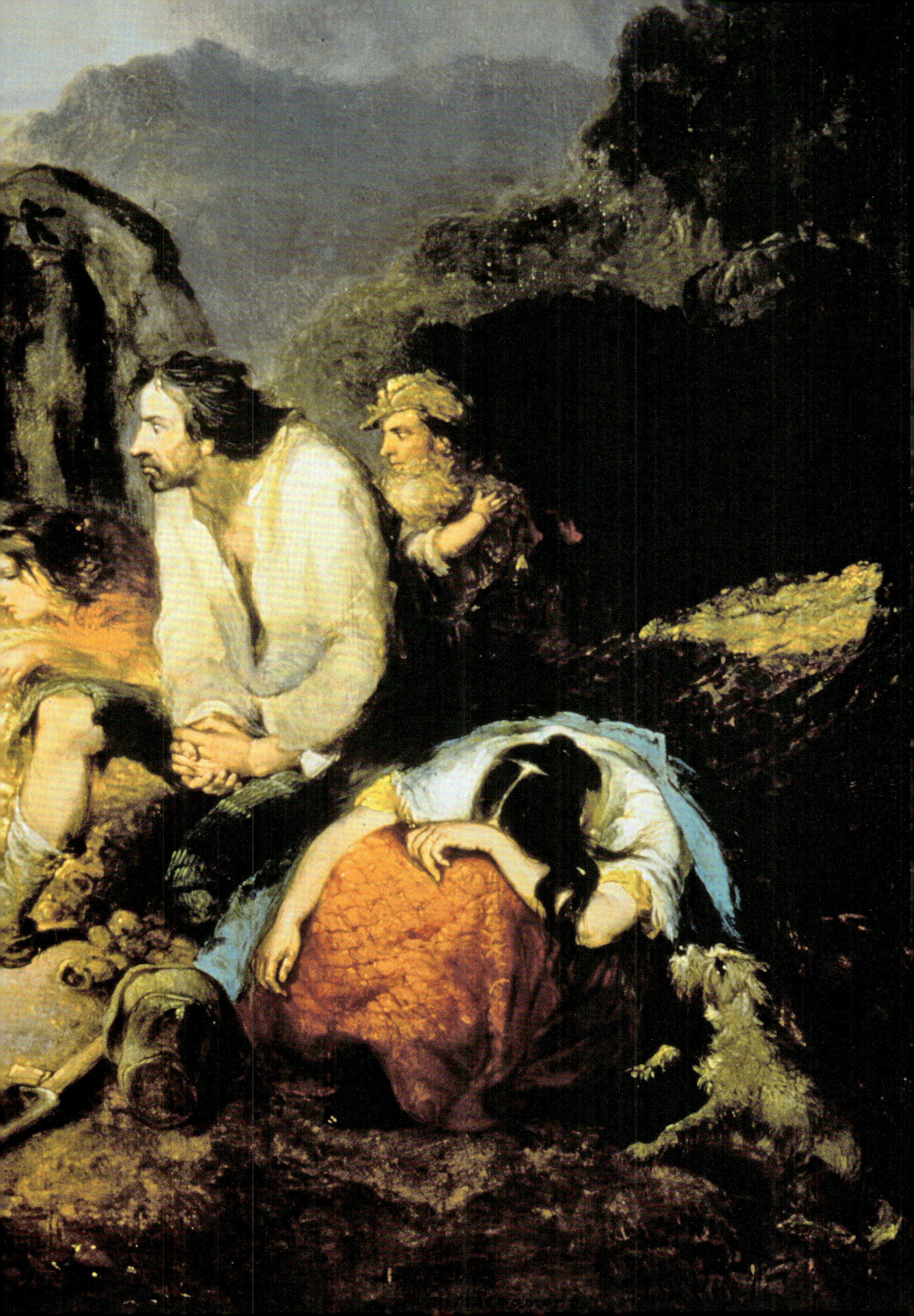

FOR BEN AND LUKE

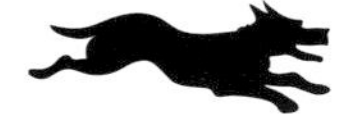

CONTENTS

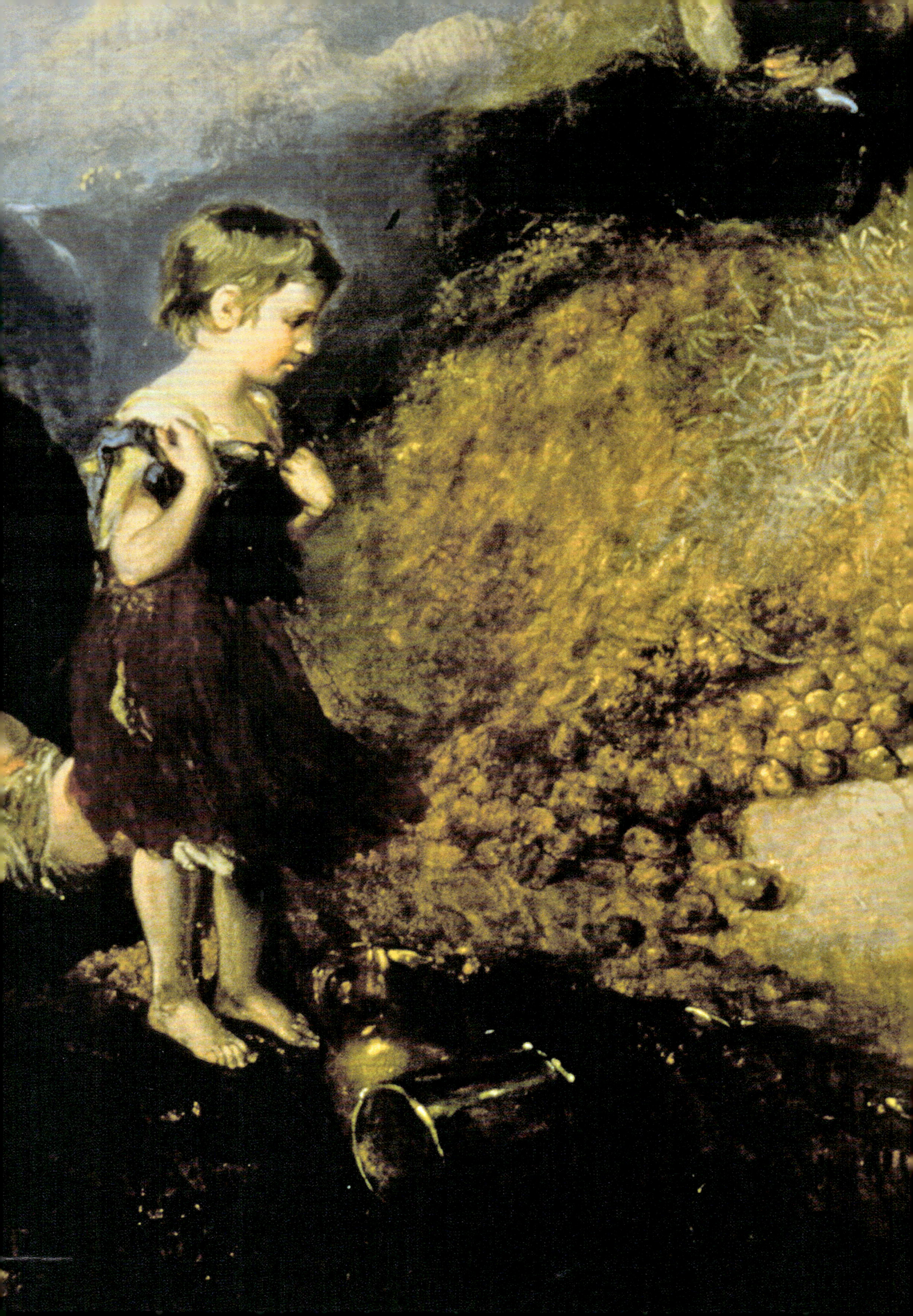

INTRODUCTION

In 1847, a harrowing painting, *An Irish Peasant Family Discovering the Blight of their Store* (**Fig. 1**), was hung in the British Institution in London. It was a prestigious venue, and the painter, Daniel Macdonald (1820–53), still only twenty-seven years old, had recently moved to London. This was the first time he had exhibited at a London salon, and the work has the invidious distinction of being the only known painting directly dealing with the Great Irish Famine itself.

By 1847, the death rate in Ireland was so great that corpses were disposed of without wake or prayer. Evicted families such as the one depicted in Macdonald's *Eviction*, often made their own way to the cemetery to die, because they knew there would be no one available to bring them there after death. But why was Macdonald the only Irish artist to tackle such difficult subject matter? Some reports of the Famine were too horrific to illustrate. Accounts of rats gnawing at the bodies of people still alive, but too weak to fend them off, and dogs feeding at shallow graves, could never make it into art, but there was an abhorrence to conveying the Famine in any way ... His painting, therefore, challenged not only polite society but also the most basic aesthetic conventions of the time.

Macdonald had a notable, if not well-known, cultural lineage. His father, James McDaniel (1788–1865), was an erudite painter, caricaturist, inventor, folklorist and musician, deeply involved with the vibrant cultural life of early nineteenth-century Cork. There existed a burgeoning, and bickering, community of remarkable intellectuals in the city — ethnographers, philosophers, folklorists, antiquarians, poets, satirists and classicists — all competing for attention, and James was a significant figure in these circles.

James had four children: the prodigy artist, Daniel, whose life was cut tragically short; Jane, who exhibited in Ireland under the name Macdonald, and in London, under her married name, Jane Masters Rogers, was also an artist of note; James Alexander was a prominent Wesleyan Minister; and the redoubtable Dr. Prof. Sir John Denis Macdonald K.C.B., F.R.S., M.D. St. and, M.R.C.5.Eng., R.N., Inspector-General of Royal Navy Hospitals and Fleets, explorer, natural scientist, microscopist of international repute, and a dab hand at art himself.

To understand Macdonald's challenge to convention and to appreciate the uniqueness of his artistic vision, we need to take a close look at his formative influences in Cork where he grew up among a privileged but enlightened intellectual elite. Long assumed to be from Irish artisan stock, the Macdonalds were actually scions of Scottish aristocracy. When Daniel was a boy, his father, James McDaniel, was informed that he was in fact a Macdonald, and so, in the mid 1830s, he reverted to the family name Macdonald, as did his children. As well as being the 8th Macdonald of Castleton, James had a claim to the important Annandale and Hartfell peerage, dormant since 1792. Given irresolvable complications of legitimacy and lunacy, he remained a claimant and never an heir. Nevertheless, there was prestige still attached to the name, which became apparent when the family relocated to London in the mid 1840s.

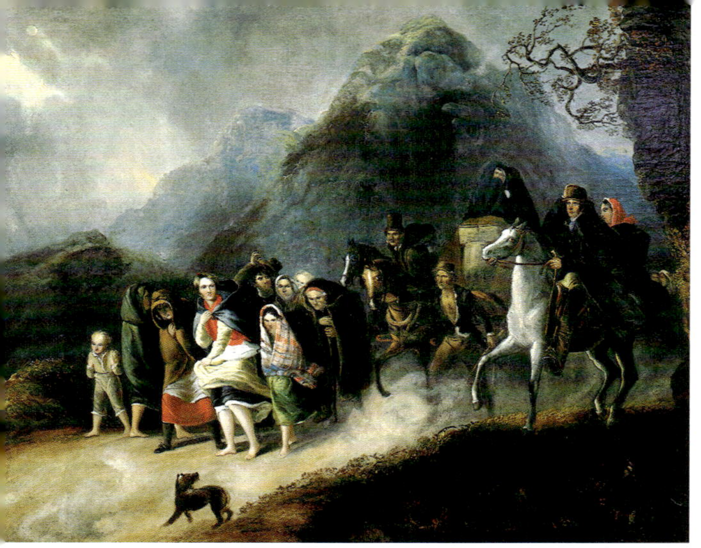

Daniel Macdonald made his debut as an artist at the age of thirteen when he contributed two sketches to a literary work, *The Tribute* (1833), a volume of prose and verse by Joseph O'Leary, journalist and balladeer. Less than twenty years later, he was dead. But in that short time, he produced an impressive number of works of striking originality, insight and skill.

Figure 2

*Sidhe Gaoithe/
The Fairy Blast*

Daniel Macdonald

1842

By the age of 21, he was on the exhibition circuit at the Cork Art Union, in its first year. The following year, in 1842, he exhibited four works at the Royal Hibernian Academy in Dublin, and he was on the managing committee of the Cork Art Union, where he exhibited eight works, including the important *Sidhe Gaoithe / The Fairy Blast* **(Fig. 2)**, a painting remarkable for its knowledge of Irish folklore, and indicative of his friendship with Thomas Crofton Croker (1798–1854), the first to publish material on fairy legends, and the beliefs, superstitions, manners and customs of the Irish people.

In the eighteenth century, a number of antiquarians began to gather Irish folkloric material. Their numbers grew in the nineteenth century, with Crofton Croker — aided and abetted by James McDaniel — to the fore. The motivation of the folklorists was largely ethnographic — the documentation of the life and customs of rural Ireland — yet, as with any ethnographic project, there was a concomitant political motive, in this case a desire to promote the 'civilizing' influence of the English ways while seeking to confine the Irish ways of life to the museum. Irish barbarism tamed and preserved by English civility. And yet despite his Protestant and anglicized background, a tolerance for things Irish and Catholic is discernible in Daniel Macdonald's art throughout his life.

In the lead up to the Famine, oath bound secret societies — from the Whiteboys to the Rockites — organized nocturnal raids against land grabbers, tithe collectors, and landlords with lethal effect. The grounds for protest and resistance were many. The fallout from 1798, the post-Napoleonic economic crash, tithe taxes, the 1817 famine, and the threat of another in 1822, precipitated outbreaks of violence, motivated by seditious intent and personal vendettas, extending to maiming, rape, arson and murder. The police and yeomanry distributed harsh justice, meting out prison sentences, deportations and executions. Rural fairs and patterns were marked by pitched battles, known as faction fights. Factions were led by flamboyant characters, such as Macdonald's *Fighter* (1844), who assumed powerful leadership positions by virtue of their prowess. Other forms of lawlessness included illicit distilling, scenes of which were also painted by Macdonald.

The colonized Irish had long been ascribed with negative stereotypes: violent, indolent and degraded. Following the Act of Union in 1800, some minor efforts were made to adjust the stereotypes to reflect a little less unfavorably on the people. The national character now became a matter of political importance, especially among the Anglo-Irish ascendancy whose own position was as challenged by the Union as any other class. Macdonald, showed the plight of the Irish poor as it was, with a certain tinge of humor but no discernible malice or prejudice in his work. From Daniel O'Connell to Harry Badger, his sketch *Public Characters* **(Fig. 3)** features politicians and boccaughs, dog executioners and ballad singers, nosy parkers and fools, dandies and temperance champions. *Public Characters* takes a graphic swipe at the high and mighty, the down and dirty, the corrupt and disreputable of Cork city in the early 1840s.

Throughout his work, Macdonald's characters play music, dance, court and marry; they make poitín and get drunk; they go to school and Mass; they pray to God, and fear the fairies; they fight, they die, are waked and buried. The beautiful and winsome; the strutting and cowering; the ridiculous and brave; the cringing and devil-may-care; musicians and actors; fools and lunatics; undertakers and stone masons; laborers, farmers and gentlemen; the military, in all its guises; priests and merchant princes; and, on more than one occasion, the devoted followers of Daniel O'Connell, the uncrowned King of All Ireland — in other words, the cut and thrust of everyday life in Cork in the 1840s. Macdonald's work is wry and deadpan, droll and farcical, ironic and mordant, parodic and satirical. Above all, he tells a good story with verve and energy, knowing his subjects generically and individually. As times got darker in the mid century, however, his work took on more ominous tones, as empathy and outrage, indignation and shock, acquired visual form on canvas.

Between 1840 and 1844, prior to his move to London, Macdonald produced a prodigious number of paintings and sketches, across a range of subjects and genres, and he received high praise from Irish newspapers. His work was reviewed as 'unrivalled', 'excellent' and 'faultless'. His subject matter included landscapes, literary subjects, still lifes and portraits, but it was his subject pictures, as we shall see, that broke new ground.

The move to London in 1844 was an immediate success. Within a year, many members of the royal family and the aristocracy had sat for him, including Prince George and Princess Mary of Cambridge. Around this time, Queen Victoria herself acquired a drawing by Macdonald, *Returning from a Funeral,* which she kept in a precious album (Royal Collections), a companion to which hangs in Ireland's Great Hunger Museum. In London, many Irish artists chose to suppress their Irishness in the effort to get ahead, but for all his success, Macdonald remained true to himself, simultaneously painting the aristocracy while working on his Irish subject pictures, not least *An Irish Peasant Family Discovering the Blight of their Store.* While his star was rising, he never lost sight of his roots.

Macdonald's hometown of Cork, produced more than the national average in artists. Many, like James Barry, Daniel Maclise and John Hogan achieved international reputations, whereas others, such as 'Honest Dick' Millikin, Charles Scottowe or Henry John Noblett, also prominent in their day, faded fast. However, reconsidering the canon can often retrieve the reputation of undeservedly forgotten artists and cultural figures, and the McDaniel/Macdonald dynasty is a case in point. Macdonald was pre-eminently a painter of national character, arguably the folkloric artist of his day, but understanding his art requires a keen appreciation of his family upbringing, and the Cork milieu into which he was born. His background was one of social, political and cultural flux, and his responses to this and to the ghastly events that unfolded up to and during the Famine, have not received the attention they deserve. The Crawford Gallery, Cork, is home to many of Macdonald's paintings and drawings that feature here, and this book coincides with the first retrospective exhibition of Daniel Macdonald's work, held at Ireland's Great Hunger Museum, Quinnipiac University, in 2016.

Figure 3

Public Characters

Daniel Macdonald

1843

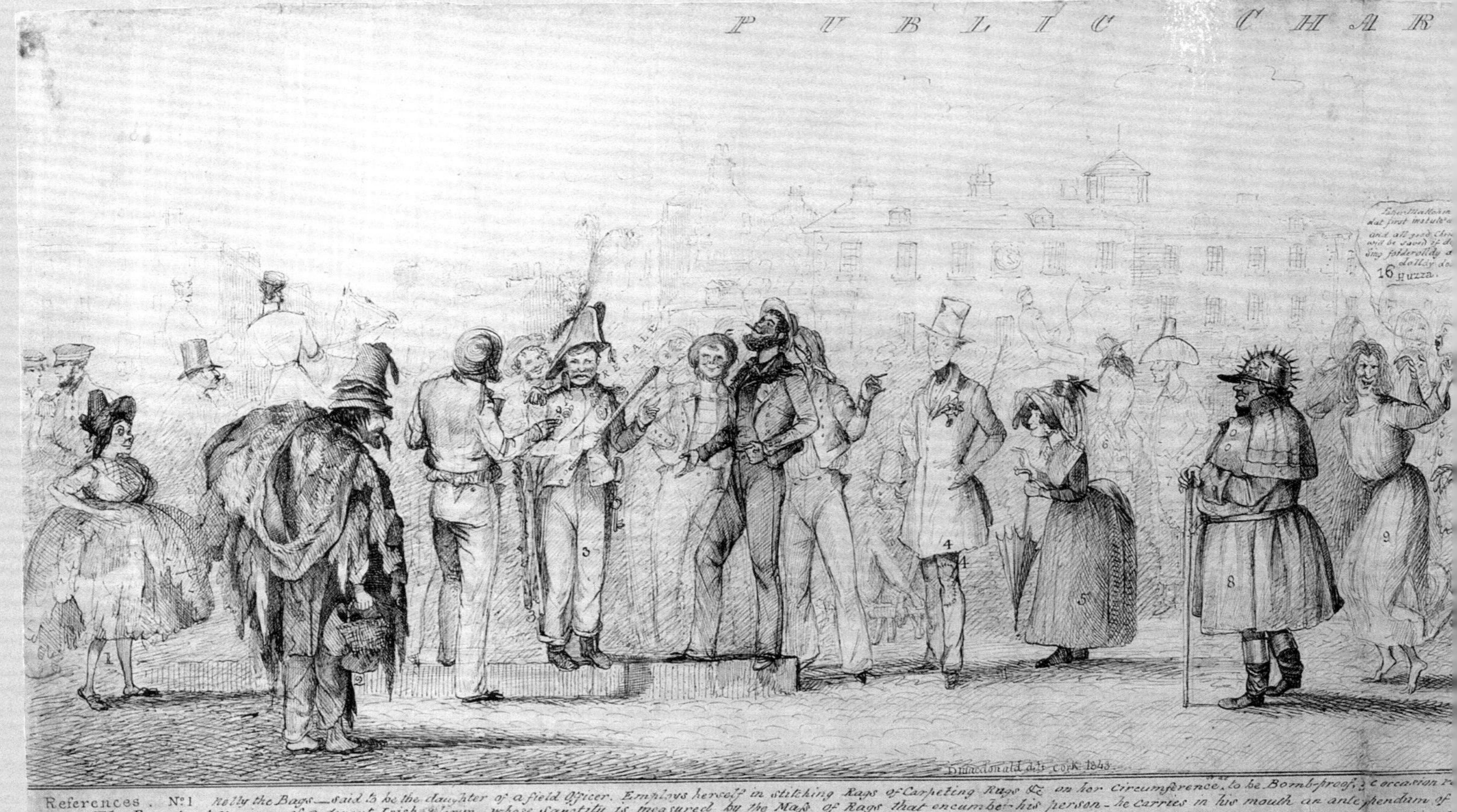

PUBLIC CHARACTERS (CORK) 1843
REFERENCES

No. 1 Nelly the Bags said to be the daughter of a field officer. Employs herself in stitching Rags of Carpeting Rugs &c on her circumference, so as to be Bomb-proof, as occasion required

No. 2 The Rag-ut A specimen of a devout Irish pilgrim. Whose sanctity is measured by the Mass of Rags that encumber his person – he carries in his mouth an antependum of the same

No. 3 Bother'd Dan The King of all Ireland denoted by the Keys of his Kingdom pendant, & inflicts the Order of Knight-hood by such a hearty thwack of a sprig of his Shillelagh that the honor he confers is received & duly felt. His Majesty attends all public meetings in the Kingdom, distance no object

No. 4 Flood Esq Whose first appearance in Cork was on the Stage, Singing a Duetto with

No. 5 He next set up as member for Cork, in the liberal interest & appeared with a sunflower in his button-hole on the hustings addressing the Wags who cheered him notwithstanding his defeat, "by bribery & corruption"

No. 5 Miss Harding the Irish Catalani, the owner of all COVE & Glanmire, up to the crown of her bonnet in Law. She waited on Danl O Connell M.P. on the death of his wife to offer him her hand & heart, it being in his power to recover her long lost rights & that she knew no man more worthy of the Offer. Her robes are of Glazed Muslin, its satin'y appearance spotted by rain

No. 6 Capt Fitton called Dot

No 7 His brother Spot. An advocate for the omnipotence of TAR, as a cure for all diseases. He hanged a dog for being guilty of Hydrophobia & collected an assembly of the Canine Species to witness the Execution, haranguing them on the advantages of good conduct and Sanity

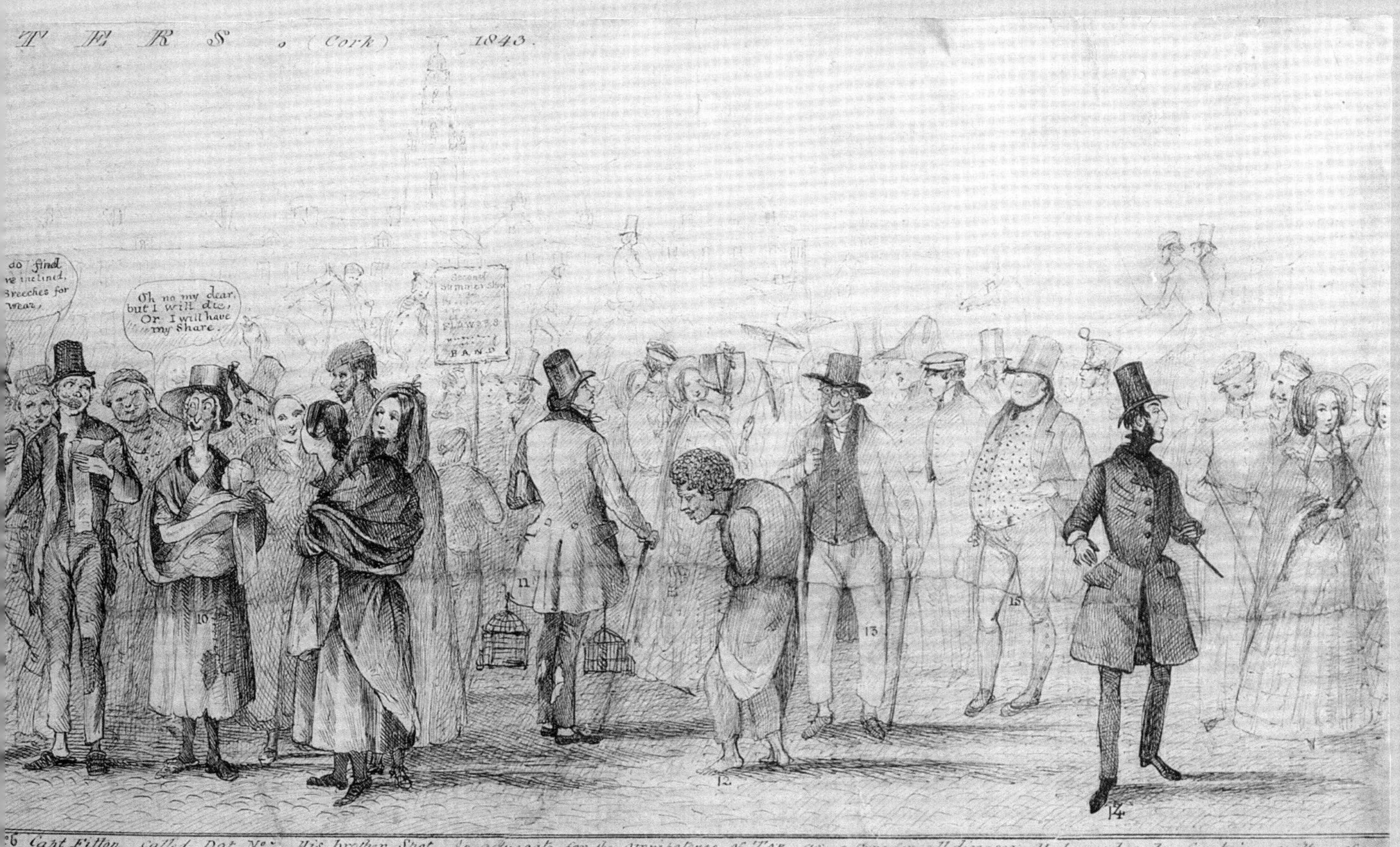

No. 8 Harry Badger. A dust who suffered so much from boys, in the article of Slating, that his friends provided him with an old helmet, studded with 2 shilling nails to save his cranium. His capacity of stomach was such that he eat an old leather inexpressibles [?], cut up & dressed in the form of Tripe

No. 9 Crazy Norry execrating the City Police

No 10 Recitatievo Ballad Singers
He sings As I do find,
You are inclined,
The Breeches for to Wear,
she responds Oh no my dear,
but I will die, Or I will have my share

No. 11 Mr. Tobin who appears balanced by a pair of Bird Cages. He is excellent Value, as his pranks are new every day, from a disinclination to repeat his own ideas, he stands as in his later appearance on Town

No. 12 Tom the fool

No. 13 Paul Pry, an inquisitive mischief maker

No. 14 Kill the Ladies, a fascinator of the first water who must ere now have a gold chain strung with the hearts of young ladies

No. 15 The wit of the Weigh-House, his Vest, a la Plumb pudding

No. 16 A Temperance Champion
[sings from a broadsheet]
Father Mattchin is de man,
dat first instuted de Holy plan,
and all good Christians will be saved,
if dey can Sing folderolldy dolldy
dolldy doll. HUZZA

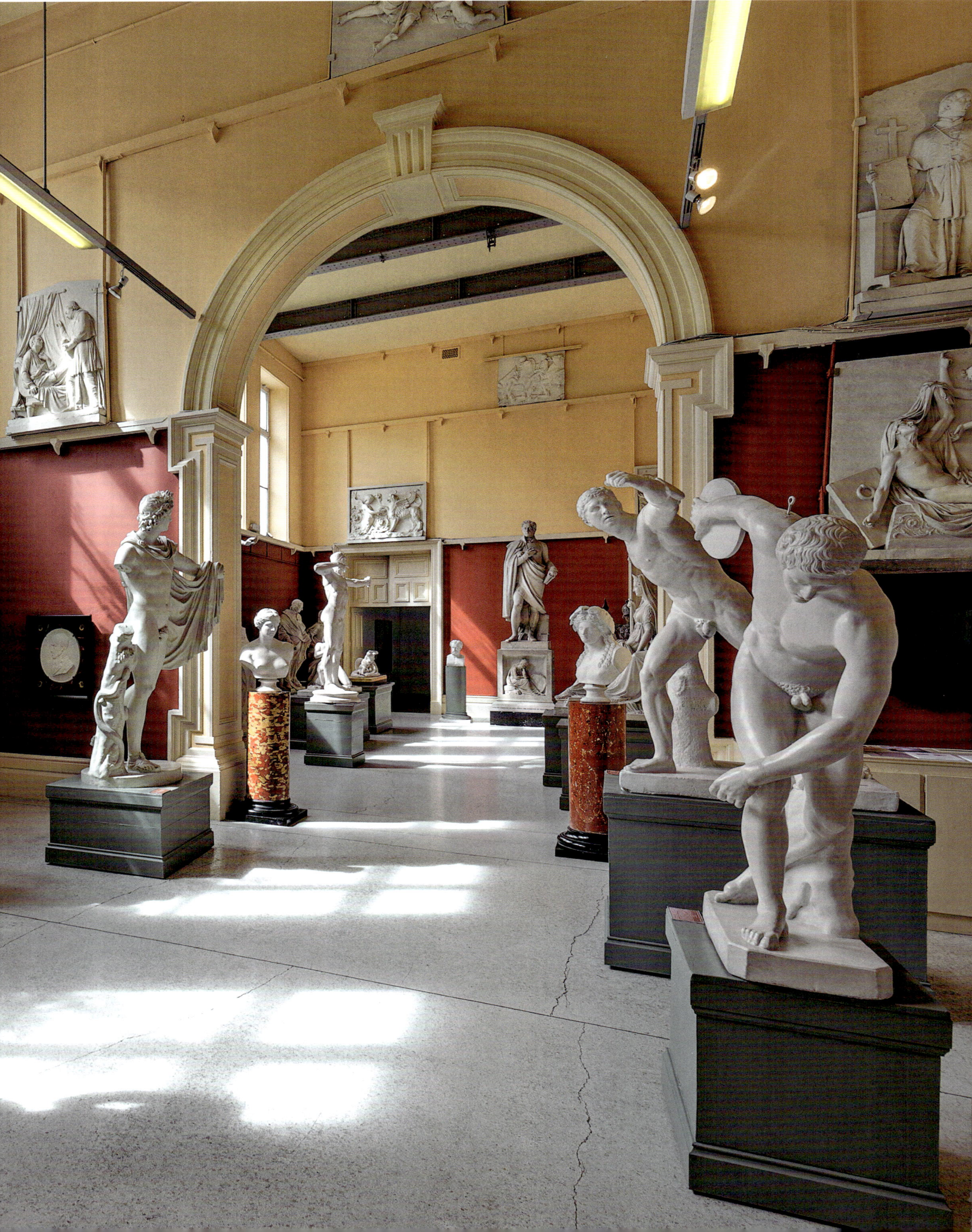

CHAPTER 1

THE CORK CRUCIBLE

During the Napoleonic Wars, vast British fleets were supplied and provisioned in Cork harbor. Business boomed. The city boasted wide streets, new churches and splendid bridges across the River Lee. Architects, writers, artists and scientists promoted the development of a progressive city, where a huge range of literary, philosophical and scientific societies thrived. The business men and new professionals became scholars and collectors of international repute. Literary life centered around Bolster's bookshop on St. Patrick's Street, and extended into the homes and clubs of the elite of Cork. Richard Sainthill, the wealthy wine importer, held literary evenings at home, frequented by writers, artists, men of science and medicine, collectors and antiquarians. It was a time of intense creativity and scientific brilliance.

Starting with the Cork Library Society in 1790, an intelligentsia emerged in Cork where literary, artistic, philosophical and scientific societies competed and collaborated. According to Dolores Dooley, Cork had more than 1,170 such societies.[1] The Cork Institution for the Diffusion of Knowledge was founded in 1803 for improvement in the arts and manufactures and the application of science 'to the common purposes of life'. In 1807, a royal charter and a parliamentary grant was conferred, creating the Royal Cork Institution, an incipient university which boasted a number of 'professors', including James McDaniel, Daniel Macdonald's father. Lectures on natural philosophy, natural history, chemistry, mineralogy, botany, music, art and literature made for a vibrant intellectual life. The Cork Library Society also maintained a museum of natural history and mineralogy, and a scientific and medical library, and it offered classes in art, science and technology. The Society for the Promotion of the Fine Arts, founded in 1815 by the lawyer and poet Richard Milliken (author of the song 'The Groves of Blarney'), amalgamated with the Royal Institution in 1825. It ran annual exhibitions, years before the Royal Hibernian Academy was founded in Dublin. McDaniel was one of its prominent exhibitors (alongside Nathaniel Grogan, Henry Kirchoffer and John Corbett).

Cork Literary and Scientific Society, founded in 1820, had its origins in earlier societies, such as the Cork Philosophical and Literary Society. It fostered antiquarianism and literature, philosophy and technology, and the sciences. This learned group heard papers on a wide range of literary, artistic, scientific, engineering, philosophical, classical, etymological, folkloric and linguistic subjects. It required its members to produce in rotation an essay for each meeting. Topics included the muscular motion of birds' wings, courtship, the French language, meteorology, the rules of perspective, fever in tropical climates, phrenology, morality, truth, poetry, music, guns, meteors and the death penalty. Essays by William Maginn, Charles Dodd, Richard Dowden, Charles Porter, Abraham Beale, Thomas Deane, Samuel Carter Hall, Henry John Noblett, William Jones, Michael Collins, Samuel Hobart, John Marks and others, attest to the originality and standards of the contributors. Daniel Macdonald's father James McDaniel once more attracts attention here, contributing a significant number on art, music and printing.[2]

The Sculpture Gallery
Crawford Art Gallery, Cork

The Mechanics' Institute was founded in 1824. It had a library of 1,500 volumes, a reading-room, and two schools, one for instruction in the arts and sciences, and one for design; it offered lectures on scientific subjects and also numbered among its teachers the brilliant young artist, Samuel Forde. The Society of Native and Resident Artists was founded and held its first exhibition in 1835. The Cuvierian Society was also formed in 1835 for the promotion of science, literature, and the fine arts. Its luminaries included Dr. Richard Caulfield (antiquarian and librarian), Richard Sainthill (numismatist and collector), John Windele (antiquarian, historian and editor of *Bolster's Quarterly Magazine*), Richard Dowden (minor wit and major botanist), Dr. George Boole (founder of pure mathematics and Boolean algebra), Robert J. Lecky (marine engineer), and Abraham Abell (banker and antiquarian). Cork had two theaters and a circus for equestrian exhibitions, a number of libraries, a museum, a dramatic society (the Apollo), and even a school for poets. As most of these co-existed, and the same names pop up in each organization, the gentlemen of Cork must have been out every night of the week as they strived to bring culture, commerce, science and industry into alignment.

The big breakthrough for artists came in 1841 when Cork set up an Art Union, giving a huge impetus to the art scene in the city. The art unions organized exhibitions and lotteries for subscribers, with paintings as prizes, thereby providing a modicum of support for artists.[3] Ten years later, in 1851, the Great Exhibition in London provided the inspiration for the major exhibition that took place in Cork in 1852, to which Daniel Maclise and Daniel Macdonald, then seen as Cork's most illustrious artists, were personally invited to exhibit. In the deep post-Famine depression of the 1850s, the exhibition was a major fillip for both art and industry. And between these two dates, Daniel Macdonald emerged as an artist with a new engagement with vernacular culture.*

However, from its heyday in the eighteenth century, Cork experienced a deep downturn in the early decades of the nineteenth. As Terry Eagleton observed, 'Cork hit its cultural stride just as it was economically declining … not the first time that a civilization had briefly, brilliantly flowered on the very threshold of its decline'.[4] Following the end of the Napoleonic Wars, agricultural prices slumped, trade decreased and credit contractions led to the collapse of many banks. Unemployment rose, but so did the population (due to the influx of migrants from depressed rural areas). While brewing, distilling, shipbuilding, tanning and butter making continued to flourish, and the harbor continued its trade, poor living conditions in the densely populated city were increasingly prevalent. By 1831, Cork had a population of 107,000, but only 8,000 houses. A series of minor but nonetheless deadly famines in 1817 and 1822, and an outbreak of cholera in 1832 (part of the European-wide pandemic), were already serious setbacks for the city, before it entered the more calamitous decades of the mid-century.

In 1841, the population of Ireland was recorded as 8,175,124, one third of whom depended almost entirely on the potato. In Cork, the rich and the poor, Protestant and Catholic, lived cheek-by-jowl. The middle classes, '[l]ocked in ferocious sectarian combat, warred for the prize of the city's economy, as new commercial interests confronted age-old political allegiances'.[5] Even before the Famine, 20,000

    *See Daniel Macdonald, Exhibition Record, and Interim Catalogue, Appendices 1 and 2

Corkonians were unemployed, and some 6,000 were utterly destitute. Food riots and demonstrations were commonplace. Inevitably, the arrival of the blight in 1845 had calamitous consequences for the city, enduring for the next seven years and beyond. As the wealthier merchants and now prosperous middle classes left the inner city for the salubrious suburbs of Montenotte, Tivoli and Blackrock, their vacated homes became tenement houses for the working classes and unemployed. Living conditions in these tenements were appalling. Although Protestants constituted only 12,000 of the population, they dominated the city. Class and religious tensions were such that Cork's premier artist, Daniel Maclise, did everything possible to draw on his Scottish and religious background to distinguish himself from his Catholic milieu. No such disdain is evident in the life or work of Daniel Macdonald.

Notwithstanding Margaret Oliphant's oft quoted dismissal of Cork as 'a place more associated with pigs and salted provisions than with literature', Mr. and Mrs. Samuel Carter Hall insisted that Cork was feted more than any other city in Ireland 'for the production and fosterage of genius'.[6] Arguably, Maclise's vast decorative scheme for the British Houses of Parliament, Thomas Crofton Croker's pioneering *Fairy Legends* (1826), Francis Sylvester Mahony's hilarious *Reliques of Father Prout* (1836), and the Halls' own landmark work, *Ireland, its Scenery and Character* (1841–43), and the combined wit, originality and brilliance of the Irish writers on *Fraser's Magazine*, could all be said to have had their origins in Cork. The Protestant intelligentsia of Cork were a creative, roistering, jealous, caustic and witty lot. Much time was passed in the many drinking clubs of the city. Dr. William Maginn, 'a tap-house sot' with an even greater appetite for alcohol than the rest (according to the sanctimonious Samuel Carter Hall), was undoubtedly the star of this particular corner of the intellectual firmament.[7] The 'cranky Cork genius', entered Trinity College Dublin at the age of 11, winning the Hebrew prize at the entrance examination.[8] Maginn knew Greek, Russian, Turkish and Sanskrit, not to mention several European languages. He was also fluent in Latin, into which he translated the Irish ballads of the day to preserve — or elevate — them for posterity. Feared for his caustic wit as much as he was admired, he was a staunch Tory who parodied the Whig Thomas Moore unmercifully for his pseudo-Irish verses, and dismissed the self-regarding Hall as a 'prig'. Although most found Hall insufferable, and they all had a go at Moore, it didn't stop them being in and out of each other's pockets. Hall retaliated in a similar spirit, attacking Maginn and friends — 'the Talents'. Each of the twenty-four sworn members of the Deipnosophists — 'the Talents' — had a personal Greek motto (providing but one explanation for the sobriquet of Cork as 'The Athens of Ireland').[9] When the Deipnosophists split, according to John Boyle, one half (highly improbably) joined the secret agrarian society, the Whiteboys, who went about 'gagging tithe-proctors, rescuing cattle, sending threatening notices, and assisting the ill-used peasantry in other illegal practices, while the other half joined the Brunswick Club, and became the most inveterate foes to their former associates'.[10] From this split, the unreliable Boyle dated the downfall of Cork.[11] Cork, more than anywhere else in Ireland, was according to Maginn '… on the verge of a civil war'.[12] Maginn left Cork. Eagleton contends that while Maginn's flight from Ireland 'may have been inspired by personal self-advancement', it was just as much 'the bellicose response of a politically washed-up Protestantism to encroaching Catholic power.'[13]

Notwithstanding all the cultural activity, patronage was almost nonexistent. As the economy was shriveling, and the population exploding, leading figures in Cork cultural life — Croker in 1818, Hall in 1821, Maginn in 1823, Maclise in 1827, and Father Francis Sylvester Mahony, among others — moved to London, resuming original friendships and animosities. Others went elsewhere. John Hogan, one of the greatest sculptors of his day, went to Rome in 1823; Jeremiah Joseph Callanan, author of 'Gougane Barra', went to Lisbon; and John Augustus Shea went to a glittering literary and journalistic life in America (where he took an interest in the young cadet, Edgar Allan Poe, at West Point).

LONDON

In London, these Corkonians brought Ireland, its history, geography, topography, culture and character to the attention of a wider cultural world. Their successes were such that in 1845, *The Art-Union* (edited by Samuel Carter Hall) was confident enough to declare, somewhat prematurely, that Irish inferiority was at an end. Citing Martin Archer Shee, Francis Danby, Jonathan Fisher and the foremost talent, Maclise, it declared that the fame of Irish artists 'has gone forth from London, throughout the world.'[14] Notwithstanding such hyperbole, the importance of the Cork contribution to Victorian cultural life was immense. Maginn, the Halls, Dr. Edward Vaughan Kenealy, Croker and Father Mahony were forcible presences in the world of letters, but many of them were also authors of their own destruction, While they lived a hell-raising émigré life of distinction for a time, all too soon — awash with drink and debt — they sank under the weight of their own disappointment.

Hugh Fraser and Maginn set up the high-profile *Fraser's Magazine* in 1830. For the next twelve years, with the connivance of Thomas Carlyle, William Makepeace Thackeray and Samuel Taylor Coleridge, the magazine was dominated by Irishmen, especially Croker, Maclise and Mahony. Edited by Maginn, it was an eclectic mix of brilliant writing, erudition and doggerel, invective, scandal and satire. Its contributors savaged each other's work, sometimes even their own, bringing the concept of plagiarism itself to art-form. Maginn, of daunting wit and learnedness, was, perhaps, too clever for his own good: his review of Sir Grantley Berkeley's *Berkeley Castle* in 1836 was so ruinous that *Fraser's* publisher was beaten almost to a pulp by the author.

Maclise's contribution to *Fraser's* was enormous. His *Gallery of Illustrious Literary Characters* **(Fig. 4)**, under the punning pseudonym of Alfred Croquis, comprised some eighty biographical illustrations, and was highly successful. As a serial biography of literary London, it combined written and visual — mostly satirical — characterizations, included some notably *uncelebrated* writers, and ensured the non-complacency of anyone who *was* included in the Gallery. The sketchers wrote and the writers sketched, and everyone, it seems, ventured into verse, or 'metrical effusions' as Bernard Barton called them.[15] The poet Richard Milliken painted; the folklorist Croker etched; Mahony, the 'spoiled priest', wrote travel notes for Croker; the antiquarian, John Windele, drew illustrations for the Halls; and the Halls reviewed them all. Tightly tribal, collectively they performed what Eagleton calls a type of 'carnivalesque overturning of the isolated writing ego' and, in the process, Maginn and Mahony, in particular, knocked the traditional concept of originality on the head. As Eagleton sees Mahony, he was 'potentially a major writer striving very hard to become a minor one.'[16]

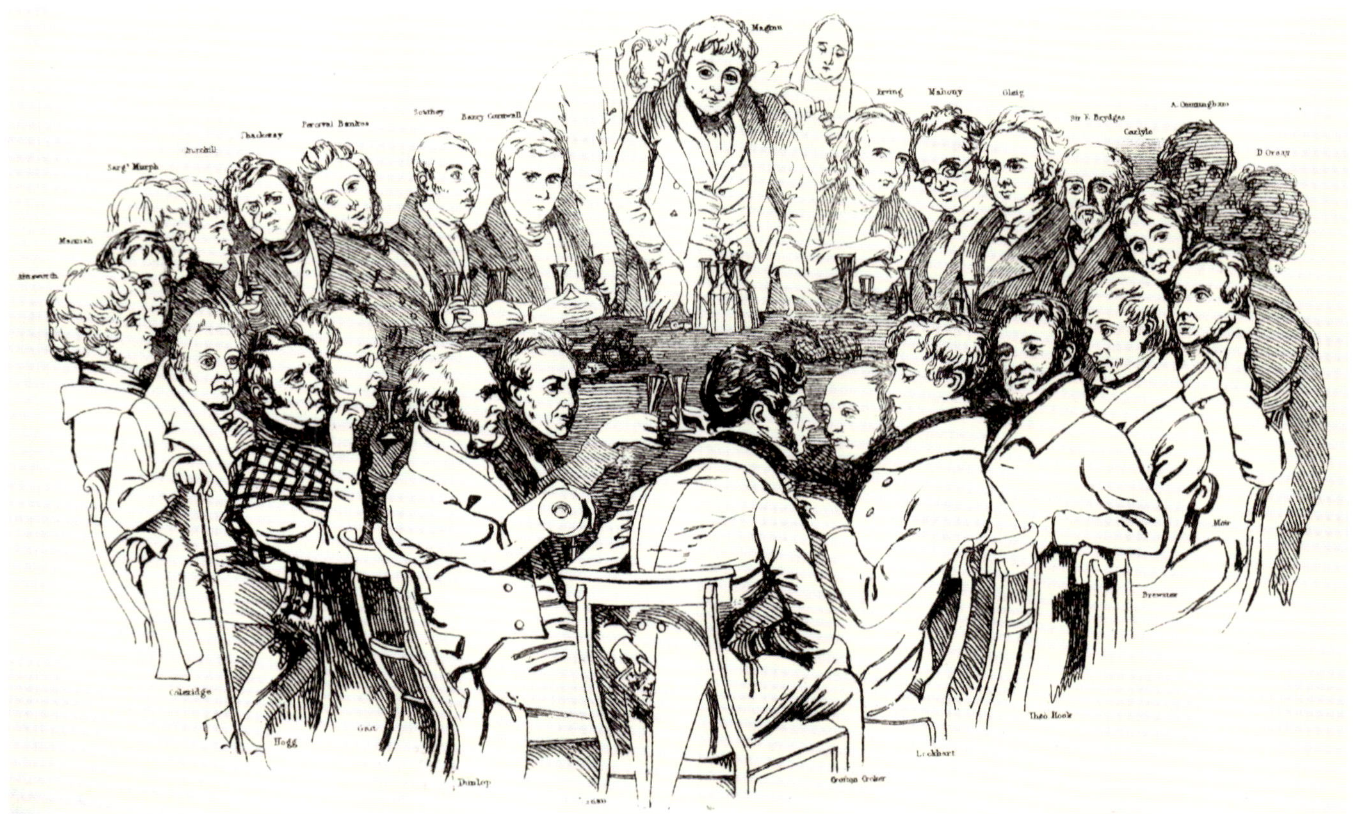

Figure 4

The Fraserians
Daniel Maclise

Politically, too, they were a conflicted lot. Many of the Protestant minority opposed Catholic emancipation, fearing Catholic power, but in time converted to Repeal. In London, at a safe distance, many Orange Ascendancy/Tories professed a newfound interest in the Irish poor, where they largely opposed *laissez faire* economics, on the basis that such policies beggared an already destitute country. It is against this background that the family of Daniel Macdonald is best understood.

As a young man, James McDaniel was torn between the sciences and the arts. His father, Daniel McDaniel, had a grocery on Grand Parade in Cork in the 1790s, and when he died James took over the business.[17] James's wife, Catherine, acquired a bustling millinery and fashion business at 113 Patrick Street in 1828 (from Miss Hall), and regularly advertised fashions 'just arrived' from Paris or London. As it was for Robert Day, Richard Sainthill, Richard Dowden and the other merchant princes of Cork, business was good, but James complained of living a mundane life. By 1815, although he continued with various scientific experiments (some of which were submitted to the Admiralty in London), McDaniel was exhibiting his art.* By 1819, he had a studio and a long list of students, and by this time, his letters to Croker **(Fig. 5 a-b)** abound with commentary on the manners and customs of the Irish peasantry, ancient poetry, and the melodies and music of the past. He was now a figure of some importance.

On April 20, 1821, *The Freeholder* published 'A Song touching and concerning the Variance among the PHILOSOPHERS of Cork' by the acerbic William Maginn:

> *Did you hear the Philosophers fought,*
> *And how one party ousted the other?*
> *They parted (at least so 'tis thought)*
> *With a great deal of bustle and bother …*

108 Patrick St, York. September
Friday Eveni[ng]   107

All accounts of this Marquis corrobate [corroborate]
this Statement — Neither is there a [word] mentioned as [...]
of the Branches of the family of Johnstone, during or about the
period [...] referred to in this letter

My Dear Friend

As I am sure that you would readily assist me
in any enquiry that would turn to my account, I write
to acquaint you of matters respecting my origin, which
I never had occasion to mention to you hitherto.

From about 1758 to 1760 My Grandmother who
was Lady Jane Johnstone, married my Grandfather
Alexander Macdonald, and came off with him from
Scotland to Ireland, and lived in Cork (calling
themselves McDaniel for purposes of concealment)
until they had four Children, namely, Daniel, William,
Mary, & Alexander. After the birth of Alexander, my
Grandfather sailed with a Captain Templeman for Scotland,
[...] made arraingements for their return home. And was
[lost at] Sea, and my Grandmother survived the Shock
but Six months. During the period of her sad affliction,
in a strange place, She confessed her history to those
about her, and Stated, that hers was a Love Match with
her late husband, that her Maiden name was Jane Johnstone,
that She was the Daughter of a Nobleman in Scotland,
(and as well as I remember) an Only Child. And no doubt
she revealed Particulars that I had no opportunity of
being acquainted with. She died, leaving two surviving
Orphan Children, Daniel, who was my Father, & Alexander
an Infant in his Cradle. Their history to Manhood

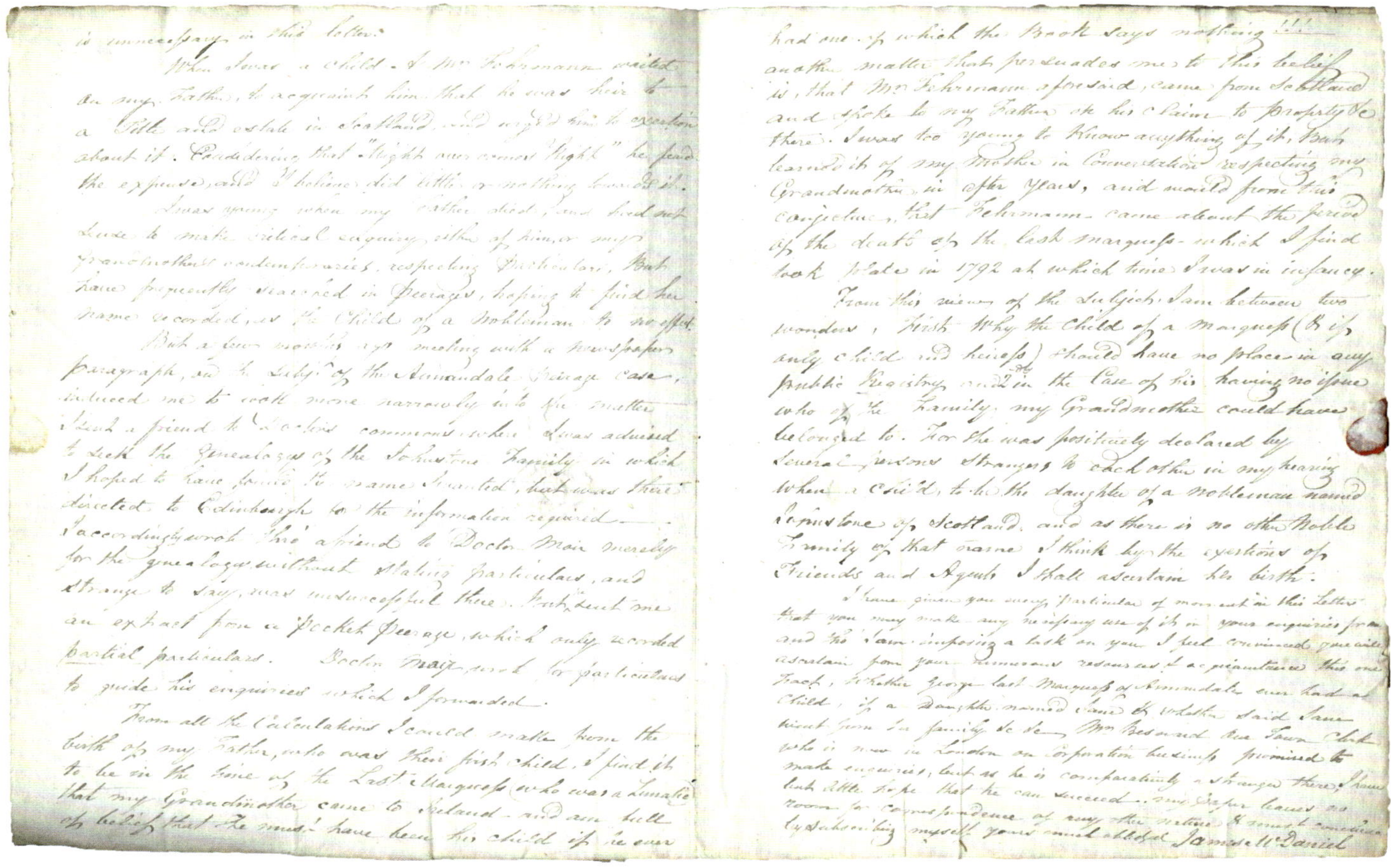

There follows several stanzas on the 'sweet smelling gang of banditti', at which point the poem addresses James:

> Then a bag-pipe with any bags,
> McDaniel described in a canter,
> And the ladies they all laughted like wags
> At the thoughts of the length of his chaunter,
> But they owned that they wished for the bags.[18]

Figure 5 a–b

Letter from James McDaniel to Thomas Crofton Croker

September 9, 1835

Whatever about the literary merits of the poem, it attests to James's involvement in everything Cork. He was a key member of the Philosophical Literary and Scientific Society, the Society for Promotion of the Fine Arts and the Cork Institution, among others. Versed in the arts, accomplished in the sciences, pioneer in ethnography, inventor,[19] artist, teacher,[20] architect,[21] translator,[22] and, by all accounts, talented musician, James was quite the polymath.

Robert Day, Sr. described McDaniel as a caricaturist who 'excelled in his pen and ink drawings'.[23] James illustrated business cards, and designed book-plates (much in vogue at the time). Day described how his father's book-plate had the name 'James McDaniel, Professor of Drawing and Painting' in several branches, on the face of a sculptured fountain.[24] Another, signed 'James McDaniel Sculpt.' was a pictorial frontispiece for a Cork imprint of Sir John Moore's *Introduction to the Use of the Globe*. 'I have some of his drawings, which show his keen sense of the humorous, and are characteristic of the man', wrote Robert Day, Jr., by then a renowned collector and Fellow of the Royal Society of Antiquaries, who

FAMILY HISTORY

Family history comes from several sources, is neither fully consistent nor always verifiable, and is beset by complications, not least the interchangeability of Daniel/Donald as both christian and surnames.[1] According to Mackenzie's History of the Macdonalds and Lords of the Isles: With Genealogies of the Principal Families (1881)[2] — the most accurate — James's father, Daniel/Donald McDaniel/Macdonald (died 1804) was the son of Alexander Macdonald (lost at sea in 1758). He married Jane, supposedly eldest daughter of the Hon. Captain John Johnstone of Stapleton, second son of James, second Earl of Hartfell, who had been created Earl of Annandale and Hartfell in 1662 by Crown Charter.[3]

Daniel/Donald married Johanna Manning, and had three children, James McDaniel (father of our artist), Daniel and Jane/Johanna. James McDaniel married Catherine McCarthy (1797–1877) on 7 May 1816. In 1827, James's brother, Daniel (67th Regiment) married Catherine's sister, Susan(na) (both daughters of Denis McCarthy of Kilcolman, Co Cork), and they had three children, James, Donald/Daniel and Jane). Daniel died 30 September 1834. And James's sister, Jane, married George Gwynne, of whom nothing is known.[4]

James McDaniel and Catherine McCarthy had four children: Daniel (1820–53),[5] Jane (1824–1909), James Alexander (1826–1907) and John Denis (1826–1908). Far from the Irish artisan stock they are assumed to be, the claim to be scions of Scottish lineage, the Macdonalds of Sleat, Isle of Skye, is verifiable. But arguments that they descended from an even more illustrious line — resulting in James becoming an Annandale claimant in the 1830s — are more problematic. Dormant since 1792, the Annandale and Hartfell peerage dispute spanned 193 years. During that time, successive members of the Hope Johnstone family, the ultimate victors, claimed the 1662 title. But it was not until the House of Lords determined the outcome in 1985 that James's connection, through his grandmother, Jane, daughter of the Hon. Captain John Johnstone of Stapleton, would appear to have gained some retrospective credibility, although the current Lord Annandale refutes any such possibility.[6] In the 1920s, further efforts were made to establish connections, but the Stapletons were not having it.[7]

In September 1835, James wrote to Thomas Crofton Croker:

… I write to acquaint you of matters respecting my origin …. From about 1758–1760 my grandmother who was Lady Jane Johnstone married my grandfather, Alexander Macdonald, and lived in Cork (calling themselves McDaniel for purposes of concealment) until they had four children, names Daniel, William, Mary and Alexander. After the birth of Alexander, my grandfather sailed with a Captain Templeman for Scotland to make arrangements for their return home and was lost at sea, and my grandmother survived the shock but six months. During the period of her sad afflictions in a strange place, she confessed her story to those about her, and stated that hers was a love match with her late husband, that her maiden name was Jane Johnstone, that she was the daughter of a nobleman in Scotland (and as well as I remember) an only child. And no doubt she revealed particulars that I had no opportunity of being made acquainted with. She died leaving two surviving orphan children, Daniel, who was my father, and Alexander, an infant in his cradle. Their history to manhood is unnecessary in this letter.

When I was a child, a Mr Fehremann waited on my father to acquaint him that he was heir to a title and an estate and urged him to exertion about it. Considering that 'might overcomes right', he feared the expense and I believe did little of nothing towards it. I was young when my father died and had not sense to make critical enquiry either of him or my grandmother's contemporaries, respecting particulars. But have frequently searched in peerages, hoping to find her name recorded as the child of a nobleman to no effect.

But a few months ago meeting with a newspapers paragraph, on the July of the Annandale peerage case induced me to look more narrowly into the matter. I sent a friend to Doctor's commons, where I was advised to seek the genealogy of the Johnstone family in which I hoped to have found the name I wanted, but was there directed to Edinburgh for the information required. I accordingly wrote thro' a friend to Doctor David Moir merely for the genealogy without stating particulars, and strange to say was unsuccessful there. But he sent me an extract from a pocket peerage, which only recorded partial particulars. Doctor Moir wrote for particulars to guide his enquiries which I forwarded.

1 The names Daniel and Donald, Jane and Johanna, and Susan and Susana are used interchangeably throughout the genealogy, as are the names Macdonald, McDonald, and McDaniel.

2 Alexander Mackenzie, *History of the Macdonalds and Lords of the Isles: With Genealogies of the Principal Families* ([1881], reprint. London, 2013), 282–83.

3 William, the 3rd Earl, was promoted to Marquess of Annandale in 1701. His son, James, the 2nd Marquess had died in Naples in 1730. George Vanden Bempde, 3rd Marquess of Annandale (1720–92), his half-brother, became 3rd Marquess, but in 1747 was declared incapable, and a curator was appointed. When he died unmarried in 1792, there being no next in line, the titles were declared dormant (and the estates were passed to his grand-nephew James the 3rd Earl of Hopetoun). For nearly 200 years there were attempts to re-instate the titles, but it was not until 1982 that the Lord Lyon recognized Major Percy Johnstone of Annandale as an heir to the dormant titles; the case was brought to the House of Lords in 1985 and the court found in favor of the Major's son Patrick, Earl of Annandale and Hartfell to the 1662 Earldoms by Crown Charter and Chief of the Clan.

4 I am enormously grateful to Karol Defalco for her generous genealogical expertise in tracing the very complex family lineage.

5 Baptized July 2, 1820, Church of Ireland, Church of the Holy Trinity, Cork.

6 According to Lord Annandale, there was no such person as Jane. Stapleton died in 1715 in Poland. He married, had one daughter who died in infancy, and had no living legitimate descendants on his death. Correspondence with author, July 2015.

7 I am grateful to Lord Annandale for corroboration, correspondence July 2015. For an official account of the claim, see *http://hughpeskett. co.uk/003GENEA/Annandale%20 and%20Hartfell%20Peerage%20 Claim.pdf* (accessed 2 December 2015).

8 James McDaniel to Thomas Crofton Croker, Cork City Library, September 1835. A pencil annotation to the letter reads: 'George who became third Marquis of Annandale — this George was never married, he became insane shortly after his succession. He lived to a great age and died on April 29, 1792. Ext. from Pedigree obtained from the Lion College at Edinburgh. All accounts of this Marquis corroborate this statement. Neither is there a Jane mentioned as a member of the family of Johnstone during or about the period referred to in this letter.'

9 On an earlier occasion, in relation to an unspecified topic, James mentioned to Croker that 'his papers were at Castle Mahon, home of

From all the calculations I could make from the birth of my father, who was their first child, I find it to be in the time of the Last Marquess (who was a lunatic) that my grandmother came to Ireland and am full of belief that she must have been his child if he ever had one of which the Book says nothing!!! Another matter that persuades me to this belief is that Mr Fehremann aforesaid, came from Scotland and spoke to my father of his claim to property there. I was too young to know anything of it, but learned it of my mother in conversation respecting my grandmother in after years, and would from this conjecture that Fehremann came about the period of the death of the last Marquess which I find took place in 1792 at which time I was in infancy.

From this news of the subject I am between two wonders. First why the child of a Marquess (his only child and heiress) should have no place in any public registry, and 2 in the case of his having no issue who of the family my grandmother could have belonged to. For she was positively declared by several persons strangers to each other in any hearing when a child to be the daughter of a nobleman named Johnstone of Scotland, and as there is no other nobleman family of that name I think by the exertions of friends and Agents I shall ascertain her birth.

I have given you every particular of moment in this letter that you may make any [?] use of it in your enquiries for me, and I am imposing a task on you I feel convinced you will ascertain from your numerous resources and acquaintances this one fact, whether George, last Marquess of Annandale, ever had a child, [?] a daughter named Jane and whether said same ever went from the family secretly [?] Mr Besward, our town clerk who is now in London on corporation business promised to make enquiries but as he is comparatively a stranger there, I have but little hope that he can succeed. My paper leaves no room for correspondence of any other nature, I must conclude by [?] myself you much obliged, James McDaniel.[8]

James enlisted the help of friends, and friends of friends. As well as Croker, John Bolster, Sir William Chatterton and Sir William Betham, helped stake his claim.[9] Dr. David Macbeth Moir — a literary doctor of repute who wrote for the *Edinburgh Literary Gazette, Blackwood's* and *Fraser's Magazine*, and was the subject of one of Maclise's literary characters, also took up the case with the Lord Lyon, Edinburgh.[10] A year later, on September 5, 1836, James again wrote to Croker on the matter, asking him to intervene with Sir William Betham, the genealogist, to return documentation. Here he says that he has 'valuable evidence in addition', which he felt obliged to pursue so as not to 'leave an inferior chance to my son [Daniel] of ever recovering his birthright'; he wished to rearrange the documents to submit to Sir William Chatterton, who was also helping establish his claim.[11] Whatever the evidence, henceforth, James signed himself Macdonald.

In the meantime, James had to satisfy himself with the status of the 8th Macdonald of Castleton, Isle of Skye, the representative of the family. Had Daniel, his eldest son, lived, he would have inherited — but the distinction went down through Rev. James Alexander Macdonald, the second son — the Macdonalds of Castleton being a cadet house of the greater territorial Macdonald of Sleat (although here were several matrimonial links between the two houses).[12]

Arms were recorded in the Public Register of All Arms and Bearings in Scotland in 1918 in name of the Reverend James Alexander Donald John MacDonald, minister of the parish of Ullapool, wherein he narrated his descent from his grandfather, James Macdonald, artist of Cork, and his wife Catherine McCarthy. The supposed descent is further narrated in relation to Donald Macdonald of Castleton, youngest son of Sir Donald Macdonald of Sleat, 1st Baronet, but as proof positive was not available in 1918, neither James Macdonald nor his son or grandson could be recognised as Macdonald of Castleton until 1956 when Major James Alexander Macdonald, son of the Reverend James, provided proof that he was the 11th of Castleton, which would indeed confirm that his great grandfather would have been 8th of Castleton, had the descent been established at that time.[13]

Undoubtedly complicated by issues of lunacy and legitimacy, a family connection with the Stapletons would seem to have some retrospective credibility. Although James remained consigned to the status of 'claimant', rather than 'heir' (as did James Alexander following the death of the eldest son, the artist, Daniel), there was prestige attached to a claim, as can be seen by the reception the family received when they relocated to London in the mid 1840s.

Sir William and Lady Georgiana Chatterton.' James McDaniel to Thomas Crofton Croker, Cork City Library, January or February 1819.

[10] According to the Lyon Office in Edinburgh: 'no record of correspondence with either James McDaniel or Macdonald or Dr. Moir in the letter books for the 1830s/40s [appear] and [they] doubt if a claim to the Annandale peerage at that date would have been made directly to the Lord Lyon. The claims at that time took place when there was considerable spotlight on the succession as a Petition of 1795 was referred to the Committee for Privileges, and this claim was followed by other petitions between the 1820s and 1840s by John James Hope Johnstone. In the 1985 case before the Committee for Privileges, mention was made of various other claims between 1792 and 1882 but none satisfied the Committee that the claim had been made out. If, therefore, James Macdonald did make a claim, presumably by virtue of a descent from a Johnstone ancestress, it would have been made to the Committee for Privileges … [at] the House of Lords Library.'

[11] James Macdonald to Thomas Crofton Croker, Cork City Library, September 5, 1836.

[12] Donald Macdonald, second son of Sir Donald Macdonald, eighth baron and first baronet of Sleat, by his wife, Janet, second daughter, by his first marriage, of Kenneth, created first Lord Mackenzie of Kintail, on November 19, 1609, and sister to Colin Ruadh, and George, first and second Earls of Seaforth (creation 1623). Donald of Castleton took a distinguished part in the civil wars of the time in which he lived. He married Margaret, daughter of John Cameron of Lochiel — father of the famous Sir Ewen Dubh, by whom he had issue:

1. John, his heir.
2. Mary, who married her cousin, Sir Donald Macdonald of Sleat (died 1718), with issue; and secondly, Alexander Macdonald, first of Boisdale, as his first wife, also with issue:

Donald was succeeded by his only son: John Macdonald, second of Castleton. He fought at Killiecrankie, and married Mary Maclean of the family of Ardgour, with issue...

I am grateful to Jonathan Macdonald, Curator, Museum Clan Macdonald for this information.

[13] For this information, I am very grateful to C. G. W. Roads, LVO, FSA., Snawdoun Herald, Lyon Clerk and Keeper of the Records, Court of the Lord Lyon, Edinburgh.

recalled his father talking about McDaniel as talented, witty, clever, entertaining and artistic. Indeed Day recalled his father bringing him to have his portrait done by Daniel Macdonald, who was barely more than a boy himself at the time.[25]

In the first Munster Exhibition in 1815, McDaniel exhibited *Music, Painting and Poetry — Humorous Pen Sketch* (engraved by R. Dorman), which shows a number of well-known local characters, and occasioned a comparison with James Gillray and Thomas Rowlandson.[26] Set in Blarney Lane with the Shandon steeple in the distance, the sketch features classical muses. Music is represented in burlesque by the blind fiddler, poetry by the ballad singer delivering a sorrowful lament, and painting by the hunchback painter decorating a tobacconist's sign. Prefiguring Father Theobald Mathew's attempts to dry out the citizens of Ireland, the sign 'Dry Lodgings' — warmth without the comfort of alcohol — ties in with a letter from McDaniel to Croker in which he describes a 'Muggery Club' in Sunday's Well (featuring men dressed as women).[27] In McDaniel's *Muses and Bacchus*, the blind peddlar, carrying papers marked 'Controversy' and a bottle of booze, also features in *Poeta Nascitur* as 'equally a disciple of the Muses and Bacchus'[28] The identity of this man is very likely Roger O'Connor, the errant patriot and eccentric.

Even when he declared for the arts, James McDaniel remained fascinated by science, a duality he sought to resolve through research into the nature of color and color compounds, lithography and etching, and a number of inventions involving signalling and telegraphing systems that he submitted to various bodies — all advanced for their time.[29] McDaniel was as friendly with the artists as he was with the antiquaries and scientists. His letters to Croker exhibit an idiosyncratic range of references, including examples of classical learning, native irony, Irish pronunciation, the construction of steam engines, military quickstep, the economy of phraseology heard in the criers of Cork set to music, how to sleep in two counties simultaneously, a 'God Save the King'–singing parrot, cross-dressing, the sound, sense, weight and measure of syllables, and myriad other whimsies of life.

In his letters to Richard Dowden, James poked fun at the Catholic Church and the Oxford Movement, Mariolatry, the Pope and the Papacy — the 'mirth and jollity' and other 'damn nonsense' of life. He planned a series, *The Nursery Rhimes of Mother Church,* which he kicked off with 'Volo Episcopare', illustrated with a sketch of a papal or ecclesiastical coat of arms, which takes swipes at Nicholas Patrick, Edward Bouverie Pusey and Cardinal Wiseman, and clerics climbing the greasy clerical poles to their Bishoprics (sung to the tune of 'Dance to your Mammy').[30]* As well as his own endeavors, James immersed himself in the creative and intellectual lives of his children. When the family moved to London in 1844, he lived with his daughter (and her husband and children) and his son Daniel, then establishing their reputations as artists.*

   *See Appendix 3

A CONTEMPTIBLE TRIFLE

In London, other than one painting, *The Bird's Nest* (1852), traces of James McDaniel's work go cold.[31] Perhaps. The appearance in 1849 of the second edition (no trace being found of the first) of what might well be a variation of his episcopal nursery rhymes, was published. In 1848, there appeared a much publicized, anonymous publication, *A Modern Visit from the Devil* (**Fig. 6 a-c**), by 'One in Babylon', published in pale blue wrappers, with ten illustrations by Daniel Macdonald. It caused much indignation.[32] Of the first edition, *The Era* wrote:

> We condescend in noticing this contemptible trifle, but as it is evidently published for the author, and at his own expense, and the ebullition of a conceited scribbler who can afford to pay for the printing of a few hundred copies, and indulges himself in circulating them, in the fond and erroneous belief that there is merit in his rhymes — moreover as they are advertised, and from taking nature of the title people may be induced to throw away sixpence in the purchase of the production, we give our candid opinion in reference to it. The scribe writes from 'Belgravia', and says, 'as the lines came into his head, so he wrote them' — this is saying but little for the head in question; the lines themselves show a want of every requisite but the art of spelling (the MS. was perfect in that respect) to entitle him to be styled a poet. He gives us a string of jingling rhymes, false rhymes, and lines that do not rhyme at all, such as two men out of three could talk off hand to please a child, but expressive of that would-be satirical disposition which is contemptible, because there is neither originality nor power belonging to it. Some half-witted idler and antiquated lounger seems to have done this. There is all the conventional slang of the club and dining room poet about it. We have not patience to select a sample; it is all alike vile in thought and construction, twaddle of the rankest kind, and pretension most disgusting. (October 15, 1848)

The following year, on the appearance of the second edition, *The Era* resumed:

> This is mere pretension, and therefore sorry stuff. The author would be a lampooner — half wag, half poet — a sly satirist and caustic censor — a modern Juvenal, or something of that kind, but he lacks all the necessary qualifications. Anybody now-a-days could scribble such bad rhymes and common place remarks as these … . His doggerel rakes up every hackneyed topic and event of the day, and that is all, for he neither points a moral, nor adorns a tale. The illustrations too are atrociously vile, even in intent; and this *'Modern Visit from the Devil'* is what the devil himself would be ashamed to own, because what no man of anything approaching talent would be capable of writing. We were about illustrating the truth of these remarks, but we have not patience to mark an extract for the printer. (July 1, 1849)

But worth purchasing it must have been, given that it went to a second edition. And the repetition of certain phrases, nine months apart, would suggest the same reviewer was on the case, or, just as likely,

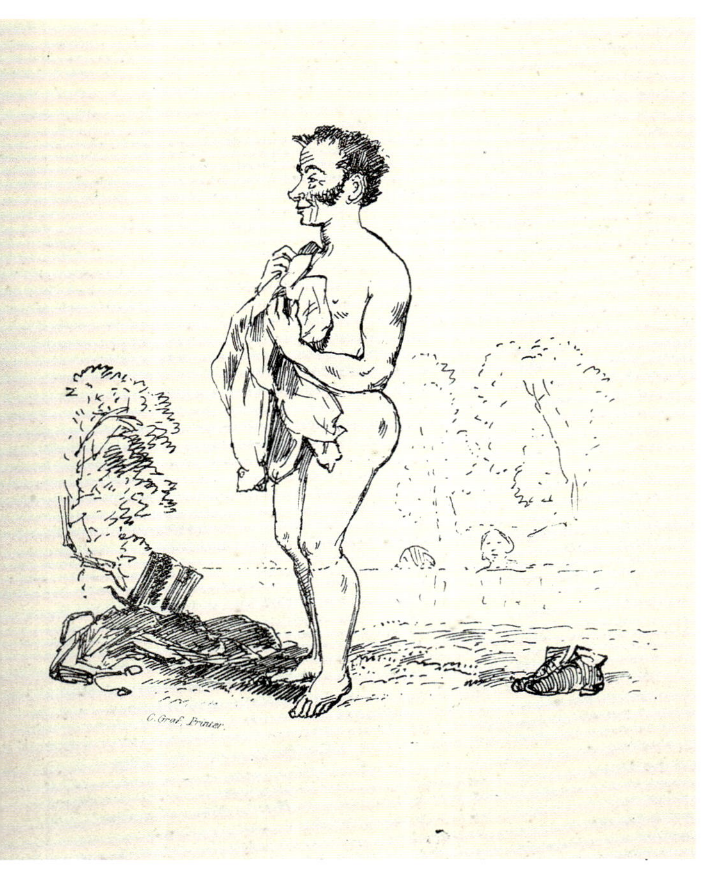

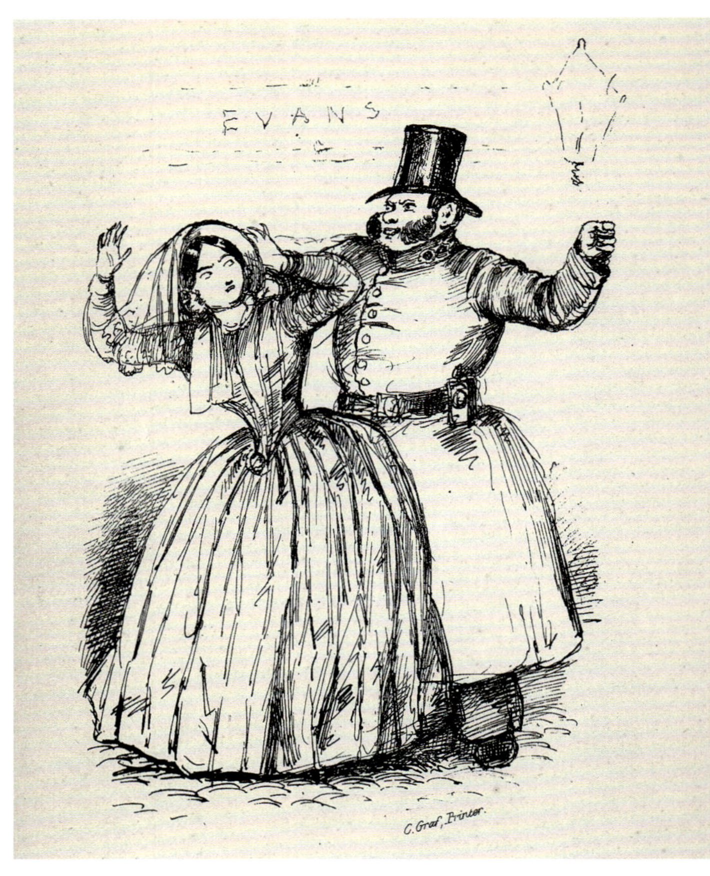

Figure 6 a–c

Images from One in Babylon's A Modern Visit from the Devil

Daniel Macdonald

London, 1849

that the author himself wrote the review to fuel controversy. That notion that James McDaniel (or one of the Fraserian set) was the author, becomes more plausible when we consider that the illustrator was Daniel Macdonald.

In the preface, the author notes 'the mildest asperient is sometimes very bitter, whilst many poisons are tasteless.' It is difficult to *précis* the poem, as it skitters with eccentric erudition from topic to topic, and person to person, including Sir Robert Peel, Lord John Russell, Lord Brougham / 'Lord Quixote of Vaux', Joseph Fussell, Pierre-Joseph Proudhon, François Guizot, Charlotte Corday, Daniel O'Connell, William Smith O'Brien and the Widow McCormack; the French Revolution and the Irish Rebellion, slavery, trafficking and emigration, Chartism, and the Oxford Movement, and so on. Behind the highly wrought satire, it is difficult to follow the narrative, laced with obscure references and allusions. It imagines the Devil nefariously infiltrating various elements of the empire: 'I summoned the Devil — and forthwith he came / But he said that of late he had alter'd his name … .[33] It pillories philosophers, artists, writers and prominent political figures. It takes on the higher echelons of the Catholic Church, especially Newman, Pusey and the Oxford Movement:

> *O Oxford! O Exeter Hall! O Hypocrisy!*
> *Respectable elders of Cant's aristocracy!*
> *O Bishops, O Big-wigs, O N-wm-an, O P-s-y,*
> *Let the world find ye out, if it can, and abuse ye,*
> *My glorious high-priests in church and in chapel,*
> *As ye pocket the price for which Eve stole her apple.[34]*

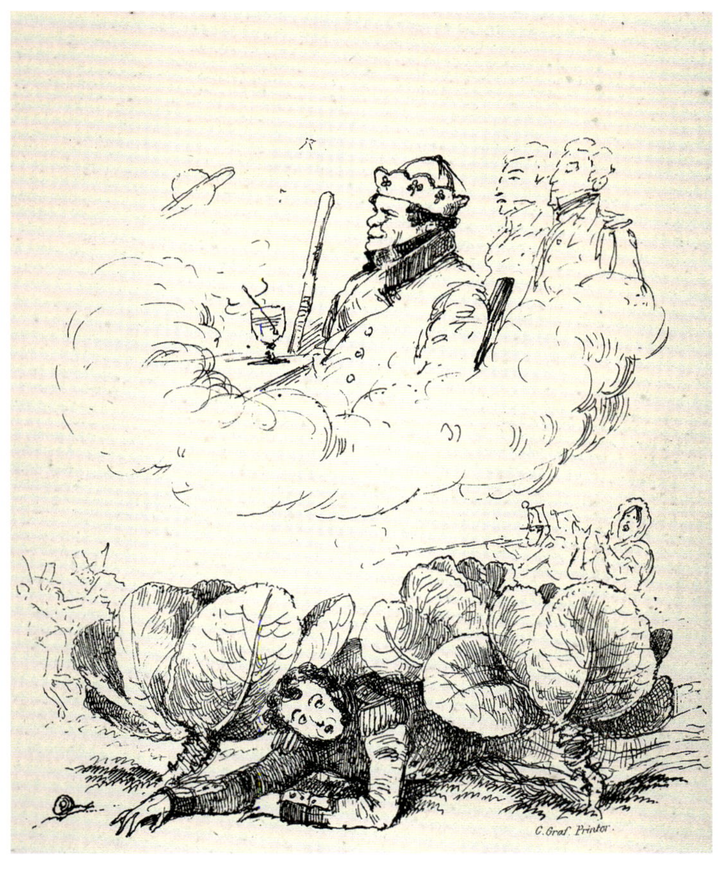

The Irish Chartist, Fergus O'Connor, features (son of Roger O'Connor, patriot polemicist, previously sketched by James McDaniel). Joseph Fussell (the veteran revolutionary) appears in the nude: 'A diminutive Chartist with Mammoth intentions — sanguinary as a flea; a kind of *Bottom* the weaver, in the farce of Universal Suffrage.'[35] However, only some of the illustrations are now recognizable: the finger wagging Lord Brougham; the skinny-dipping Joseph Fussell; the recently deceased O'Connell in his famous chariot (with grave robbers William Burke and William Hare riding pillion); and the unidentified man sketched by Macdonald at the Tracy Peerage case, the previous year. Undoubtedly hares were raised, gauntlets thrown down and scores settled, and Macdonald, as illustrator, was up for it all.

ARTISTIC FORMATION

It is against this colorful background that Daniel Macdonald emerges in his own right. Apart from home tuition, some local art classes and more than a smattering of science, literature, history, archaeology and anatomy acquired at the Cork Institution — the latter lectures given by Dr. John Woodroffe of the South Infirmary (where Macdonald's brother, John Denis, studied medicine) — he seems to have been self-taught. Woodroffe founded Cork's School of Anatomy in 1811. Gifted with great eloquence, he identified the link between anatomy and art as essentially *visual*, to which medical and art students responded with equal enthusiasm. His repertoire included lectures on the anatomy of expression, the philosophy of the human body, and phrenology (a subject on which James McDaniel also lectured, wrote and illustrated). Maclise, Samuel Forde and John Hogan attended demonstrations in anatomy at the Infirmary, and all spent hours copying casts. Woodroffe was a military surgeon who argued that an understanding of anatomy was critical to being both a good surgeon and a successful artist. Many of his students went on to become famous artists as well as anatomists and surgeons, painting and modeling the body, writing and illustrating anatomical atlases and saving lives through surgery. Among these was Joseph Maclise and John Denis Macdonald, brothers of Daniel Maclise and Daniel Macdonald, respectively. Woodroffe thus embodied the combined interests of the Maclises and Macdonalds — artistic, military, medical and scientific.

Daniel Macdonald's education, then, was one of happenstance. Early attempts at printmaking by father and son were hampered by the lack of a lithographic press in Cork. Moreover, the general lack of decent art materials in provincial Ireland also inhibited artistic development. But the young Macdonald had access to a number of private collections of Old Master paintings in and around Cork where he saw work by James Barry, Angelica Kauffman and Jacques-Louis David, owned by Lord Ennismore in Convamore, Cooper Penrose at Woodhill House, and George Newenham at Summerhill, amongst others. But it was undoubtedly the arrival in Cork of some 200 casts of Canova sculptures that transformed the education of the young artists of the city.

Viscount Ennismore (later Lord Listowel) was instrumental in organizing a gift of a fine collection of casts from the Antique for Cork in 1818. Pope Pius VII had them made under the supervision of the great Antonio Canova as a gift to Britain in gratitude for support in securing the return of treasures looted by Napoleon. When the Royal Academy declined them, Ennismore, a Member of Parliament, and then president of the Cork Institution, suggested that they should go to the Society for the Promotion of the Fine Arts, founded in 1816, where they were welcomed with enthusiasm. In the absence of a school of art at the time, their influence was inestimable. In August 1819, McDaniel wrote to Croker of copying from the casts, and the magnificent volumes of etchings donated by Ennismore, as well as attending Woodroffe's lectures.[36] With some Hibernian hyperbole, he went so far as to declare that the casts had a 'miraculous effect' on Cork, to the extent that 'the jarring discords in taste, politics, and religion were suspended'.[37] It was further argued that this incipient school of art in Cork would save young artists from having to go to London where

> in addition to the temptations with which every young person there is surrounded, an additional and great one, occurs in drawing from living models, before the morals are matured, and the mind annealed, so as to endure without warping or cracking, the ordeal to which it must be thus necessarily exposed.

It was also believed that the casts would encourage the new rich to invest in the arts, and he went on to suggest, rather optimistically, that arising therefrom:

> A trade new in Ireland would appear, which would afford subsistence to numerous artificers dependent on it. Men would return from fairs and markets bearing ornaments to their dwelling, amusing instruction to their families, with cheerfulness in their aspects, not as now filled to excess with these deleterious liquors, by which health and strength are destroyed, domestic union dissolved, cottages reduced to ruin and cheerfulness driven far away.[38]

Like Maclise, Forde and Hogan before him, Macdonald had access to this collection and so, in addition to anatomy, was able to study the human form aesthetically, a crucial factor in his formation as an artist. Such influence is evident in his work, especially if we consider the *Apollo Belvedere*, *Hercules* and *Laocoön* in the context of the mass, beauty and power of his striking male figures. Many writers, from Oscar Wilde to W. B. Yeats, perceived analogies between Greek and Celtic mythology (indeed Yeats believed that the classics were the builders of his soul).[39] The ultimate accolade for the collection, and the links between Ireland and classical antiquity, is found in Thomas Davis's influential essay, 'National Art,' in which he argues that the casts provided the basis for a new Irish school of painting, capable of building on the achievements of James Barry:

The casts … are perfect, they are the first forms from Canova's moulds, and embrace the greatest works of Greek art. They are ill placed in a dim and dirty room — more shame to the rich men of Cork for leaving them so — but there they are, and there studied Forde and Maclise, and the rest, until they learned to draw better than any moderns, except Cornelius and his living brethren.[40]

An added value was the Hellenism of some of these works in terms of their emotional power and sensuality, translated by Macdonald, as we shall see, into powerful images of Irish masculinity. [41]

Macdonald was drawn to two types of artists, those who demonstrated superior draftsmanship, and those who evinced humor, and he himself was often at his best when he combined the two. When David Wilkie saw Forde's drawings, he declared that they could have been painted by an Old Master; his monumental *Fall of the Rebel Angels* (1828), from John Milton's *Paradise Lost* — a source also mined by Macdonald — made a major impact. Nathaniel Grogan, on the other hand, was noted for his humorous genre scenes of Irish life (managing to support nineteen children on the proceeds); according to Nicola Figgis, his figures 'lack substance', being more interested in 'the representation of character and the injection of humour', his *Itinerant Preacher* (c. 1783) being a case in point.[42]

Three of the most talented artists of the time, Samuel Forde (1805–28), Samuel Skillin (1819–47) and Daniel Macdonald himself, died prematurely. Forde died at twenty-three years. Skillin and Macdonald were almost the same age and lived on the same street (their parents being fancy haberdashers and mercantile salesmen); they painted the same people; both were involved in the running of the Cork Art Union; and both moved to London in the 1840s (but Skillin returned to Ireland to die). He was described as a 'national ornament',[43] erudite, witty and sociable, as was Macdonald, and his death must have been a major blow. Skillin's boccaugh painting, *King of the Munster Beggars,* was exhibited alongside Macdonald's *Sídhe Gaoithe/The Fairy Blast* in 1842. Who knows what they might have achieved, and how they might have spurred each other on, had they lived.

It was predominantly in Maclise's footsteps that Macdonald traveled. Their early experiences were almost identical, although in one crucial regard they deviated. Maclise, coming directly under the influence from a young age of Sir Walter Scott, engaged in many imaginative recreations of the past, realistic in detail and romantic in conception, and although Macdonald made forays into literature, he did not share Maclise's medievalizing tendencies. Nevertheless, there was much to cleave these Macs of Cork. The Maclises, like the McDaniel/Macdonalds, claimed descent from the powerful Highland Scottish Macdonald Clan. Following an internal clan dispute, Maclise's family had converted from Catholicism to Presbyterianism. In Cork, dissenters and established church members worked together to counter Catholic influence. Both families (albeit for different reasons) took assumed names: the MacLeishs chose Maclise, and the Macdonalds temporarily chose McDaniel before reverting. Like the Macdonalds, the Maclises also had long associations with the British Army (particularly the medical wing). Maclise's father was at the Battle of Bantry Bay in 1798, facing the threat of invasion by French force and United Irish rebels led by Theobald Wolfe Tone, many of whom were also Presbyterian. Maclise's mother was from Bandon, Macdonald's from nearby Kilcolman. The relatively low social status of the Maclises led to their insistent efforts to distinguish themselves from the native Irish. When Maclise opened a portrait studio, it was on St. Patrick's Street, the street on which the McDaniels lived, and it was here too that young Daniel Macdonald opened his portrait practice, a few years after Daniel Maclise went to London. In a letter from James McDaniel to Croker in 1835, mention is made of a journey to be undertaken by McDaniel and Maclise (although we do not know if it ever transpired).[44]

Both Maclise and Macdonald, therefore, came out of the same Cork cultural milieu, and both fitted rapidly into the upper levels of London society, where Maclise, it would seem, extended the hand of friendship to the McDaniel/Macdonalds, just as Croker had supported him on his arrival in London in 1827. In Maclise's diary, McDaniel — described as a poet and a 'gifted brother of the brush' — was one of the few artists to be identified by name. [45]

Alongside many similar works, Maclise executed a painting of an artist selling a picture to an old Jewish cognoscente. The theme was derived from Lady Morgan's romantic biography of the seventeenth-century Italian painter, poet, patriot and philosopher, Salvator Rosa, published in 1824.[46] The biography followed her two-volume book on Italy which exposed the corruption of various Italian regimes, causing a major scandal: 'the kingdom of Naples exhibited a spectacle of rapacity and missrule in the government, and of misery in the people, which even unhappy Ireland, in her worst days, has perhaps never surpassed', she wrote.[47] She depicted the artist, Salvator Rosa, joining the banditti of Abruzzi, providing opportunities to draw parallels between Ireland and Italy, comparing Salvator to the Irish musician Turlough O'Carolan, for example. The wild landscape of Naples, and the rampant lawlessness, reminded her of the west of Ireland, indeed her own hero assumed many of the characteristics ascribed to romantic rebels in her Irish novels, as it would Macdonald's *Fighter*, for example. [48] Her work inspired many Irish artists, such as Maclise. Maclise selected a less dramatic scene than other artists: early in his career, Salvator sold paintings to *rivenditori* (dealers) who sold art from the Strada della Carità in Naples. Maclise's painting shows the handsome painter watching anxiously as the Jew studies his picture. His beautiful daughter, taking down the miser's moneybox, looks coquettishly at the artist. From the reviews, Daniel Macdonald's unlocated painting, *The Connoisseur in a Jew's Shop*, would seem to echo the Maclise. But, if so, the connection would appear to have been overlooked.[49] The painting was exhibited twice, once just before and once just after the artist's death, first in the National Exhibition of the Arts, Manufactures and Products, Cork (1852), and then in the Royal Institution, Manchester (1854).

At the first venue, the reviewer described:

> A gentleman of the old school, who seems to pride himself on being a connoisseur, is inspecting the merits of a picture in the studio of a dealer. A comely looking girl is seated in the foreground, and a Jew, with all the cunning of his race strongly marked on his countenance, seems to chuckle at the bargain he is about to effect. The subject is a matter of everyday life, but the story is told very effectively and forms a very attractive picture. (*Coleraine Chronicle,* June 26, 1852)

John Francis Maguire, Mayor of Cork, declared *The Connoisseur in a Jew's Shop* Macdonald's best painting:

> a clever satire on that pretentious class of artists, who discover 'the learning of Poussin and the Corregiecity [*sic*] of Correggio' in every work which is palmed by artful fabricators of the Old Masters upon their credulity. With some characteristic faults, especially a degree of harshness in colouring, this picture was full of merit, and told the story with great humour and effect. [50]

The *Southern Reporter and Cork Commercial Courier* considered it clever:

> representing one of the genus in question, criticizing with knowing air, a picture, just purchased by a friend, while the Jew 'manufacturer', behind with his tongue thrust in his cheek, and his laughing eyes, evinces his accurate appreciation of the judgment passed upon his 'furniture' piece — doubtless proclaimed by the critic to possess 'all the Corregiosity [*sic*] of Corregio'. (July 1, 1852)

But at the second venue, the *Manchester Courier and Lancashire General Advertiser* announced the painting 'a mistake':

> Jews, when they fancy they have got hold of a customer who is green and may be fleeced, do not go behind him to express their intention by pantomime to passers by, as the Jew is doing in this case. We cannot make out what the youthful female form in the foreground has to do with what is going on in the rear, though we suppose we are to look upon her as the Jessica of the story. The picture, however, is not to be wholly condemned, the connoisseur is well done; we see that he thinks he knows an original from a picture dealer's imitation, and is prepared to give the price asked 'if he likes the subject'. He occupies so much of the front of the work to be inspected, that his friend is fain to be satisfied with a glimpse in such a corner. The costumes are excellently given, and we mention it as a fair specimen of drawing and manipulation, but faulty in point of conception. (October 21, 1854)

There were many instances of shared subject matter, as well as a shared concern for draftsmanship between Maclise and Macdonald. In this case, given that the painting remains unlocated, the extent to which the Macdonald resembles the Maclise is hard to say. As previously mentioned, Maclise and Macdonald were personally invited to send works to the 1852 exhibition in Cork, and this then may have been an opportunity for the younger artist to pay tribute to the older one. If so, even though the reputations of the two painters were increasingly favorably compared at this time, none of the reviewers seem to have picked up on the Maclise / Lady Morgan association with Macdonald, although a tiny pen sketch by Macdonald including many elements of the Maclise painting would seem to confirm Macdonald's knowledge of the older artist's version of this work. [51]

Being professionally untrained would appear to have been more of an advantage than disadvantage in that it left Macdonald unconstrained by academic conventions, unfettering his considerable originality, and allowing influences other than iconographical ones to inspire him. It was this lack of convention that led perhaps to his study of Irish folklore, country life and customs through his father, and, with unusual acuity for his age and times.*

ANTIQUARIES

Joep Leerssen has identified an interesting inversion in nineteenth-century Ireland: rather than assuming a 'top-down civilizing offensive,' the high culture of the Anglo-Irish elite rejuvenated itself 'through an osmosis with the unspoilt, primitive energy and ebullience of native low culture': song and verse, folklore, and the Gaelic. [52] In the eighteenth century, a number of antiquarians, among them Charles O'Conor, General Charles Vallancey and Joseph Cooper Walker began the quest for an authentic Gaelic past. Their discovery of Irish folkloric material led to what Clare O'Halloran calls 'an early identification of the perceived link between popular culture and national identity formation, and of the inexorable connection of both of these to antiquity as a kind of valorizing agent.' [53] In the early nineteenth century, Thomas Crofton Croker (**Fig. 7**) travelled around Ireland, observing and collecting stories of the beliefs and superstitions, as well as the manners and habits, of the people. His interest and the interest of James McDaniel, and later of his son, in the world of Irish antiquity and folklore should be read as a kind of co-option of national identity. As Leerssen sees it:

> Popular native culture is one of remains and relics; it is yet another mode of establishing a filiation between the post-Union, indeed post-Famine present and the ancient roots of Irishness. It is also a reservoir of raw material to be mined and cultivated: to be relieved from its illiterate repository, the peasantry, who hoard this cultural heritage with spontaneous and unreflective naivety, without the necessary intellectual refinement to appreciate its higher interest. [54]

The new interest in antiquaries and vernacular culture did enormously important work in reclaiming Ireland's heroic past, although, as Leerssen suggests, most of the researchers were keen to distance themselves from the distasteful habits and habitats of the native Irish. The majority of folklorists were

    *See Appendix 2

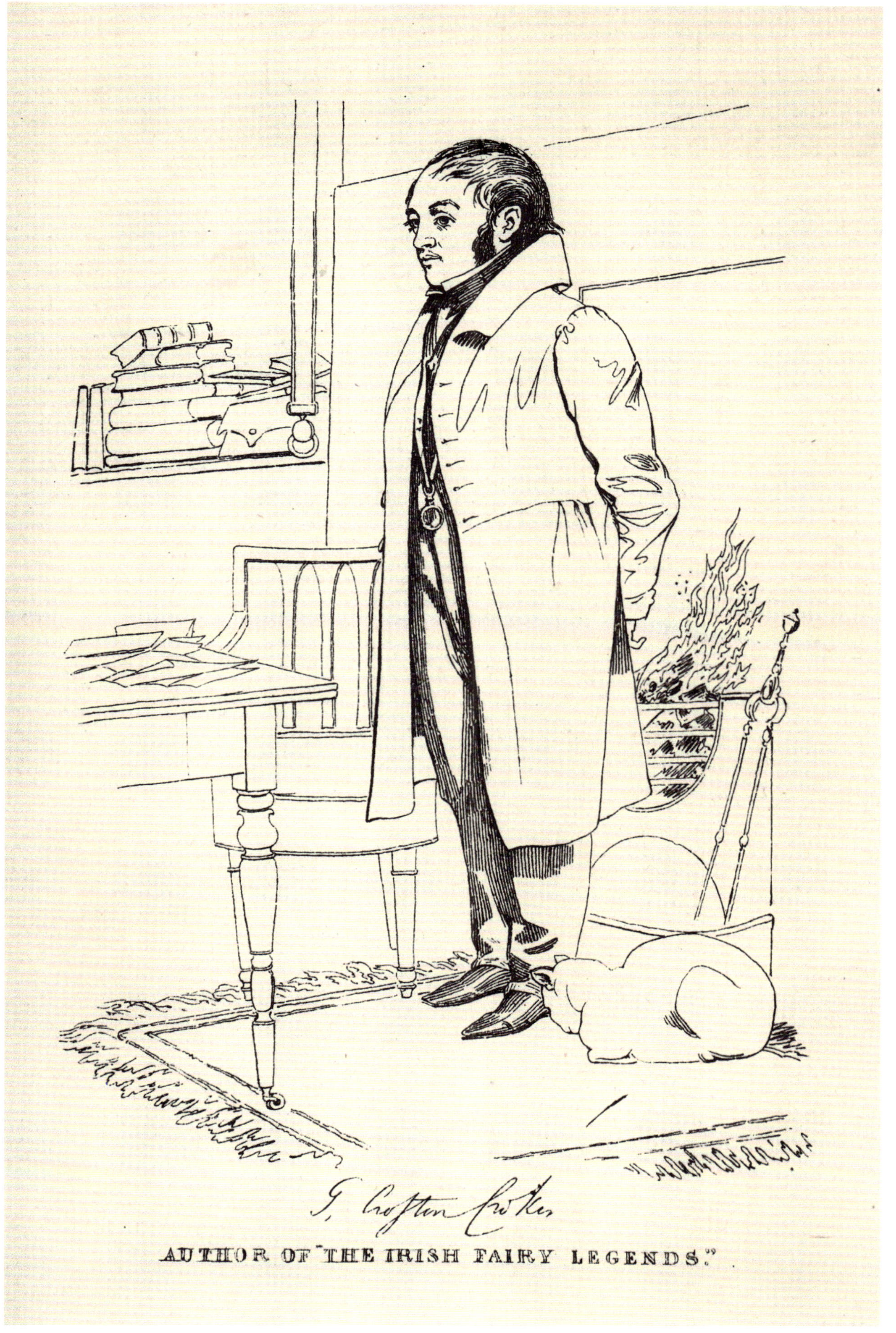

AUTHOR OF "THE IRISH FAIRY LEGENDS."

well-to-do Protestants, mainly descendants of settlers, from English or Scottish stock (like McDaniel), engaged in what might be called the first phase of the Celtic Revival. They were interested in the early history and culture of Ireland, developing also a parallel interest in the beauty and wildness of the Irish landscape. But while the most intrepid of the new researchers, Samuel Carter and Anna Maria Hall, may have done wonders for the tourist industry, they did not do much for the reputation of the Irish peasant. Catholic antiquarians took a different angle. By referencing early Christian and medieval learning prior to the Anglo-Norman invasion, Catholic antiquaries argued for the superior culture of the Gaelic elites, and a golden age of learning and culture, dismantled bit by bit since the 12th century. Each had a political subtext. Focusing on the vulgar ways of the lower orders provided justification for the 'civilizing' mission of the invader, while resurrecting the high culture of the Gael served to undermine that mission.

Approaching the art of Daniel Macdonald in this light, we find no such oppositions, but an open mind, an inclusive vision embracing Irish and English, Catholic and Protestant, lower and upper classes. His grasp of contested concepts in culture seems unusually advanced, and owes much to his relationship with his father, and his father's relationships with others, particularly Thomas Crofton Croker. Sir Walter Scott described Croker as 'little as a dwarf, keen eyed as a hawk, and of an easy and prepossessing manner'.[55] Less than five feet tall, skinny, and facially disfigured, Croker was a charming and important figure in antiquarian circles in London: a fellow of the Society of Antiquaries of London and the British Archaeological Society, the Society of Noviomagians (dedicated to archaeology and to 'sciences comical and gastronomical'), as well as numerous prestigious international societies. In 1824, he published his pioneering *Researches in the South of Ireland: Illustrative of the Scenery, Architectural Remains, and the Manners and Superstitions of the Peasantry* and, the following year, *Fairy Legends and Traditions*, the first collection of oral legends ever assembled in the British Isles.[56] The reactions to Croker's 'twilight tales of the peasantry' led to accusations of exaggeration and untruthfulness (and later plagiarism). Some welcomed him as recording local superstitions before their demise, others feted the prospect that his work would hasten the end of peasant culture.[57] However, Croker himself, dubbed the 'Honourable Member for Fairyland' was uneasy about the impression of Ireland that his work might convey to English audiences. In *The Keen of the South of Ireland: As illustrative of Irish political and domestic history, manners, music and superstitions* (1844), he explained that 'private and political feeling are often strongly infused in such compositions,' perhaps recalling the concluding section of the 1798 rebellion in his earlier *Researches in the South of Ireland*. Consequently, he restrained himself from publishing 'spirit-stirring' songs with political subtexts. His aim was to encourage his English readers to get to know the Irish, in order to better understand their grievances.[58] Croker's folkloric interests were initially inspired by the 'civilizing' impulses of the ethnographer, but his views evolved over this period, to the extent that by the 1840s he had embraced Daniel O'Connell's campaign for the repeal of the Act of Union. In time, as Leerssen put it, '[r]ustic popular culture [was] canonized into the very essence and bedrock of national identity'.[59]

It was no doubt by means of his father that Daniel Macdonald became aware of these learned debates. In time, Macdonald's own network included Edward Croft Murray, who owned quite a few of his drawings (now in the British Museum) including *Portrait of William Sandys Wright Vaux* [60] and

LONDON ENGAGEMENTS

A letter to the *Cork Examiner* (May 28, 1845) declared Daniel Macdonald 'a credit to our native city. His career in London is brilliant beyond any precedency, when his youth is taken into account, and the fact considered of his not being yet twelve months in England.' It reported that he had recently completed a commission from Prince Albert to paint his famous ox, 'justly admired for the spirit of its execution', no less than the girth of its subject. Additionally, it reported that Her Royal Highness, Princess Mary of Cambridge's portrait was executed by Daniel at Cambridge House, and was so admired that Macdonald was invited to St James's Palace to take the portrait of her brother, Prince George (and a second portrait of the Prince was done for the Grand Duchess Augusta of Mecklenburg-Strelitz, Queen Victoria's aunt). Moreover, 'for Mr Macdonald's rapid improvement and the intrinsic excellency of his portraits for truth and faithfulness in the first style of the art, orders are pouring in upon him from several of the most noble and illustrious characters in and about London.' The letter was signed 'a subscriber' and the address given was 3 Trafalgar Square. At the time, 3 Trafalgar Square was the headquarters of the Topographical Society, and from that address Edward Cresy, the celebrated antiquary, architect and civil engineer lived and worked, as did George Ledwell Taylor, also a Fellow of the Royal Society of Antiquaries, prominent architect and writer. Clearly Daniel had friends in this circle, further attested to by a number of portraits he executed of London antiquaries.

His success was also noted by the *Dublin Evening Packet* on May 17 and 25, 1845 (quoting the *Cork Constitution*). These describe Prince George, sitting in his full uniform as Colonel of the 17th Lancers, with star on breast, wearing the George. Reportedly, the royal family pronounced it 'the best ever taken of his royal highness', adding that the likeness of Princess Mary had 'elicited high encomiums from her illustrious parents for its truthfulness and finish.'

By June 1845, the upper echelons of the aristocracy were queuing for him. In one week he had sittings from the Marchioness of Anglesea; Lady Lambton, Louisa, Countess of Durham, Mary Montagu, Countess of Sandwich and Lady Sanders, one time Ladies of the Bedchamber to Queen Victoria; Lady Douro; Countess Rosebery, the Honourable Anne Margaret Anson; Lord Stanley's daughter; Princess Mary, Duchess of Gloucester and Edinburgh, wife of Prince William Frederick, fourth daughter of George III, Lady Turner; and Lady Georgiana Bloomfield, friend and maid of honor to Queen Victoria, writer of court memoirs and watercolor painter; and Prince George of Cambridge. By any standards an extraordinary achievement for a young Irish artist. So far, no trace has been found of most of these works, but around this time, Queen Victoria herself acquired a drawing by Macdonald, *Going Home after a Funeral* (1842) (Royal Collections).[1]

Further afield, he executed portraits of *Thomas Dimsdale; Lord Godfrey William Wentworth Boswell Macdonald, 4th Lord Macdonald (180963); Sir William Mordaunt Sturt Milner, 4th Bart.; Seymour Vallall Hale Monro;* and *Charles James Hale Monro*, amongst others.

Monday

Lady Lambton   Countess Rosebery   Lady Sanders

Tuesday

Lady Sanders   Prince George of Cambridge St James' palace   Mrs Oliviers

U140/E/65/3

Wednesday

Duchess of Gloster   Lady Sandwich   Duchess of Montrose

Thursday

Miss Sandys   Lady Turner   Duchess of Montrose

Friday

Honble Capt Grey Queens Palace Equerry   Lady Turner   Honble Miss Mitford

Saturday

Honble Capt Gray   Lady Rosebery   Lady Bloomfield

Engagements for this Week
June 23d 1845

James McDonald
Artist

[1] Although signed 'James Macdonald', the engagement list for June 23, 1845 was clearly Daniel's, given what we know from other sources of these sitters, Richard Dowden Papers, Cork City and County Archives, Ref. IE CCCA/U140.

Portrait of Edward Jesse (1844) (National Portrait Gallery, London), attesting to his standing among the antiquarians of London. And indeed the young painter's connections, drawing on his father's connections, to the upper echelons of London society were extensive and impressive.

A regular correspondence between James McDaniel and Croker took place after the latter's departure from Cork for London in 1818. From as early as 1819, McDaniel talked of joining Croker and made several forays to London for intellectual sustenance, perhaps testing the idea of a move there for himself: 'I have such an irresistible propensity for scientific pursuits, and am such an ardent admirer of the fine arts', he wrote, noting that London offered more than Cork in both regards. But the arrival of Daniel and three other children put a halt to his gallop.[61] James sent Croker many fascinating 'fragments Irlandais', and 'articles' for publication, to be used at Croker's discretion.[62] When Croker became an established scholar in antiquarian circles in London, he published songs and ballads for the Percy Society, many supplied by McDaniel (who remained unacknowledged). Although the longer 'articles' have not been found, McDaniel's letters abound with observations that appear with uncanny fidelity to the originals in Croker's work.[63] Even James's daughter Jane offered material to Croker *ad libitum*.[64]

McDaniel's lasting influence on Croker can be seen in his contributions — quoted at times almost verbatim from his letters — to the pioneering *Researches in the South of Ireland*. The subject of 'salutations' for example, begins with McDaniel writing to Croker in 1820: 'The custom of saluting with a benediction is almost exclusively practiced in Ireland from time immemorial. It had been an eastern custom … .' Five years later, Croker's *Researches* reads: 'The custom of greeting with a benediction is almost exclusively practiced in Ireland from time immemorial. It is perhaps of eastern origin …' McDaniel's letter continued:

> Persons on a journey through Ireland (most commonly in the morning or at the approach of night) are saluted in expressive terms peculiar to the Irish language, such as 'God and Mary attend you'. One word generally conveys several ideas and in this instance the verb implies such parental affection as a child expressed from a fond father or mother. If a traveller is apprehensive of danger, the benediction varies with 'safe home to you', such a safety also includes perfect health and divine protection.

Croker, in turn, resumed:

> Persons on a journey are saluted with various and peculiar phrases … early in the morning or on the approach of night you hear such as 'God speed you' and such as 'God and the blessed Virgin attend you'. … if the traveller has to apprehend danger on his route, the expressions are more energetic, as 'Safe home to you by the help of God' …[65]

Croker's account of how '[o]n the last night of the year, a cake is thrown against the outside door of each house by the head of the family, which ceremony is said to keep out hunger during the ensuing one; and the many thousand practical illustrations of the fallacy of this artifice have not yet succeeded in producing conviction of the same' also comes directly from a McDaniel letter to Croker.[66] Many of

McDaniel's accounts of Popery, superstition and Irish customs were transcribed almost exactly into *Researches*. McDaniel was especially interested in superstition and made some effort to explain its origins:

> In a savage state, man is degraded below the brute creation by superstitions which are both sanguinary and absurd … . Where popery prevails, as in Ireland, the various denominations of christianity may be classed into two general bodies, the Catholic (so called) and the Protestant; a prohibition of the general use of the scriptures in the one denominaton and the privilege of free enquiry in the other accounts for the surprising differences between vulgar Protestants and Papists of the same community.

Error in religious views leads to practical error in common life as in the instance of indisposition the Protestant can so suit cause to effect. He resorts to medicinals while the poor Catholic looks to charms for deliverance, which never staggers his faith even if it deceives his expectations.[67]

In *'Keens and Death Ceremonies'*, Croker's tale of a woman giving a porringer to some beggars so that her deceased child would not go without in the next world, is also taken directly from McDaniel. And Croker's 1824 account of how the clay from the graves of priests noted for their sanctity was 'resorted to' and the clay mixed with water and drank for the cure of various diseases, derives from an 1820 McDaniel letter to Croker.[68] At times, McDaniel is concise, at others discursive. His description of 'boccaughs', for example, 'wandering lame beggars as the term imports, [who] receive potatoes for charity and retail their superabundance of alms, custom warrants them the use of a bed and other accommodations' was, in this instance, elaborated upon by Croker, who went on to describe mutilated mendicants, who led an unsettled, wandering lifestyle. Some 'boccaughs' were known to have literary accomplishments, and they also functioned as match makers and arbiters of rural disputes. Croker, however, occasionally demonstrates a more jaundiced view of the Irish peasantry than McDaniel, commenting in the case of boccaughs on the venality of many healthy men who assume 'the ragged garb [and] crave the privileges of the impotent and aged.'[69] Croker's examples of 'Hibernian importance', including the residents of mud cabins speaking of their 'drawing rooms', or 'the road through their farms,' are more condescending that anything found in McDaniel.[70]

In his borrowings from McDaniel, Croker went so far as to narrate a story told to him by friend, as if he had overheard it himself:

> I remember once overhearing a contest between a poor man and his wife respecting the burial of their infant. The woman wished to have the child laid near her own relation, which her husband strongly opposed, concluding her attachment to her friends was superior to her love for him, but he was soon convinced by his wife's argument, that as her sister had died in childbirth only a few days previously, she would afford their poor infant suck, which nourishment it might not have if buried elsewhere.[71]

Croker's appropriation of the contributions of others to *Fairy Legends* became an issue, and subsequently raised questions over his work. His assertion that the book appeared 'after sundry adventures with Whiteboys, in caves and out of cabins, upon hill tops, with bootmakers and broguemakers, with pilgrims and pedlars', was as far-fetched as some of the stories themselves.[72] More problematic was the description of Croker as only its 'editor' by one of the eminent contributors, S. C. Hall; this is certainly true of the second edition when, on Croker's losing the original manuscript, Hall, William Maginn, Joseph Humphreys, [John?] Pigot, Thomas Keightley and Charles Dodd rewrote most of the stories.[73] However, in his review, Maginn specifically declared that Croker 'has been very candid in acknowledging his obligations to others': 'This is a little book, about little people, by a little author, of the height of Tom Moore — full of little stories … a book in short, all the persons and things connected with which are little, except the good humor and the research; both of which are great.'

Maginn went on to insist that the stories were ancient and universal, but their originality lay in the telling, 'with a true Hibernicism of tone and manner.'[74] Curiously, Croker did not put his own name on the first edition of *Fairy Legends*, which he *had* written, in keeping with the spirit of the oral transmission of knowledge and narrative, and the collaborative nature of folklore collection. However, he did claim authorship of subsequent editions, much of which he had *not* written himself, and he certainly pocketed the money, as he also did in the case of *Researches,* notwithstanding the extensive contribution of McDaniel and others.

Plagiarism was a particularly controversial issue at the time, manifesting itself variously as tribute, parody, mimicry, and hybridity, as well as downright venality. Even 'anti-plagiarism', or the claim that a derivative work was superior to the original, thereby supplanting it in importance, was rife. The Fraserians delighted in such sophistry, and Maginn and Mahony were particularly adept. Over-hasty questioning of their plagiaristic practices, therefore, seems to have been applied retrospectively. Even self-plagiarism was not unknown, or reviewing of one's own work, as suggested above.

A fascinating letter from McDaniel to Croker features the grotesque story of how ignorant parents can distinguish their own child from a changeling insinuated into the house by the fairies, the real child having been removed to be a playmate or, if older, a nurse of fairy children. This is directly transcribed by Croker:

> Fairies are diminutive spirits that bewitch children & when children decline their parents suppose that they are substitutes deposited with them in exchange for their offspring. Such children are frequently placed on a shovel and carried to a dunghill, where they are supposed to lie for a certain time with a view to discern whether this is the case. When children are thus exposed to cold they conclude that a natural disorder had caused the symptoms of decay & they treat the child with more tenderness from the notion that if the child had been a fairy that it would not brook such indignity.[75]

Intriguingly, Croker called some of the protagonists in *Fairy Legends* 'MacDaniel'.[76] 'The Two Gossips', for example, tell the story of a young couple from Cork who had a 'fine, wholesome-looking child' that the fairies were determined to have to themselves, while putting a changeling in its place: Mrs.

MacDaniel had a gossip (friend) who, returning home one evening, encountered so many eddies of dust on the road that she 'had pains in her bones with dropping so may *curchies* (courtesies)' in order to mollify the fairies who were about. As she muttered 'God keep all here from harm!', she saw one of the MacDaniel windows open and 'her gossip's beautiful child without any more to do handed out', she knew not by whom. She grabbed the child and brought him home with her, and returned the next morning to find Mrs. MacDaniel complaining that 'her' child was fractious and nothing would quiet it. The gossip was delighted to tell her that the problem child had been left by the fairies, but she had managed to save the real child, whom she would now reunite with its mother. The name, the changeling story, the eddies and the salutations all come from McDaniel, and indeed, as we shall see, recur when his son, Daniel, gives visual life to such beliefs. It is as if McDaniel's own words become 'changelings' in Croker's hands. Incidentally, the story (if in fact written by Croker) appeared when Daniel Macdonald was a boy of four or five years. According to Angela Bourke, redeemed changelings were often thought to return with enhanced attributes and skills, indicative of accomplishment to come. In this light, it is tempting to read 'The Two Gossips' as Croker's prophecy for Daniel's future success.

THE HORRORS OF THE ROAD

Daniel Macdonald's painting, *Sídhe Gaoithe / The Fairy Blast* **(Fig. 8)**, first exhibited in 1842, can perhaps best be seen as a visual rendition of the researches of his father and Croker in the underworld of the peasantry. The painting depicts a desolate mountain scene in the dead of night, in which a 'huddle' flee from some unseen terror. Led by a bare-footed girl, holding down her skirt against a violent gust of wind, they move in unison, each intent on their own flight through the narrow mountain pass. Shoulders to the wind, eyes anxious, they press on, driven by some sinister force **(Fig. 9)**.

Sídhe Gaoithe / The Fairy Blast was accompanied by an anonymous verse designed to send shivers up the spine, anchoring its effects in first hand as well as scholarly responses:

> *The dreaded Sídhegaoidhe marks enchanted ground,*
> *Where Fairy Elves with vicious pranks abound.*
> *The timid Peasant fearfully moves on,*
> *All apprehensive of some fate unknown.*
> *A train of hidden ills invade his head,*
> *From Fairy-strokes with visitation dread.*
> *Circles of dust in sportive eddies play.*
> *Anon a twirling column blocks the way.*
> *Brisk miniatures of men, a rambling host,*
> *Their motions active as the flying dust.*
> *Until perchance a current sweeps from view,*
> *The mystic cloud, and leaves him to pursue*
> *The journey homeward, to his safe abode,*
> *There to sum up the horrors of the road.* (Fragment)

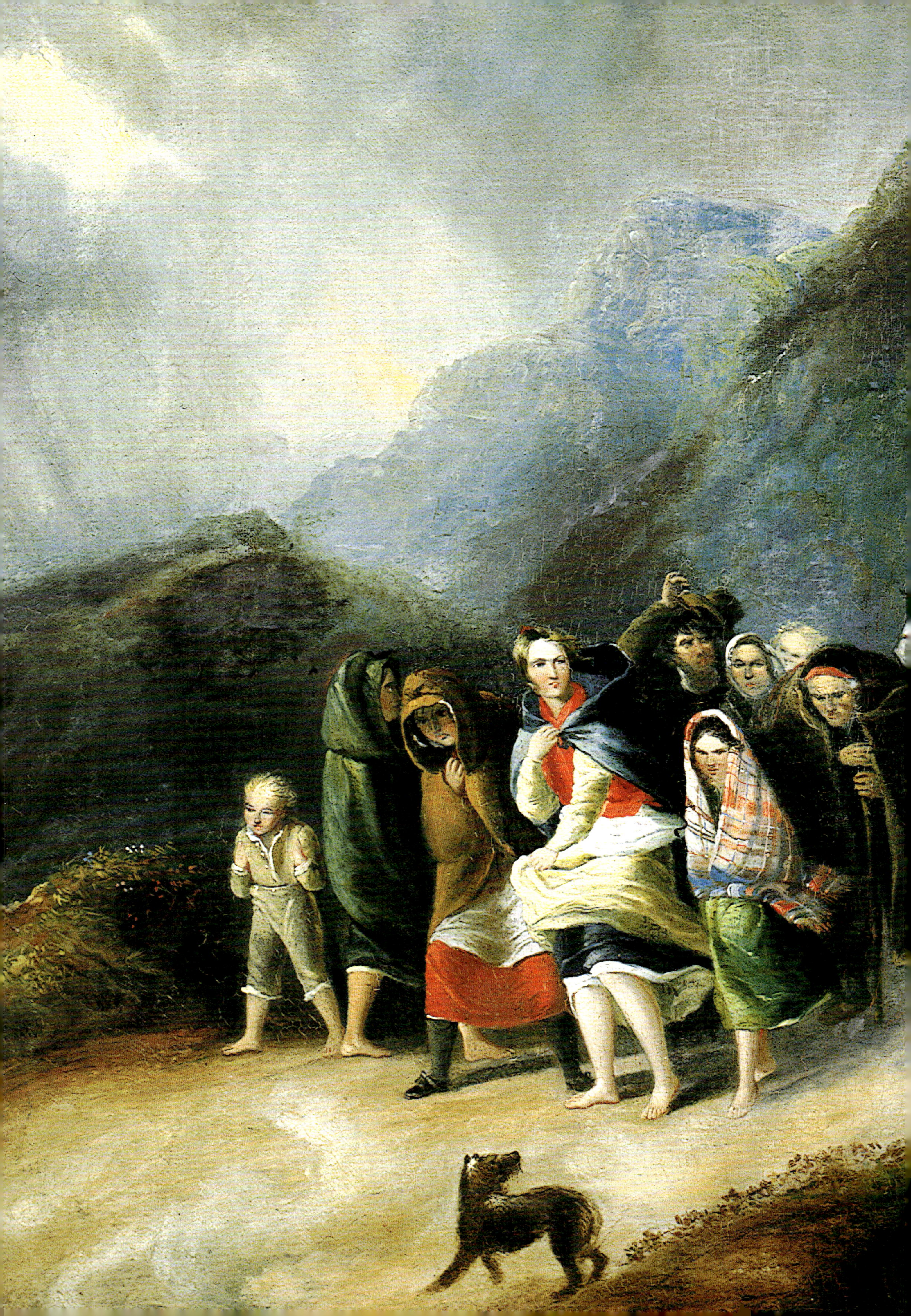

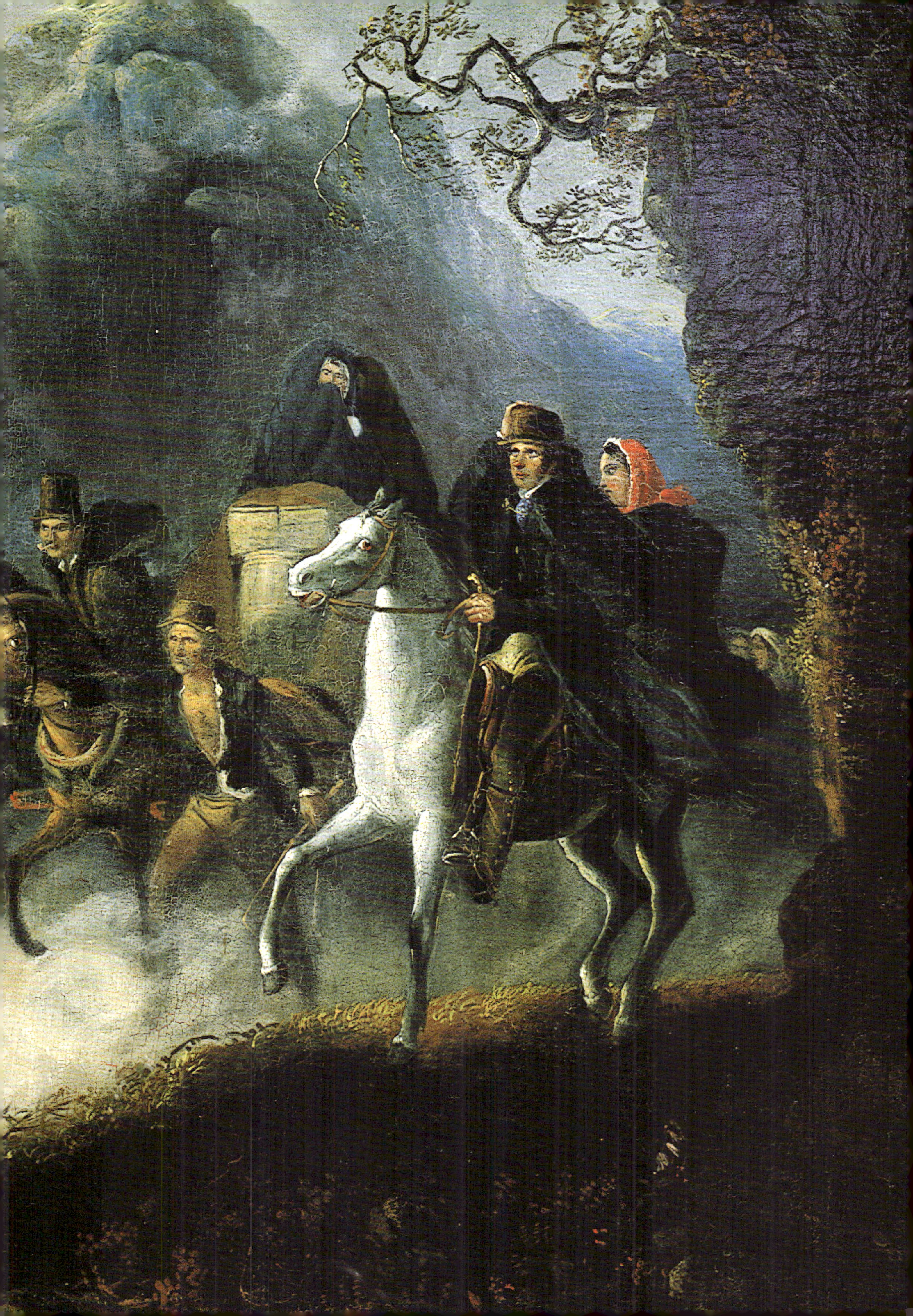

Figure 8 [CROPPED]
PREVIOUS PAGE

Figure 9 [DETAIL]

*Sídhe Gaoithe/
The Fairy Blast*

Daniel Macdonald

1842

The women in the scene are shawled or cloaked in the West Cork manner, the men hatted according to their social station. They are not, however, treated as an undifferentiated mass of ignorant peasants. Surprisingly, the group comprises individuals from across the classes travelling together: landlord, farmer and wife, and tenants on foot who, despite the reality of deprivation endured even before the Famine, look reasonably well fed and clothed. All are subject to the same evil force. The group have travelled from the other side of the mountain, having attended a fair or pattern, it would seem, laden with a barrel and boxes, intended for some communal event, a wedding, or a wake, perhaps. Unusually, two years later, in 1844, Macdonald revisited the composition, producing a sketch, based on the painting, that post dates the painting. *The Shower* (**Fig. 10**) may have a more benign title, but the sense of anxiety and threat prevails.

Stories of 'spirits' haunting strategic points on journeys home in the dark, especially from local fairs, were common. In the poem, references to the dreaded *'sídhegaoidhe'* (in modern Irish spelling: *sídhe gaoithe*) and 'enchanted ground' would have done nothing to dispel the fear that sinister beings were about. In Irish folklore, the effect of certain places, such as the *fód mearbhaill* (the stray sod), was to send a person reeling if one stepped on it, and this is closely related to the *féar gorta*, or hungry grass. Such lore was part of peasant consciousness, and while it speaks of primitivism, and suggests a credulous people, it also allowed multi-layered narratives to function at different levels: unfettering anxieties, providing opportunities for behavioral guidance, or even as omens foreshadowing future events. Moreover, as Sir William Wilde put it 'these matters of popular belief and folks'-lore, these rites and legends, and superstitions, were after all, *the poetry of the people*, the bond that knit the peasant to the soil'.[77] Such beliefs, according to Angela Bourke, marked 'symbolic boundaries, which more widely facilitate the organization of knowledge and thought outside the culture of literacy.'[78] Bourke also suggests that in painting such a scene, the artist:

> combines vernacular verbal art with ideas of the sublime and the Gothic to represent a society in tension, divided by language and culture. Mostly barefoot and female, arguably also impulsive and improvident, because shown empty-handed, the poorest people here have placed themselves almost under the horses' hooves. The leading woman's bare legs and head emphasize her vulnerability and sexuality, but she and her people endanger their more prosperous neighbors and impede the progress of the virile landlord figure the artist has made central: the only one who shows no fear. His painting anticipates the rhetoric of the Famine, and hints at how it came to be remembered and forgotten.[79]

In this vein, it is worth recalling Susan Sontag's argument that images can become 'memories' of events that have yet to occur.[80] Although painted before the Great Famine, this painting may thus be seen as a harbinger of horror ahead, in keeping with the prognostications of William Carleton's Black Prophet, who beseeched:

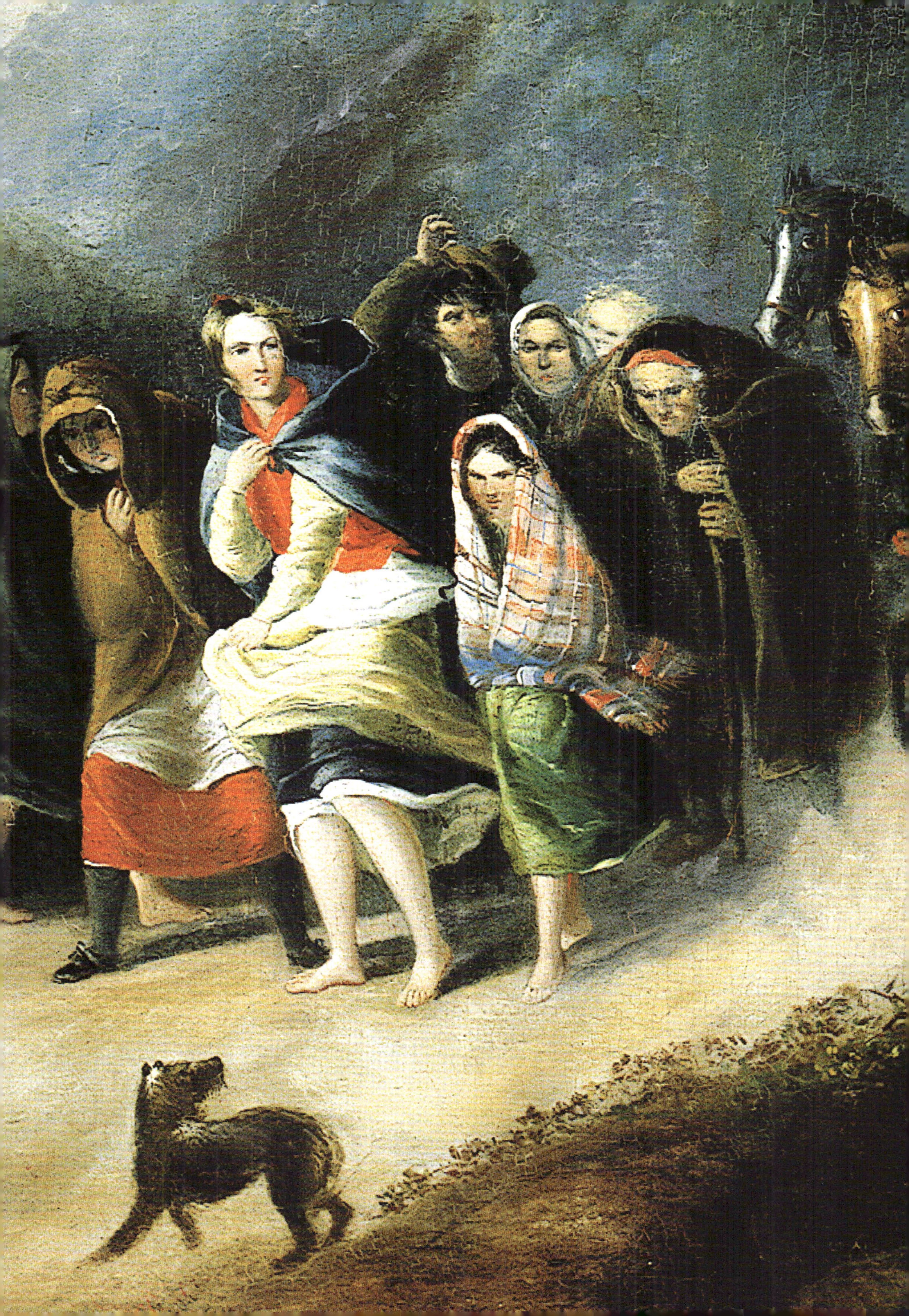

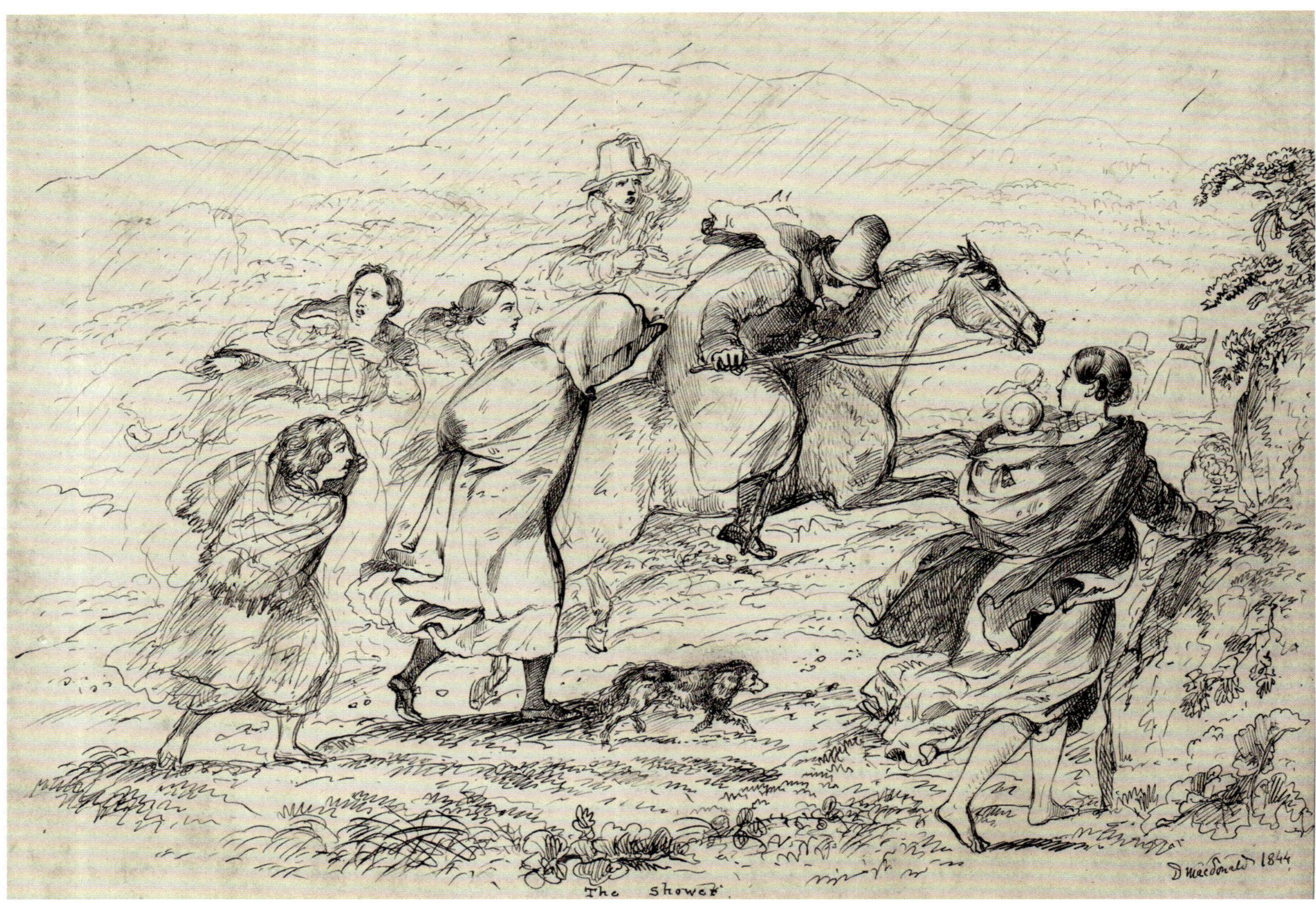

Figure 10

The Shower

Daniel Macdonald

1844

Look about you, and say what is it you see that doesn't foretell famine–famine–famine! Doesn't the dark, wet day, an' the rain, rain, rain foretell it? Doesn't the rottin' crops, the unhealthy air, an' the green damp foretell it? Doesn't the sky without a sun, the heavy clouds, an' the angry fire of the west foretell? Isn't the airth a page of prophecy, an' the sky a page of prophecy, where every man may read of famine, pestilence, an' death?[81]

A *sídhe gaoithe* is both a rush of wind or whirlwind, and *síodh-ghaoth*, a more sinister fairy wind or blast; the terms sound the same, and their meanings have conflated. In the poem accompanying the painting, references to the 'vicious pranks' and 'circles of dust' tell of a host of fairies accosting a group of travelers in the night. *Sídhe gaoithe* also speaks of crops 'blasted' by disease; after 1845, 'blast' took on a new and deadly meaning in the face of the blight, the fungus — *Phytophthora infestans* — that devastated the country, and which became, as we have noted, the subject of the most famous painting by Macdonald, that of a famine scene. Expressions of folklore are traditionally confined to oral narration; alternative expressions are rare, making Macdonald's painting all the more fascinating. In its lived form, folklore allowed people to speak obliquely of events, or conditions, or states of mind that might have been difficult to articulate by other means, and the same goes for the adaptation of literary subjects in paintings.[82]

Although invisible to the eye, Irish peasants believed (more than disbelieved) in 'the little people', and considered neither their diminutive size nor their euphemistic names any protection against their malevolence. Fairies were thought to make their presence felt at times of change, mostly at night, and as far as possible from human observation. Country people would have avoided traveling under such conditions, and the eerie scene in Macdonald's painting perhaps vindicates their fears. The little boy looks as if he has been electrified by some force from beyond. The old women are heavily shrouded, the young girls — showing their bare legs — relatively exposed. There were many stories, as noted above, about boys being kidnapped, and young women taken as fairy wet-nurses to be replaced by cantankerous changelings, thus reinforcing social restrictions on women and children being in remote places at night — a theme famously revisited by William Butler Yeats in his 'Stolen Child' (1886) with its haunting refrain: *For the world's more full of weeping/Than we can understand …*

The lines appended to Macdonald's painting have not been identified, but whoever wrote them (perhaps Macdonald himself, or his father) had a good knowledge of the fairy lore of Ireland. The specific scene seems to allude to a passage in Croker's *Researches in the South of Ireland* (1824) — much of which, as we have seen, derived from Macdonald's father):

> An eddy of dust, raised by the wind, is attributed to the fairies journeying from one of their haunts to another; on perceiving which, the peasant will obsequiously doff his hat, muttering, 'God speed ye, God speed ye, Gentlemen;' and returns it to his head, with the remark, 'good manners are no burthen,' as an apology for the motive, which he is ashamed to acknowledge. Should he, however, instead of such friendly greeting, repeat any short prayer, or devoutly cross himself, using a religious response, the fairy journey is interrupted, and if any mortals are in their train, the charm by which they were detained is broken, and they are restored to human society.[83]

In the painting, the gust of wind whips around and is watched intently by the women, while the man in the middle and the man on the white horse lift their hats as the blast passes **(Fig. 11)**. None seem to bless themselves, although they may be silently praying. The reference in Croker's *Researches* to the 'shame' associated with superstition is interesting. In the center foreground, the man with red skullcap, just behind the smaller girl, wears the cloak of a rebel (fitted with a device to hold a folded pike). Irish peasants may be superstitious, but his presence suggests, they do not necessarily accept their social fate, any more than supernatural tidings. Opposing hostile forces was a matter of rural pride, whether it be fairies, landlords, or the forces of law and order.

Macdonald's large canvas has visualized this with extraordinary perspicacity, and the *Southern Reporter and Cork Commercial Courier* (September 15, 1842) picked up on its impressive grasp of peasant life in some detail:

> This picture illustrates one of our rural superstitions — a remnant of the Pagan mythology of the early days of Ireland. It represents a group of peasantry in a mountain pass, assailed by a whirlwind of dust, supposed by them to indicate a fairy progress, and sometimes a

Figure 11 [DETAIL]

*Sídhe Gaoithe /
The Fairy Blast*

Full painting
on pages 38–39.

fairy combat: — the onslaught of two rival factions of the 'good people'. The deprecatory 'God speed ye gentlemen' of the credulous countrymen accompanies the dusty movement, and thereby they hope to avoid the evils of 'the blast', or the crimping which substitutes a sickness-wasted denizen of fairyland for a hale inhabitant of our own nether regions. Mr M. has well caught up the spirit and character of such an incident and produced a very attractive picture. There is a judicious gradation in his grouping, and his tone is generally excellent. Some of the figures are purely intensely Irish, from the brawny open-chested peasant of the center group to the smug mounted farmer on his left, who evidently bids God speed to 'their honours', as they whirl past him.

The disposition of sixteen people in motion across an imposing landscape, alternately illuminated by flashes of lightning and shrouded in the swirling dust, in the vertiginous mountains of west Cork, is compelling, but the same reviewer also noted what it considered some technical defects in the handling:

> The background, a mountain elevation, seems to us to overhang rather much: the distance in fact not being well kept and the aerial perspective to be defective. The near tints of some portions of the middle groups strike us also as a little crude and the yellow in the drapery of his principal female figure requires certainly to be toned down, in as much as the harmony of colouring is injured by it; but these are minor defects, whilst the whole, we regard Mr. Macdonald as a young artist from whom we have high expectations.

Pre-Famine belief swayed from the pagan to the religious. According to Charles Townshend, priests 'waged a deliberate or unconscious kind of theological pacification campaign to drain the energy out of popular beliefs in magic, defiant celebrations of, and wild displays of quasi-pagan faith', but the ideological cleansing of Irish popular culture, whether by Anglo-Saxon Protestant folklorists, or the increasingly powerful Catholic clergy, lingered long into post-Famine Ireland.[84]

A FATAL TRYST

In his early twenties, Macdonald took on a number of Shakespearean scenes, and in 1843, tackled John Milton's *Comus* (that same year, Maclise had participated in a trial, commissioned by Prince Albert to decorate the new garden pavilion in Buckingham Palace with frescoes based on *Comus*). Such literary compositions typically put young artists through their paces. Macdonald's efforts remain untraced, but there is an intriguing picture *Figures by a Coffin — a Scene from 'The Collegians'* **(Fig. 12)** that would appear to fit this genre.

The painting was acquired as based on the novel, *The Collegians* (1829), written in the year of Catholic Emancipation, by Gerald Griffin, who died in 1840, the year Macdonald executed the painting. *The Collegians* was derived from a true story which became a *cause célèbre* in Ireland In 1819, Ellen Hanley, a beautiful peasant girl (and orphan), was seduced by a squireen, John Scanlan, a lieutenant in the Royal Marines, and entered into a form of marriage (some said Scanlan had someone dress as a priest to perform the sham ceremony). Six weeks later, he wanted out (his mother had 'a match' for him that would bring a

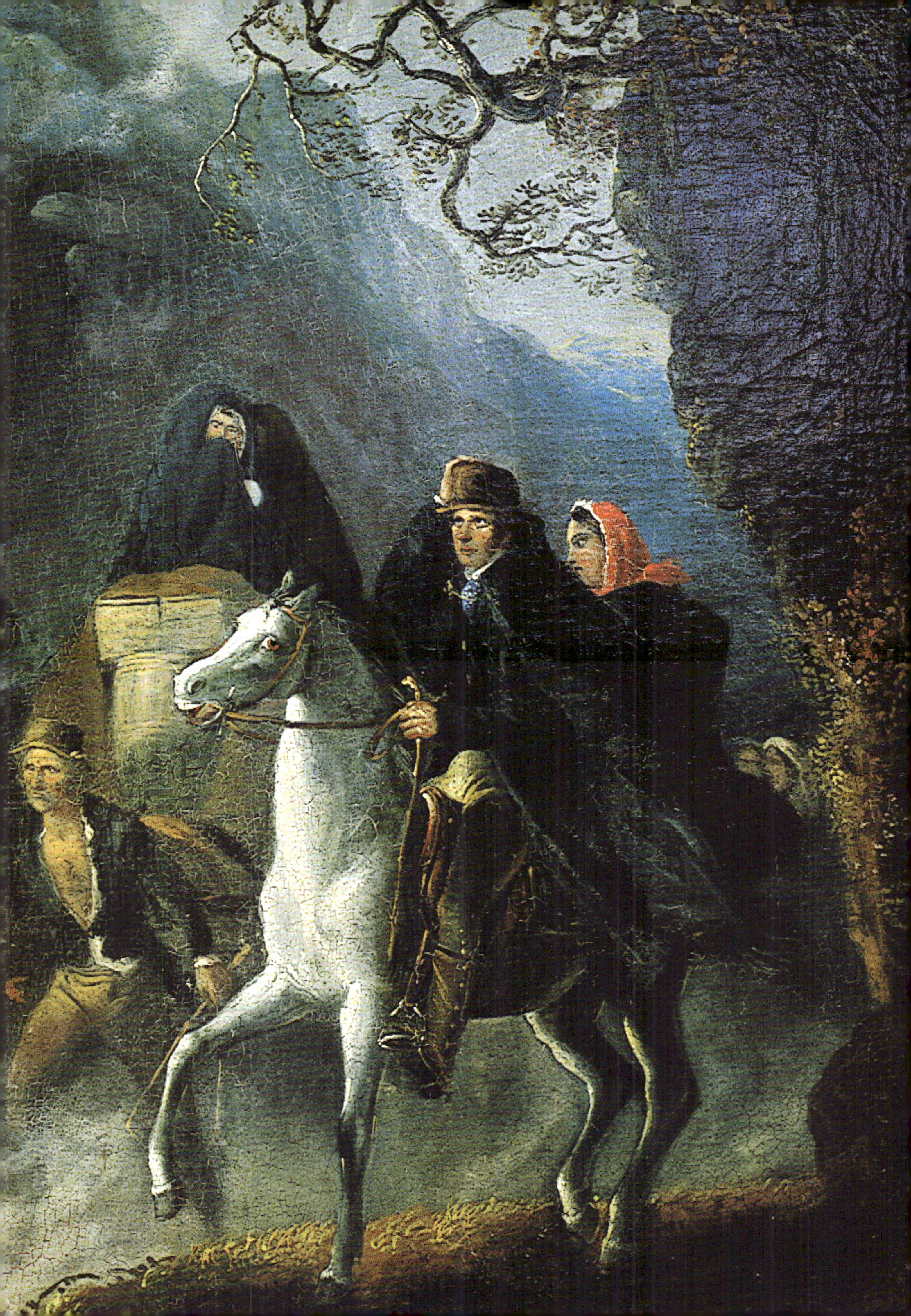

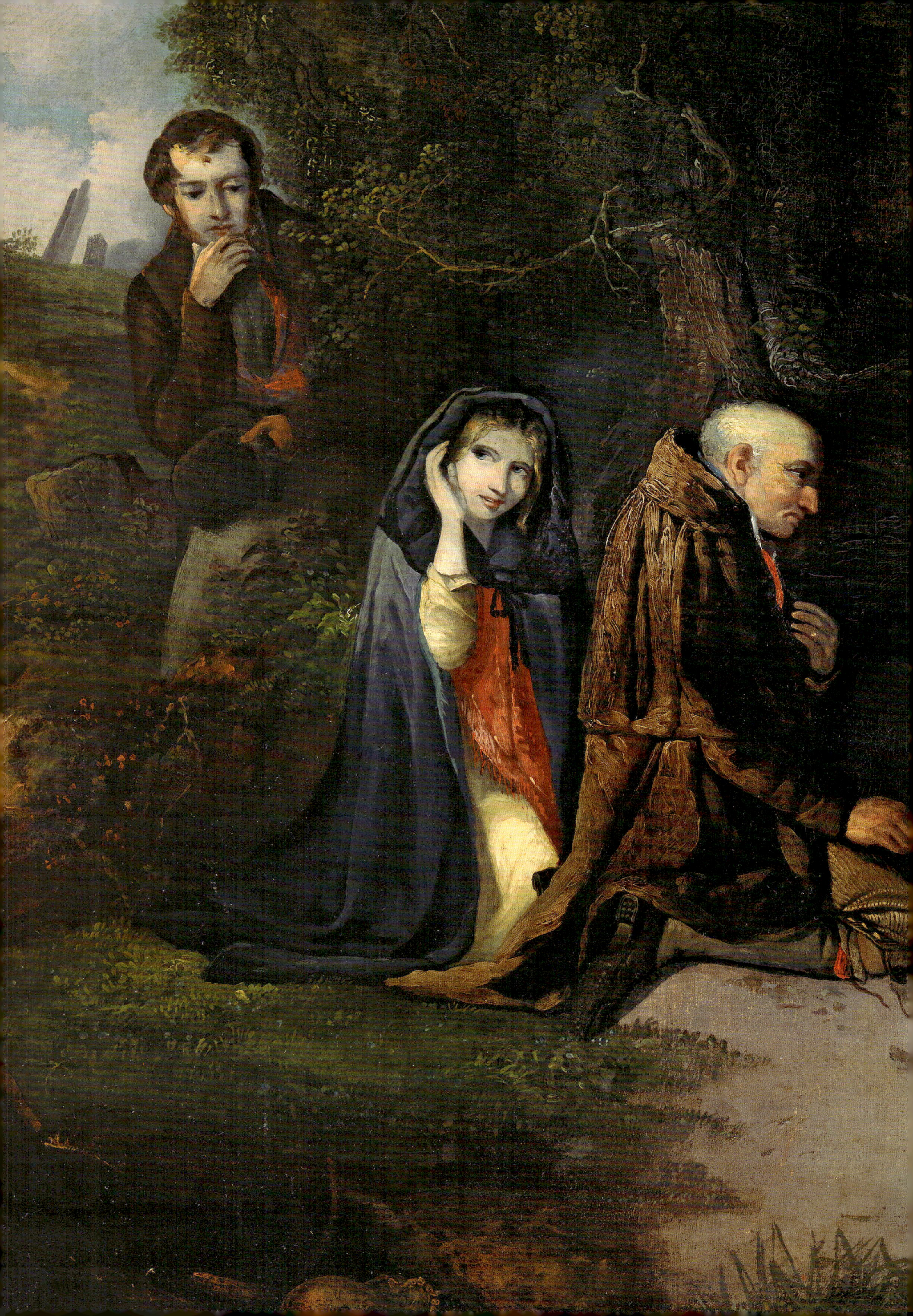

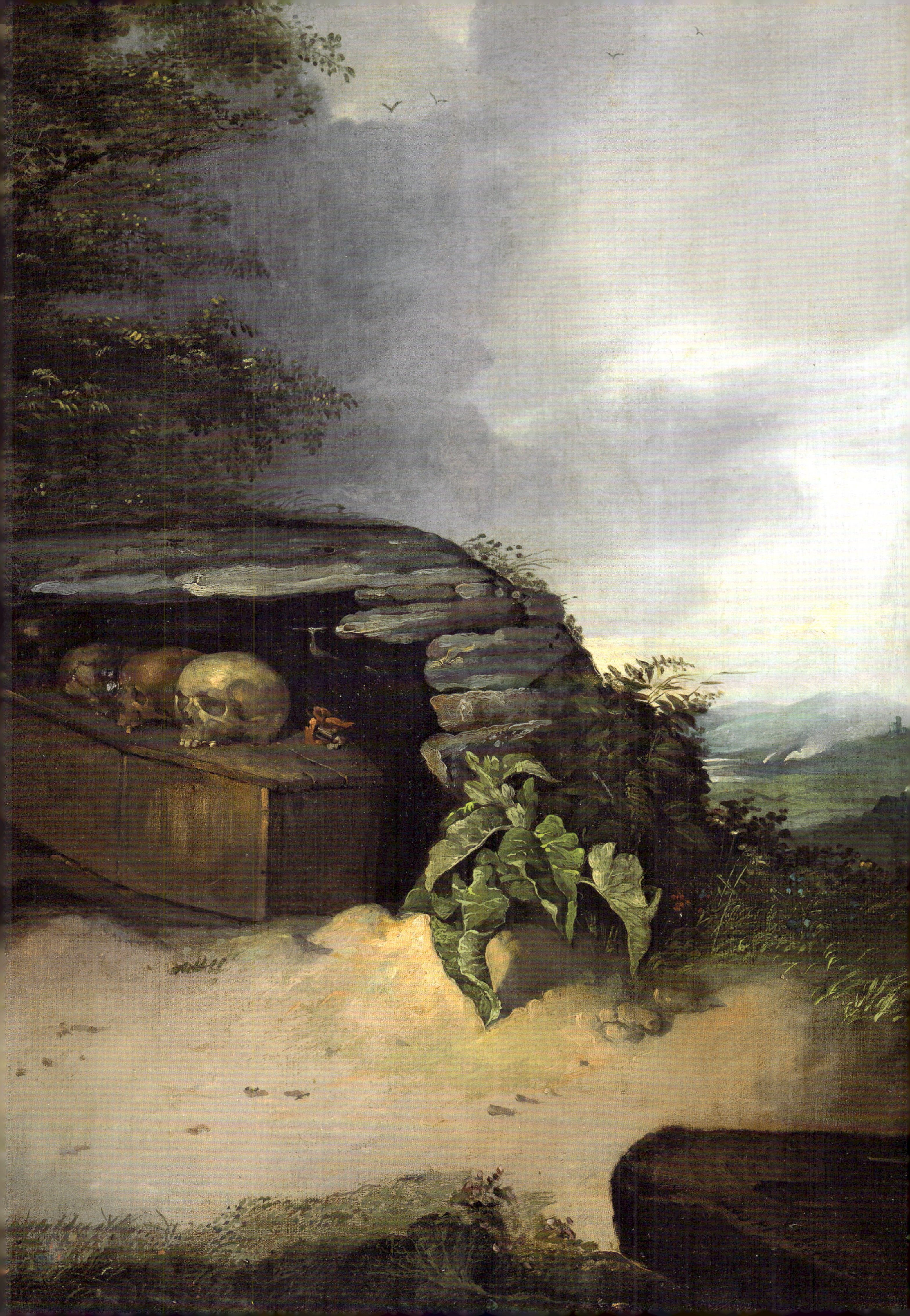

Figure 12 [CROPPED]
PREVIOUS PAGE

*Figures by a Coffin —
a Scene from
'The Collegians'*
Daniel Macdonald
1840

big dowry). Scanlan extricated himself by having his manservant, Stephen Sullivan, drown her in the river Shannon. Scanlan was arrested for murder and, although defended by Daniel O'Connell, was found guilty and sentenced to death (Griffin was a cub reporter at the trial). Sullivan met the same fate.

> 'The fictions of the Gothic romances are not so remote from credibility as is commonly supposed' mused Dr Johnson.[85] In turn, Griffin's version tells the story of a Protestant gentleman, of dubious morality, and a young pure Catholic Irish girl (who becomes the *Colleen Bawn* and, in the later operetta, the *Lily of Killarney*). The lovely Eily O'Connor, the daughter of a Garryowen tradesman, is seduced by the indolent young Anglo-Irish landowner, Hardress Cregan, who tires of her within weeks of their clandestine marriage, and hides her away in the Kerry mountains, where she is killed by Danny Mann, his manservant.

In so far as the depiction of the girl in the painting fits the doomed Eily O'Connor, the older man is perhaps her father, Mihil, a ropemaker from Garryowen — described in the novel as 'dreary as a winter churchyard' (a neighbor of the O'Connors was a coffin maker, who is seen finishing Mihil's coffin in the final scene of the novel). If indeed the painting is based on *The Collegians,* it is a composite of motifs in the novel, rather than a single identifiable scene. Alternatively, it may be a conflation of a number of literary sources of the period.[86] The novel cuts across many traditional pairings of Protestant morality, rationality and hard work, and Catholic barbarity, indolence and violence. It may thus be seen as a national allegory, exemplifying conflicts of class, culture and religion. The beautiful Catholic heroine represents simplicity and virtue in a romantic tale of national redefinition. Claire Connolly argues that *The Collegians* (1829) is

> the best representative of the new Catholic fiction: published in the year in which Catholic emancipation passed into law, it blends themes from Irish history with contemporary trial reportage and the new trend for society (or 'silver-fork') fiction … . The densely textured social landscape of rural Ireland: landowners, strong farmers, Middlemen, smugglers, lawyers, boatmen and buckeens all jostle for space in a narrative that shows how conflicting codes of conduct create moral chaos and political turmoil.

This new Catholic fiction 'shows how the literary consequence of emancipation' had implications for 'Catholic authorship for what had been a largely Protestant form.'[87]

In this connection, Sinéad Sturgeon relates 'Anglo-Irish Gothic criticism, which aligns the supernatural with either the oppressed (and vengeful) Irish or the oppressing (and guilt-stricken) Anglo-Irish', to 'the structures and practices of colonialism' in Griffin's work, arguing that 'the overwhelming scholarly convention has been to decode Irish Gothic writing as a vehicle for class anxiety, finding in the texts of writers such as Charles Maturin, Sheridan Le Fanu, and Bram Stoker, a fitful literary tradition that allegorized the troubled subconscious of the Protestant Anglo-Irish in the nineteenth century.'[88] Griffin formulated a kind of Catholic Gothic version of this literature. Just as the reckless Protestant Cregan represents moral decay, the honorable Catholic Daly in the novel signifies the rise of the new Ireland after Emancipation, in a romantic melodrama that draws on intertextual Gothic tropes of tragedy and despair, duplicity and betrayal, horror and death.

In Macdonald's painting, the tryst in the cemetery is intriguingly opaque. (Unusually the painting is signed and dated upside down). The elderly man kneels respectfully, hat in hand, hand at breast, looking mournfully and in oblation at the skulls displayed on the coffin in a low, corbelled structure, reminiscent of the opening of a prehistoric passage grave. On the mound in the left background of the lovely landscape, jagged grave stones protrude. The knowing look exchanged between the young man and women is laden with significance. It is tempting to read this contemplation of death as a foretaste of the Great Famine, but of course the Great Famine was only distinguished from *all* Irish famines by its length and severity. The most recent famine previous to the date of this painting had occurred fewer than twenty years before.

CHAPTER 2
RABID FURY

Figure 13

The Fighter

Daniel Macdonald

1844

In 1844, Daniel Macdonald executed *The Fighter* (**Fig. 13**), a startling image possessing a confrontational force unusual in Irish art history. The background to this painting shows the artist to have been highly informed about the parlous state of religious, economic and political conditions in the Irish countryside in the immediate pre-Famine period.

In the aftermath of the Act of Union, many novelists such as Maria Edgeworth, Lady Morgan, Gerald Griffin and the Banim brothers focused on the 'national tale', thereby generating a new sensitivity to the romantic unity of language, culture and ethnicity in Ireland. But it was far from an easy task. Protestant antiquarians noted the subversive implications of renewed interest in the Gaelic past, drawing connections between ethnography, folklore and agrarian unrest, thus depicting the Irish as inherently rebellious and uncivilized. Most of the rank and file of the 1798 rebels were Catholic, exacerbating Catholic-Protestant tensions, and undermining the confidence of the Anglican ruling elite. In time, Clare O'Halloran suggests, the 'discrediting of that antiquarian interest in, and extolling of, the Gaelic past and culture' became 'inextricably bound up with sedition and barbarism.'[89]

Macdonald's *Fighter* tells a complex tale indicative of many bitter grievances: tithes extracted from poor Catholics to pay the elite Protestant clergy, conacre (letting of small strips of poor land for growing potatoes on disadvantageous terms), high food prices, low wages, and putting land on the market to obtain higher rents. In general, the post-1798 fallout, the economic crash following the end of the Napoleonic Wars, and the serious famines of 1817 and 1822, were the conditions for mounting unrest. But religious as well as class differences also featured, as did issues of kinship. Moreover political explanations became increasingly prevalent, as peasant agitation assumed a form of proto-nationalism, provoking poor Irish Catholic peasants to attack rack-renting, English Protestant landlords.

Well-off Protestants feared the end of a privileged way of life, while poor Catholics had little or nothing to lose. As Thomas Crofton Croker put it, 'it becomes difficult to tranquillize those who have only one life to lose and everything to gain', and he warned that predictions of 'the overthrow of English dominion' being circulated 'by secret agency throughout the country' were fanning once more 'the embers of rebellion'.[90] Croker's *Researches in the South of Ireland* was framed by both recent and distant violence, culminating in an eyewitness account of the 1798 Rebellion, 'the excesses committed by an intoxicated multitude.'[91] Although he claimed to have avoided politics in his work, Croker did believe that good government was needed to avoid further bloodshed. The 'nobleness of savage nature', he argued, would need careful handling to avoid further rebellion; this was a subtext of Macdonald's *Fighter* — it crystallized many of these tensions.[92]

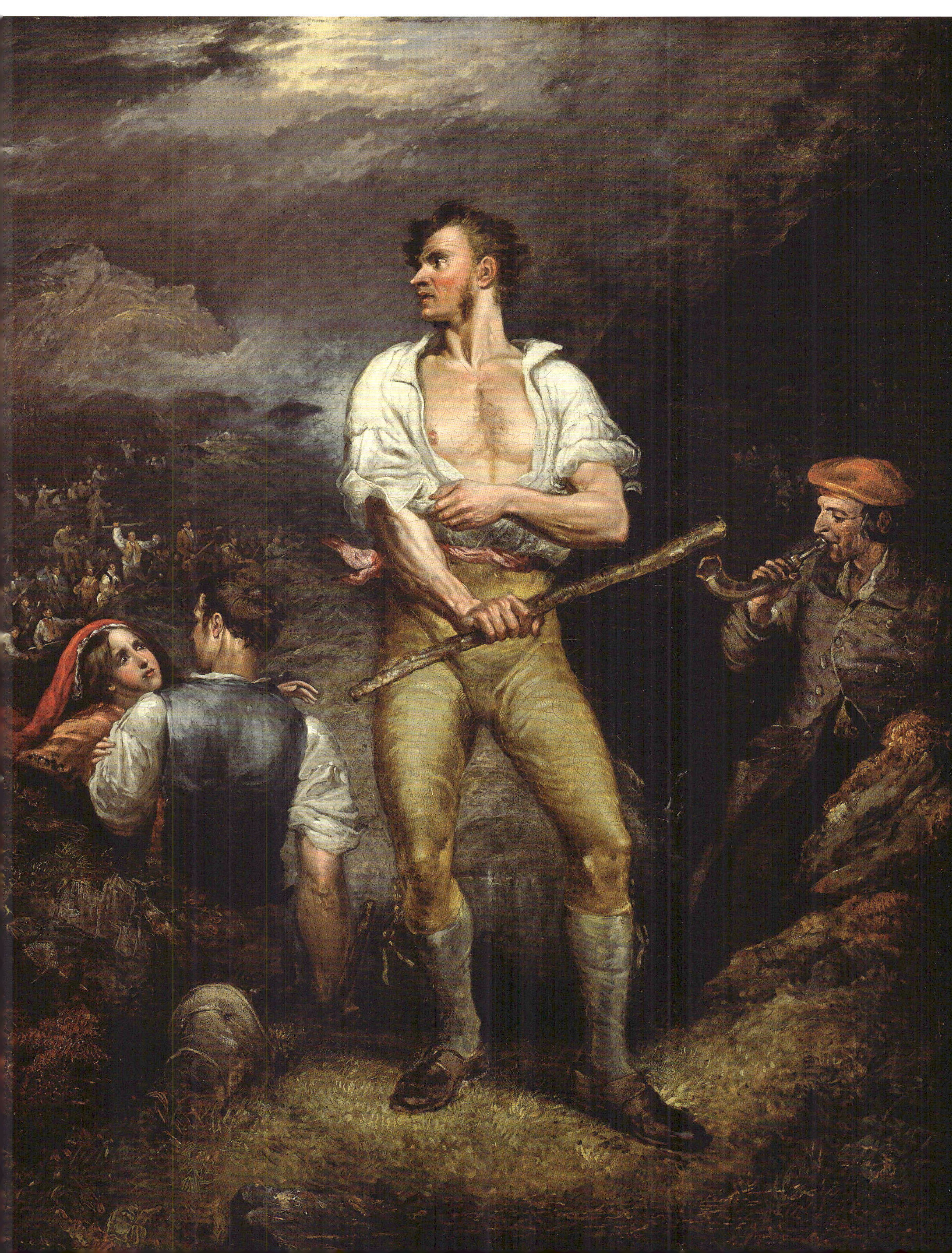

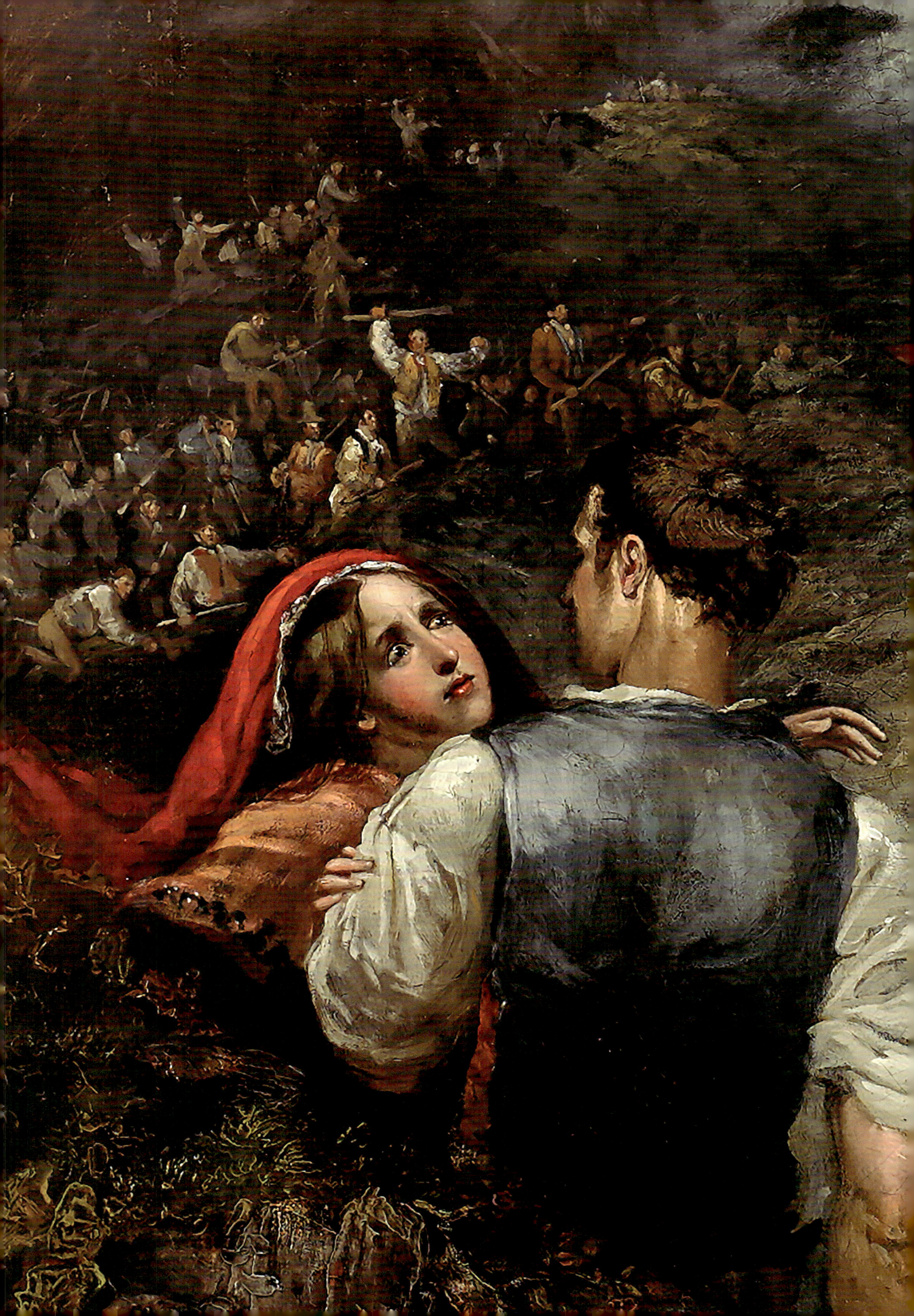

Croker's readers, however, were English not Irish, Protestant not Catholic, and although Croker was broadly reformist, he did not want to be subsumed into the culture he described. His take on the manners and customs of the Irish was often patronizing. Although he argued for the interests of the 'dependent colony', he did little to dispel the many stereotypical views of the Irish. He saw in Catholics a disturbing tendency towards superstition, and an absence of Protestant 'rationality'. In a later edition to *Fairy Legends and Traditions of the South of Ireland*, his son quotes from one of Croker's letters in which he boasted of 'bagging all the old "grey superstitions" I could fall in with,' while risking Whiteboys, smugglers and murderers.[93] He had witnessed a man who had been beaten for Whiteboy activities, singing 'songs that were rebellious in the highest degree' at a large assembly on St John's eve (midsummer eve), in the mountains of West Cork in 1813, undoubtedly followed by a faction fight.[94] O'Halloran argues that Irish folklorists '[i]n their awareness of the colonial nature of Irish history and its troubled legacies [] could neither wholly romanticize nor wholeheartedly condemn a peasant society that was considered not only barbarous but subversive, and yet which lay at the heart of the Irish problem and its solution.' [95] The 1798 rebellion had resulted in huge numbers being flogged, transported, imprisoned and killed, inuring Ireland to new levels of violence, both official and unofficial. Previous to the rebellion, agrarian unrest was mostly intimidatory; afterward, it became deadly, characterized by a self-sustaining cycle of cattle maiming, arson, assassination and brutal state repression.

The majority of the population (some 85 percent) was employed on the land. The land, however, was held by a tiny minority (some 10,000 landlords). A typical landlord owned about 2,000 acres (although one owned 115,000 acres, in five counties). A good tenant holding was 30 acres, but the majority had but a scrap of land from which to feed large families of several generations. But it was not just a matter of land, for as the English traveller Arthur Young observed in 1776:

A landlord in Ireland can scarcely invent an order, which a servant, laborer or cottier dare refuse to execute. Nothing satisfied him but an unlimited submission. Disrespect or anything tending towards sauciness he may punish with his cane or his horse-whip with the most perfect security; a poor man would have his bones broke if he offered to lift his hand in his own defense … Landlords of consequence have assured me, that many of their cotters would think themselves honored by having their wives or daughters sent for to the bed of their master; a mark of slavery that proves the oppression under which such people must live.[96]

The more substantial farmers were landlords as well, sub-dividing their holdings and renting them to under-tenants. In Co. Cork, according to the 1841 census, there were 145,000 laborers and farm servants, and fewer than 41,000 farmers. In view of the exorbitant rents charged for the hovels and patches occupied by tenants — let alone the day laborers who had to hire land on conacre — the relationship between landlord and tenant was one of tension and often hatred.

But it was not simply a matter of class: kinship also determined how peasants responded to their circumstances. The closer the relationship, the greater the possibility for conflict. Land disputes and

The Fighter [DETAIL]
Full painting on page 51.

inheritance explain much about violence in pre-Famine Ireland. From the late eighteenth century, the population of Ireland expanded at a phenomenal rate. In 1801, it was 5.2 million; by 1841, it was some 8.1 million, with the result that there was increasing competition for limited resources, in what was becoming a vastly overpopulated countryside. The wartime boom of 1793–1813, with the increase in food prices and land and rent values, brought prosperity to the larger farmers, but the ensuing slump meant disaster for the majority of tenants. Moreover, the move from tillage to pasture, with the attendant evictions, reduced opportunities for rural employment, which had a bearing on the level of rural unrest.

Harsh deprivation led to periods of agrarian unrest between 1760 and 1845. Agrarian secret societies sprang up, from the Whiteboys to the Defenders, the Caravats and Shanavests, the Ribbonmen and the Rockites. Bitter fighting between peasants and rural proprietors manifested itself in major feuds. The Caravats' and Shanavests' feud grew out of a land dispute culminating in a number hangings.[97] The secret societies were identified by emblems and personalities: Nicholas Hanley led the Caravats, and Patrick Connors the Shanavests — the poor Hanley named for his flashy cravat, and the rich Connors for his shabby waistcoat. Their membership followed suit.

Bound by a code of silence and protected by combination oaths, agrarian agitators carried out savage nocturnal raids, especially against land grabbers who took the homes of evicted tenants. Increasingly violent, they maimed, raped, abducted, burnt out and murdered. The violence, Paul Roberts argues, was 'molded by a particular culture, with a strong tradition of lawlessness.' The gangs were based on 'tightly knit, and somewhat independent communities, often with a collective economic base, whose structure positively encouraged group action and a lawless spirit, and which usually had long-standing reputations for both.'[98] In operating an alternative system of law, these movements sought to protect the poor.

Although quasi-egalitarian in structure, these secret societies — often with female sobriquets ('Lady Clare Boys') — were typically led from the top by a charismatic chief as we see in Macdonald's *Fighter*. Many became popular chapbook heroes, flamboyant men of many wives and much derring-do. Matters came to a head in Munster with the Rockite movement. Named for its mythical leader 'Captain Rock', and adapted to local circumstances, Rockism peaked between 1821 and 1824.[99] Unlike the more intellectual leadership of 1798, with a rural base in Defenderism, Rockism had grass roots in the peasantry, with strong millenarian leanings. Between October 1821 and April 1822, some 223 raids for arms and ammunition took place in Co. Cork alone. The authorities found evidence of a widespread organization, controlled by sworn oaths of the gun. Throughout January 1822, there were major clashes between the Rockites and the yeomanry with heavy losses of life. Displays of violence, including mutilation of victims' bodies and gang rape of soldiers' wives and crown witnesses, were met with state coercion and savagely put down. Martial law was established, and at least one hundred people were hanged and six hundred transported.

William Maginn spoke for many in the establishment when he expressed the view that the country was on the verge of civil war:

You would be perfectly amazed at the rabid fury of both parties, — for, accustomed as I have always been to outrageous contests, I confess I am a trifle flabbergasted. *N'Importe.* If there be a civil war I can lose nothing but my head, which is of use to no one but the owner — and may pick up something in the scramble. Old habits of authority have made it a fixed persuasion in Ireland among the Protestants that one Protestant could beat five Papists, and of course I have no fear for the result. Really, without jest, we are woefully insulted … our clergy are reviled and personally abused; our very private parties spied; our toasts controlled by authority; our churches polluted; the priests domineering, swaggering, and libelling our faith, our conduct, and our principles; and, worst of all, if we dare to say a word in reply to the most atricious calumnies or downright insults, we are denounced as not conciliatory … In a word, the question is now narrowed to this — Is the Protestant religion to be tolerated in Ireland? And the end will be that England will have to conquer the country again, which consummation I hope most devoutly to witness …[100]

Threatening warnings, often composed by wandering schoolmasters, were intended to inspire terror in the hearts of landlords. Resentment against a state that supported Protestant entitlement, evangelical proselytism and tithes was rife. Tithes were forcefully extracted by mercenary middlemen, loaded in favor of grazing and against tillage, and therefore hit the poorest hardest. Gradually, the state offered concessions, which in turn made the agitators aware of their power. Protestantism was identified with the police and the yeomanry, who wielded their power against the peasantry in myriad ways. Excesses of state violence led the contemporary historian Francis Plowden to describe the yeomanry as 'military savages', as in stories of rebels being dragged to guardhouses that kept

a supply of coarse linen caps, besmeared inside with pitch; and when the pitch was well heated, they forced the cap on his head; and sometimes the melted pitch, running into the eyes of the unfortunate victim, superadded blindness to his other tortures. They generally detained him till the pitch had so cooled, that the cap could not be detached from the head without carrying with it the hair and blistered skin; they then turned him adrift, disfigured, often blind, and writhing with pain ... At other times, they rubbed moistened gunpowder into the hair, in the form of a cross, and set fire to it. [101]

Irish Millenarianism was originated a commentary on the Apocalypse of St. John by the English Catholic cleric, Charles Walmsley, alias Signor Pastorini, who prophesied that Protestantism would be wiped out by 1825. James Donnelly argues that disempowered people are prone to millenarianism, especially those in colonial countries who have suffered defeat, or anticipate losing more, necessitating, as it were, supernatural intervention.[102] Ireland was long colonized, but the recent 1798 defeat heightened such feelings. The destruction of Protestantism now seemed to require supernatural intervention, and such prophecies among a 'credulous' peasantry were perceived as being on a continuum with superstitions about the fairies. Pastorini thus added increased religious and prophetic dimensions to already violent class differences.

Tithe grievances and Protestant proselytism brought old economic and new religious conflicts into alignment. In March 1822, in Tramore, Co. Waterford, Catholics were exhorted to pay no tithes and to fight for their religion by supporting Captain Rock. The circulation of cult tracts, handbills and even millennial ballads gained a hold in Munster, and gave solace and hope to the oppressed. Protestant evangelicals retaliated by circulating vast numbers of Bibles, declaring that Catholic priests deliberately withheld the Scriptures from their adherents. The Religious Book and Tract Society for Ireland claimed in 1823 to have circulated over 1,160,000 pamphlets and 86,000 books in the previous four years alone. Proselytism gave Catholics cause for serious concern.[103] Conversely, for wealthier Catholics, Pastorini-type Apocrypha were embarrassing at a time when rational arguments to legitimize Catholic Emancipation were under discussion. When Pastorini's predicted day of reckoning passed in 1825, the Rockite movement waned, just as Daniel O'Connell's Catholic Association rose. The gradual expansion of a rural police force and O'Connell's constitutional agitation combined to change the nature of rural unrest that had become increasingly death dealing.

O'Connell and other Catholic leaders, however, entered into a tacit co-operation with Whiteboyism during the Tithe War, and did not resume their disapproval of secret societies after the introduction of a Tithe Commutation Act in 1838. O'Connell weaned the rural poor away from agrarian insurgency into non-violent national politics, but it required some adroit political maneuvering. Initially, those who flocked to his Catholic Association believed that he would lead an armed revolt, achieving what Pastorini's prophecies failed to deliver: although he denounced violence, he took Rockite money to defend agitators. Donnelly notes the 'ease with which O'Connell, who publicly denounced Pastorini as a sort of Orange agent provocateur, was able to reap the benefit of this febrile mobilization'.[104]

Set against this background, Macdonald's sketch of *Kerry Peasantry* (1844) **(Fig. 14)** is a masterful characterization of Irish country people: young and old, men and women, reflective and hotheaded. The contrast between the beautiful vignette of the mother and baby (who feature in other Macdonald images, such as *The Shower*, *Public Characters* and *Eviction*) and the young man in the center, who slips his hand into the fold in his shirt, where presumably lies his gun, heightens the moment dramatically. The sketch, captioned 'Kerry peasantry list'ning to the account of the conviction of Dan'l O'Connell and the Traversers, at the State Trials in Dublin, Feb'y 1844', shows a group of rough and ready, but far from insensate, peasants reading *The Nation* newspaper to learn of the fate of O'Connell and the Repeal Martyrs, then undergoing trial for conspiracy. The young man's demeanor suggests that something *will* be done about the treatment of his Liberator, which Macdonald leaves in the imagination of the beholder.

In 1843 — Repeal Year — thirty-one 'Monster Meetings', as *The Times* called them, were held all over Ireland. Prime Minister Robert Peel's Westminster government banned the last meeting, due to be held at Clontarf on 7 October 1843, asserting that O'Connell's ultimate aim was to 'overthrow the constitution of the British Empire'. Although O'Connell cancelled the meeting, he was charged. In February 1844, O'Connell and his son John, along with Thomas Matthew Ray, Thomas Steel, and

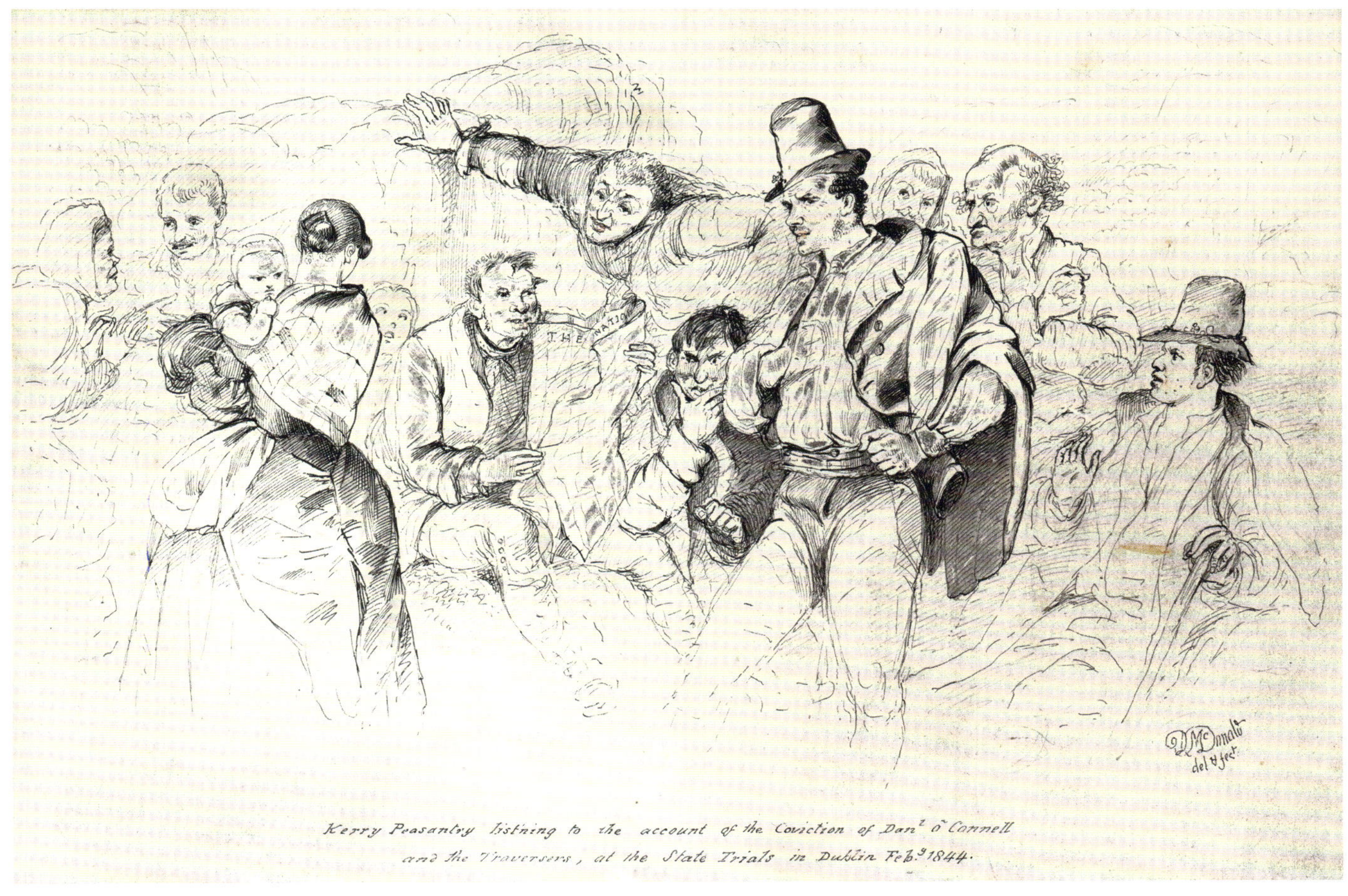

newspaper editors, Richard Barrett (*The Pilot*), John Gray (*Freeman's Journal*) and Charles Gavan Duffy (*The Nation*), were sentenced to prison in the Richmond Bridewell Penitentiary in Dublin. Thomas Matthew Ray commissioned a series of watercolors by Henry O'Neill, the antiquarian, showing the comfortable apartments in which they were incarcerated.[105] One picture shows the indulgence allowed the prisoners — a banquet, no less, with O'Connell, wearing his 'Milesian' or 'Repeal' cap, attended by associates, their wives and guests. Self-conscious of his expanding girth and increasing baldness, O'Connell wore a wig, which in the Macdonald sketch appears to be bursting free, in curly profusion, from beneath what looks like his bed cap.

O'Connell was famous for his Milesian cap of green velvet and gold threads created by artists John Hogan and Henry MacManus. At the open air meeting on the rath of Mullaghmast in 1843, the cap was borne through the crowd in a special open carriage, drawn by four gray horses and escorted by postilions, dressed in green velvet, embroidered with gold. Six men accompanied the cap inside the carriage, all wearing versions of it, including the two artists who had designed it, and a youth with a cornet perched on the box seat, playing the air 'Don't You Remember the Place Where We Met, Long, Long Ago?', recalling the slaughter of Irish leaders on that historic site in the sixteenth century. O'Connell wore this 'cap of liberty' during the remainder of his life, even in private, declaring that he would wear it to his grave.

Figure 14

Kerry Peasantry
Daniel Macdonald
1844

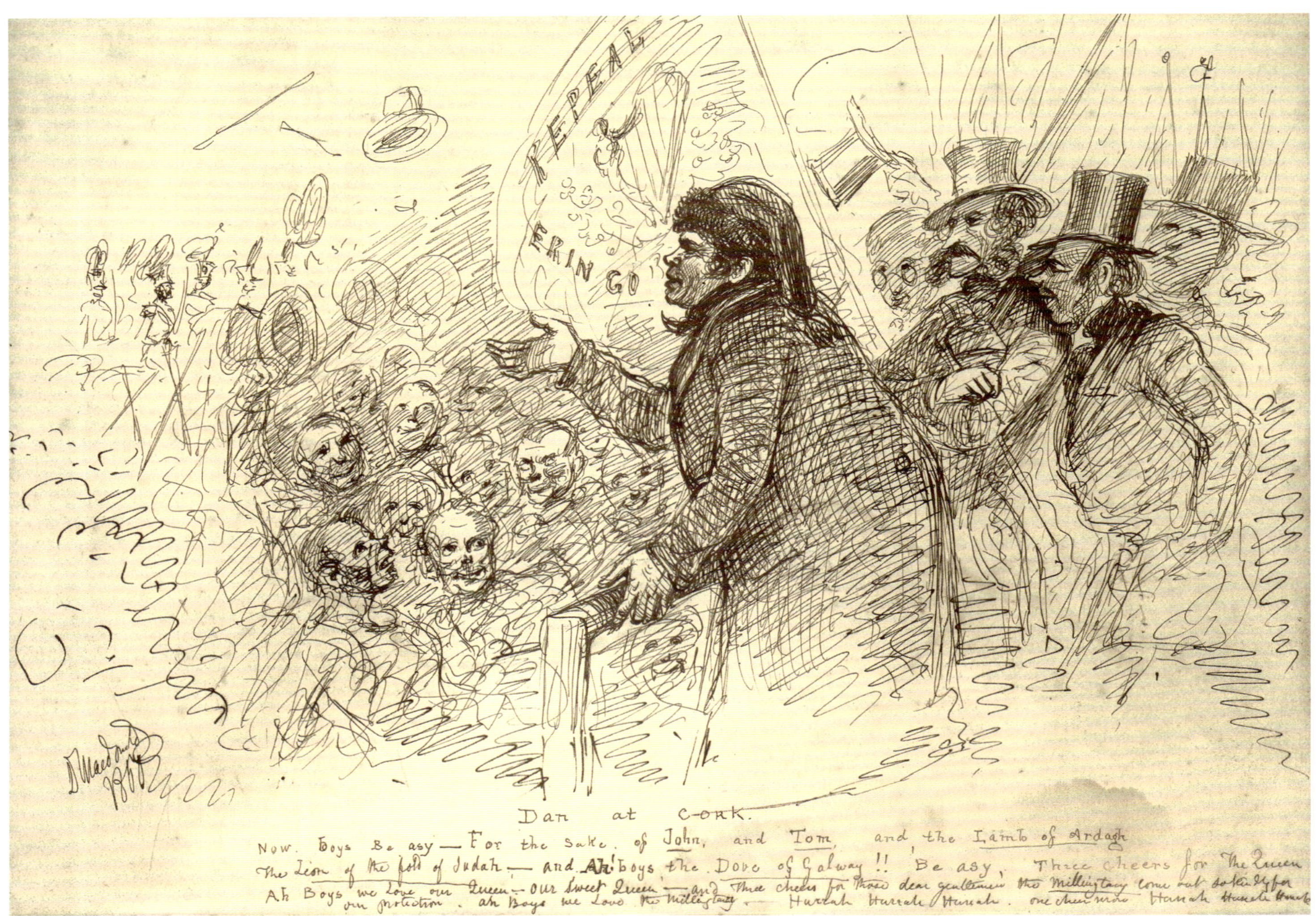

Figure 15

Dan at Cork

Daniel Macdonald

1850

The Liberator was highly image conscious. The O'Connell myth was fostered through paintings, etchings, lithographs, woodcuts, medals, ceramics and buttons intended to concretize O'Connell as leader and liberator.[106] So ambitious was the construction of his image that the artisans of Cork created a float that bore O'Connell through the streets of the city in a mass Repeal demonstration in 1845, captured by Macdonald in *Dan at Cork* (1850) **(Fig. 15)**. Twenty-foot high pillars held aloft a large green canopy, emblazoned with an enormous shamrock. Large replicas of his Milesian cap surmounted each pillar, while an even larger version of it topped the canopy itself. According to Gary Owens, to O'Connell's opponents

> the Milesian cap represented nothing less than a modern-day Irish crown and was symptomatic
>
> of its wearer's brazen audacity. His followers, on the other hand, drew inspiration from the cap's
>
> suggestion of Irish royalty — friendly journalists in fact referred to it as O'Connell's 'Crown-Cap'
>
> — and they easily related it to his popular sobriquet, 'Ireland's uncrowned monarch'.

The cap was based on an ancient gold crown that had been excavated in Co. Tipperary in the late seventeenth century, and brought to France by a dispossessed Catholic landowner, thus linking it with 'both the heroic and the tragic elements of Ireland's past and was a tangible reminder of her legendary kings who ruled their country as independent sovereigns.'[107] Macdonald's *Dan at Cork* shows the Liberator managing the crowd, with the caption:

> Now boys be asy — For the sake of John, and Tom, and the Lamb of Ardagh — The Lion of the Fold of Judah — and Ah! boys, the Dove of Galway !! Be asy. Three cheers for The Queen. Ah boys, we love our dear Queen – our sweet Queen — and three cheers for those dear gentlemen of the Millingtary, come out today for our protection. Ah boys, we love the Millingtary. Hurrah, hurrah, hurrah. One cheer more. Hurrah, hurrah, hurrah.

At a large dinner in his honor in Galway, a replica of a dove fluttered down on O'Connell as he took his seat — a spectacle that entranced the hundreds who witnessed it, and which was reenacted in Cork (unless Macdonald, deliberately or erroneously, set it there).

In this sketch, O'Connell's cap is noteworthy, for it is not his usual Milesian cap, but it could be one that also draws on age-old symbols of freedom, from the Antique to the French Revolution: the Phrygian cap, a soft conical cap, with the top pulled forward, indicative of liberty; the *pileus*, a felt cap presented to manumitted slaves of ancient Rome, symbolizing their right to vote (following the assassination of Julius Caesar in 44 BC, the *pileus* came to signify Republicanism); and the

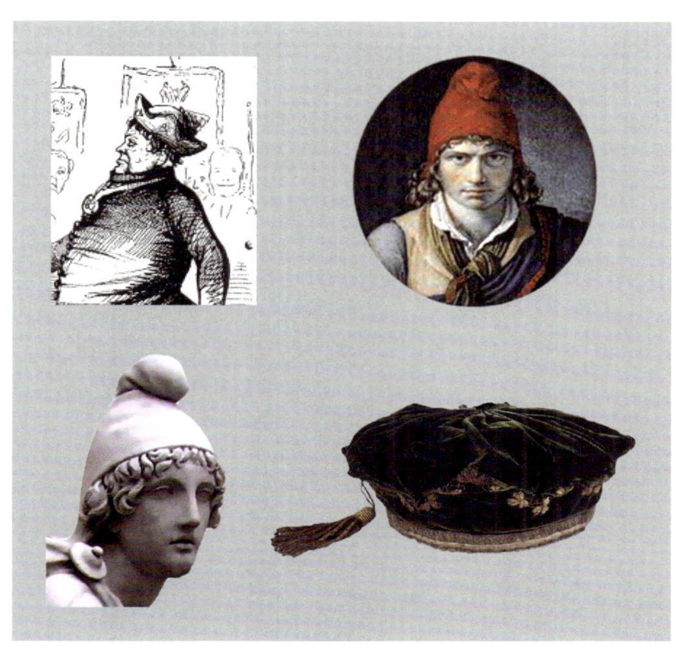

bonnet rouge, first worn in the anti-nobility Stamp-Paper Revolt in Brittany in 1675, and then adopted by the working classes to become the symbol of revolutionary France in the late eighteenth century (when caps were knitted by *tricoteuses* during public executions by guillotine in Paris) **(Fig. 16)**. In artistic representation, Marianne, the national symbol of France, wears a red Phrygian cap, as in Eugène Delacroix's *Liberty Leading the People* (1830). Given the tone of the Macdonald sketch, however, and the pride with which O'Connell usually wore his cap of liberty, one should not rule out that Macdonald is thinking satirically, and this is a mere bedcap. But for all its humor, the post-Famine, post-O'Connell sketch, executed in 1850, is disturbing. The pen work is frenetic, the adoring spectators skeletal, the military, as ever, pervasive, and the figures behind O'Connell sinister. Repeal remains elusive. Erin is far from *go bragh*.

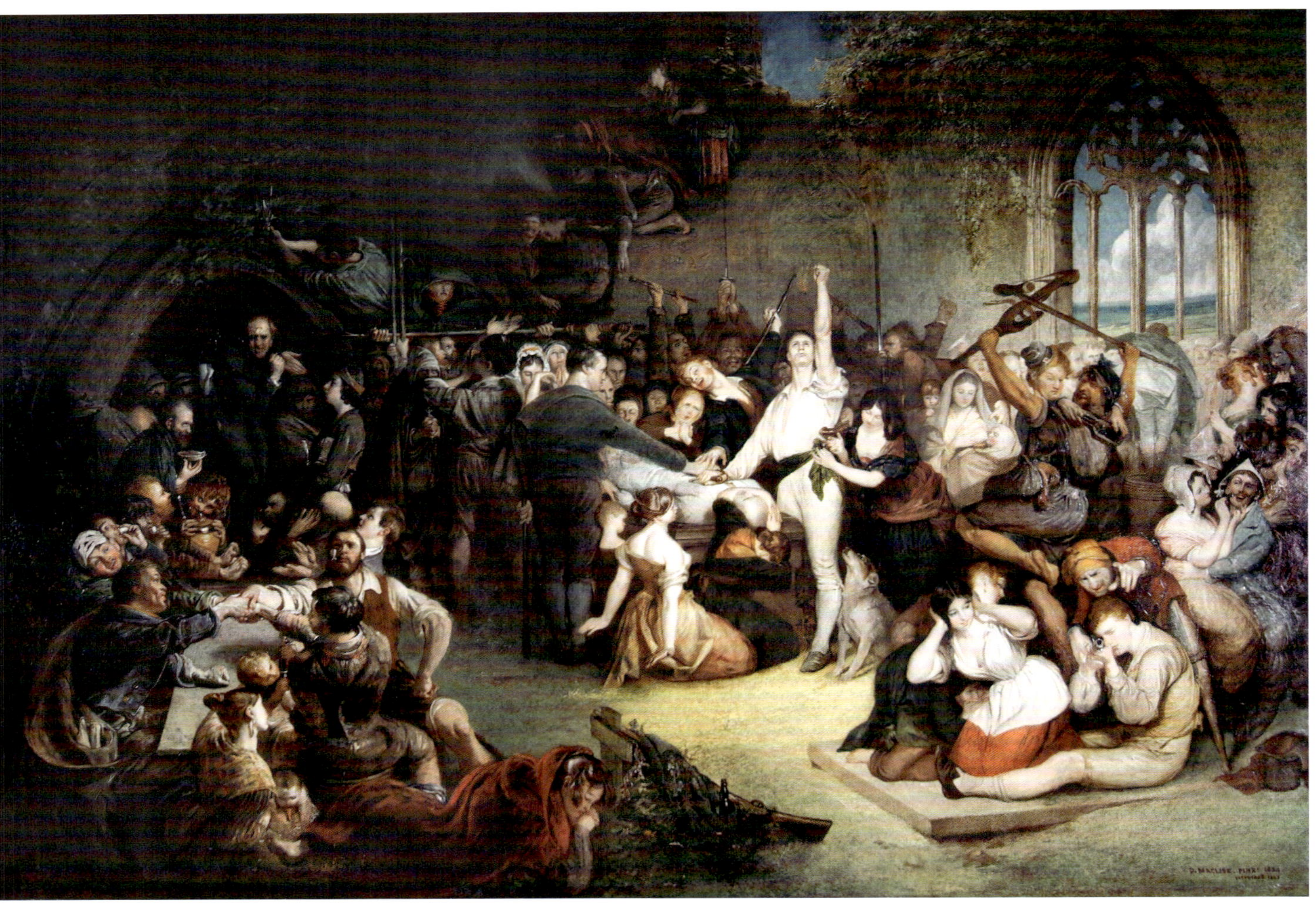

Figure 17

The Installation of Captain Rock

Daniel Maclise

1834

ROCK ART

If O'Connell appropriated popular insurgency for middle-class political ends, he was supported by a number of artists and writers. Just as many have observed how in Thomas Moore's *Irish Melodies* something wild was tamed, equally in his *Memoirs of Captain Rock,* many of the most extreme aspects of Irish popular culture were 'civilized' in order to dissuade the poor away from violent agrarian movements into nonviolent, national politics. Gerald Griffin observed that the Rockite movement created a demand for narratives about Ireland and that it was the 'subtle and murderous insurrection of 1821, 1822, so wonderful in its unity of purpose, so fearful and mysterious in its mode of operation' that 'first excited in England an alarmed interest and a strong curiosity respecting the habits of the [Irish] people'.[108]

It was Moore's tour of the south of Ireland in the summer of 1823, and his discussions of the state of the country with O'Connell, that prompted the writing of the (fictional) *Memoirs of Captain Rock* on his return to England. On its publication, one of his critics noted that he had failed to capture the spirit of how 'individual Irishmen are worked up into that state of excitement and ferocity of which we see the daily fruits in almost every part of Ireland', perceiving a lack of 'reality' and describing Captain Rock as 'but a sort of abstraction of Irish riot'.[109] According to Emer Nolan, 'Instead of detailing rapes, maimings and killings, Rock insists on the "recreational", or even the *artistic* nature of insurrection — treated here as joyful self-expression, or as a great "harvest of riot".'[110] Part history, part fiction, and part political satire,

'Moore analyses the spirit of popular protest … to decipher the complex articulation of agrarian insurgency with folk culture, ritual, and 'subversive law'.[111] The *Memoir* was a huge success and spawned a host of others versions of Captain Rock in various art forms, both contesting and emulating his story. Not least of these, albeit carrying its own enigmas, was Macdonald's *Fighter*.[112] If Moore refused to pander to the moral panic that surrounded the issue of agrarian violence, Macdonald addressed it head on.

Irish novelists struggled to find new ways to depict Ireland within the conventions of literary realism, and the same went for the even more conservative painters. Exceptionally in visual culture, Macdonald found a convincing expression for such a complex set of ideas. Before this, however, Daniel Maclise had also flouted aesthetic protocols in his vast canvas, *The Installation of Captain Rock* (1834) **(Fig. 17)**, interweaving high art and popular culture in a manner that confounded his critics, and which elaborated a darker version of Moore's articulate agrarian leader.

Set in a ruined abbey, Maclise's painting is replete with references to proto-nationalist agrarian insurgency, religious sectarianism, and cultural annihilation. The death of the old leader and the installation of his successor, the new Captain Rock, confirms Irish resistance as ever ongoing. An officiating monk holds a crucifix aloft; there is a hunchback; a 'boccaugh' patriot has unbuckled his wooden leg and waves his crutch in the air; a schoolmaster is sermonizing sedition (accompanied by some new recruit carrying books, possibly Pastorini's *Prophecies*); there is drinking and cavorting, as well as the 'wild Ullalooh' of the keening women. Together with the sashing of the new leader, all these contributed to a sense of contrived chaos — a lack of control, at both the form and content levels. Moreover the kissing and the courting drew the lip-licking censure of the *Fraser's* reviewer, 'Morgan Rattler', who conceded that all the women, and especially 'the delicious little minx who is affecting to dread the report of the gun, are most exquisitely depicted'— so much so that, he doubted they could be Irish.[113] According to Luke Gibbons, however, this suggests that

> social elevation is required to explain the ease with which women occupy public space … whereby the colonized male is deemed to be, at most, the social equivalent of the metropolitan or upper class female. This is, no doubt, intended to diminish both, but it may have the opposite effect of bringing gender and the physicality of the body to bear on colonialism in a way that calls for a total transformation of domestic and political space. By combining public and private spheres into its dissident version of the hidden Ireland, *The Installation of Captain Rock* attests to one of the most important aspects of popular insurgency, the integration of rituals of resistance into the everyday rounds of folk customs of rural life. Agrarian secret societies organised at wakes, weddings and seasonal festivals so that the persistence of folk culture itself, even in its apparently most innocent guise, became charged with political significance.[114]

For all its superstition, drunkenness, and eroticism, the painting was politically disquieting in the end, prompting Rattler to regret that Maclise had even attempted it:

Figure 18 [DETAIL]

The Installation of Captain Rock

Full painting on page 60.

for if I am not much mistaken he will be taken for a radical, or still worse, a Whig: the fact being that he has never dabbled the least in politics, and has nothing of political feeling, excepting that instinctive disposition to free and gentle Toryism, which is proper to high-minded gentlemen.[115]

Fraser's — the magazine Maclise himself contributed to — pronounced itself dissatisfied on a number of counts: 'If the visitor … be Anglo-Irish, what are the feelings towards the Rockites? The most intense contempt and hatred commingled — the feeling of the man towards the poisonous reptile: he knows that the Rockites are the most treacherous and cowardly rascals in the wide world, excepting only the agitators by whom they are incited.'[116] Not least of its ironies is that the painting paid obeisance to various neoclassical models, such as Henry Fuseli's *Oath on the Rutli,* but it also broke with convention, leading Rattler to argue that Maclise should have changed the setting

Figure 19 [DETAIL]

The Fighter

Full painting on page 51.

> to some other country and some other age … in the ruins of some ancient temple, vowing vengeance against imperious Rome and the Roman name, over the body of some fellow-slave, done to death by the cruelty of his Patrician master, and surrounded by the multitude of slaves, male and female, belonging to some great household.[117]

In other words, the distancing mechanisms considered essential to great art should have been respected. The most disturbing vignette is the figure on the lower right, taking aim, and shooting at the spectator **(Fig. 18)**. But the cardinal offense — the defective composition — was even more disturbing than the inappropriate subject matter. The painting was deemed to have no unifying features, so necessary for a successful history painting to lend itself to a detached 'aesthetic' vantage point. The contemporary setting and story, the local detail, the mix of high and low culture, and the scale of the treatment of inferior people, seemed to be transgressions forced by wayward Irish experience on acceptable standards of taste. The presentation of an agrarian agitator, historicized

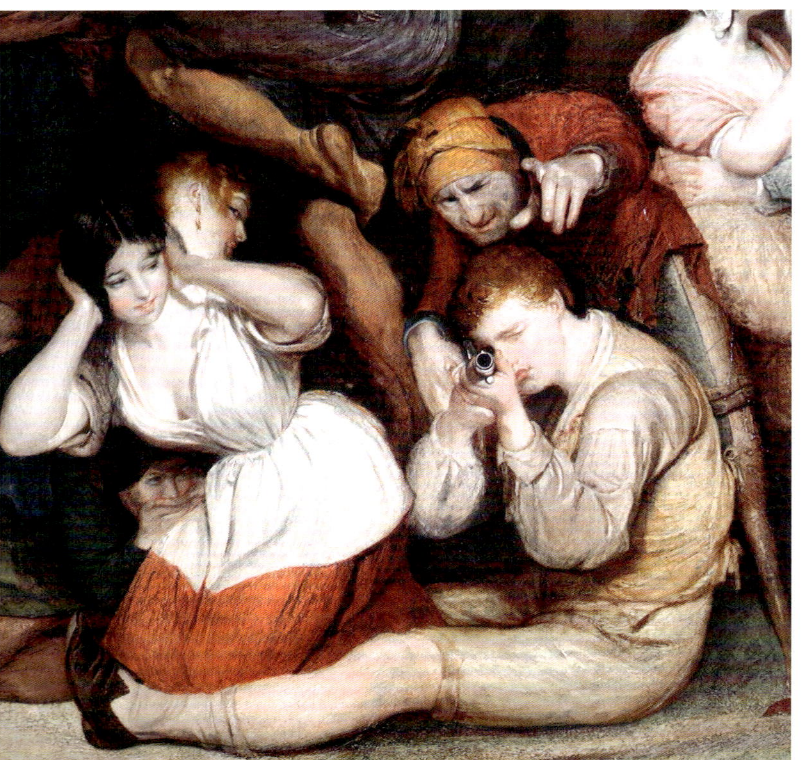

and psychologized, was enough to draw hostile criticism from metropolitan audiences. Indeed, the criticisms of *The Installation* were such that Maclise reworked the painting in 1843, making it at least partially contemporaneous with Macdonald's painting of *The Fighter*, which could also be said to evince sympathy with Irish violence, insubordination and sedition, manners, customs and rituals.

Moore and Maclise's controversial works can be seen as antecedents of Macdonald's *Fighter,* in which the conventions of representing the Irish were flouted once more. It was not alone in its contestation of

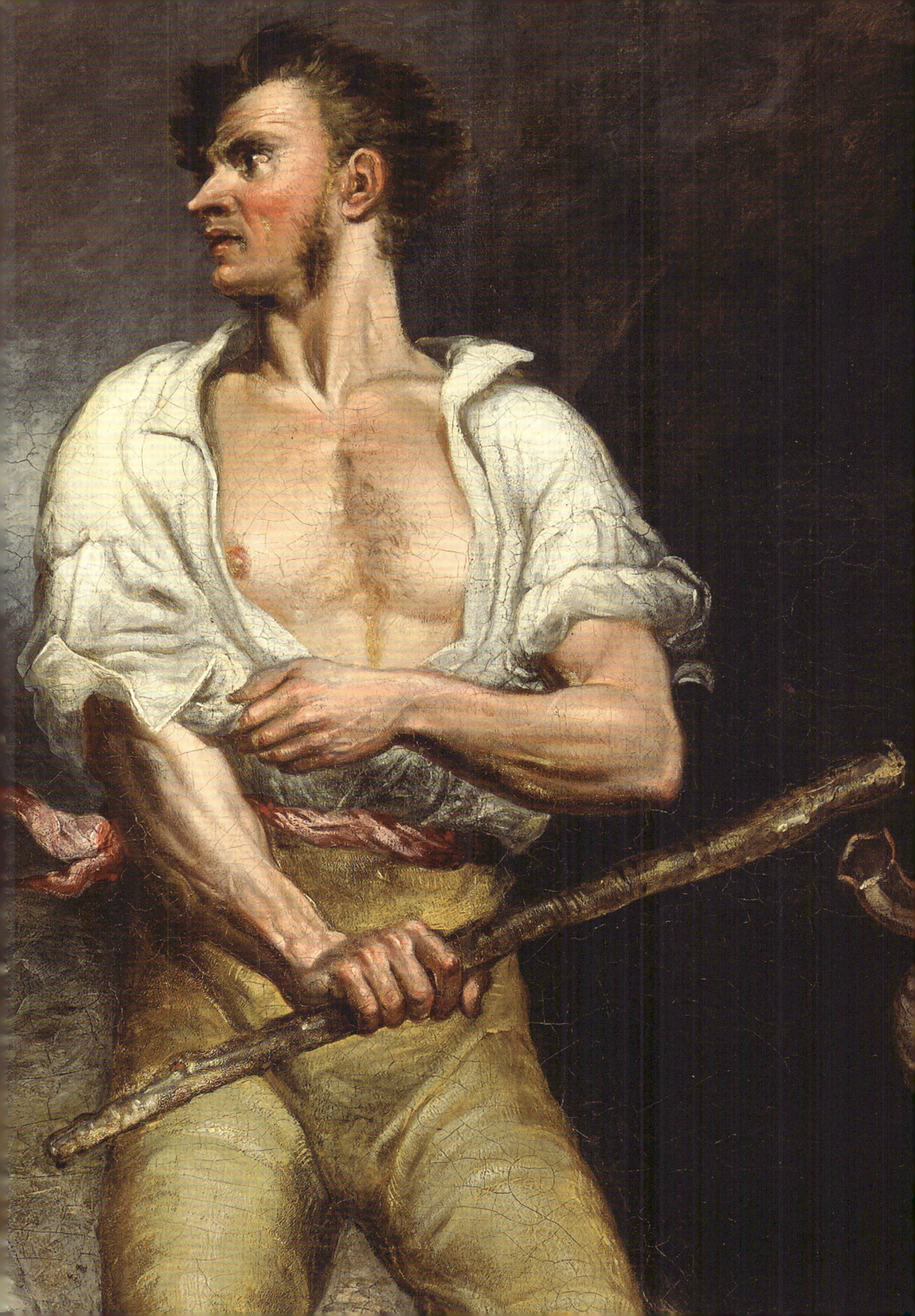

form but also in its treatment of subject matter that *The Fighter* challenged contemporary taste. If Captain Rock was the apotheosis of Irish Catholic resistance, Macdonald's fighter was the embodiment of peasant leadership and popular agency, just as disturbing to Irish Protestants as it was to the British establishment. *The Fighter* echoes Maclise's diploma piece, *The Woodranger* (1838) (Royal Academy of Arts) in its focus on a single male figure. *The Woodranger*, with his all but vibrating brace of capercaillie, is elated by his kill, but it is the more serious matter of the loss of human life, or at least social violence, that is implicit in the Macdonald painting.[118] Not even Gustave Courbet attempted such an audacious presentation of a peasant figure as Macdonald; Courbet's stonebreakers were abject creatures, given unusual prominence perhaps, but their siting *in* the landscape kept them in their place. Predating Courbet's figures by five years, Macdonald's vigorous peasant has stepped fully into the visual field, if not the spectatorial space of the viewer.

Whether forming a tribute or a challenge to Maclise, Macdonald's *Fighter* strained even further the bounds of convention. He brought his rebel forward and aggrandized him, so that he dominates the space and towers above the spectator. His chest is bared, his sleeves rolled, his stick clenched. Every muscle is strained, his face is contorted with the effort of holding his men in check until, frenzied and beyond containment, he unleashes them on the enemy **(Fig. 19)**. Unlike the diffusion of action evident in Maclise's *Installation*, this painting demonstrates Macdonald's understanding of Hellenistic principles, and although there are other figures — a multitude in the background — the power is concentrated on the central figure who is paramount. Macdonald has absorbed the lessons from classical Greek sculpture, such as *The Fighting Gladiator* **(Fig. 20)** and *Laocoön and his Sons*, and applied them to nineteenth-century Irish visual culture, producing a figure heroic for its age and time, but in a most unlikely setting.

Stick fighting was a martial art requiring skill, agility, fitness and psychological nerve. Far from the wanton chaos that the authorities perceived, the participants were often well trained, initially by fencing masters, and then by army deserters and veterans. From the seventeenth century, when recruiting was undertaken in Ireland for Irish brigades and regiments abroad, recruits trained with sticks, building up skill and discipline. Many sought to keep such expertise alive for use in agrarian insurgency — given the prohibition of arms to the native Irish. Such skills were as effective as swordsmanship. Indeed, faction fighting, as the enforcement of local law and custom, was on a continuum with the grounding of agrarian movement, such as Rockism, in the cultural codes of class and political conflict.

In the early decades of the nineteenth century, fairs and patterns were marked by ferocious pitched battles, with sticks (the use of knives was seen as unmanly and un-Irish). In some cases, the traditional ash stick was upgraded to a *clogh alpeen,* weighted with iron or lead ferrules. Sticks were always carefully primed: buttered, polished and seasoned up the chimney, until they had the right feel and heft. Fights broke out for many reasons: territorial, personal, communal, political, and even sometimes for the sheer fun of it. Often the reasons were complex and intertwined: resistance to usurping grabbers, agents or rapacious landlords resulting in guerrilla class-warfare; revenge for family or neighborly slights; Romeo and Juliet–type friction between feuding families — all of which kept readiness for sedition alive to serve the business of 'the nation'. At one fair alone in 1807, twenty were killed — such fights became the stuff of local legends. Of course, outsiders saw such fighting as barbaric, but the protagonists saw it as honorable, patriotic and as a time-honored form of social regulation. Fighting also had the psychological benefit of enabling men, otherwise emasculated by domination, to demonstrate their virility, and faction fights, displaying not only individual strength, but social organization and mobilization, gave comfort to a downtrodden and disheartened people. Accounting for of the impact of faction fighting, moral force, passive resistance, boycotting and intimidation on different levels of Irish society, Charles Townshend states that '[i]t seems almost impossible that such widely observed manifestations of popular energy as faction fights, whatever their original causes, could have persisted for so long without drawing political color from the constitutional and ideological issues of the period.'[119] The cultural framing of faction fighting is evident from the fact that it was customary at the feast of Lughnasa in August. Rural villages would fight, sometimes to the death, but it was often as much about observance as winning. There was an old folklore belief that the success of the harvest was dependent on the fairies, and was decided by a battle between two neighboring troops. Máire MacNeill suggests that success in factions was thought to bring fruitfulness to the winning side, and that such fights were symbolic re-enactments of fairy battles.[120]

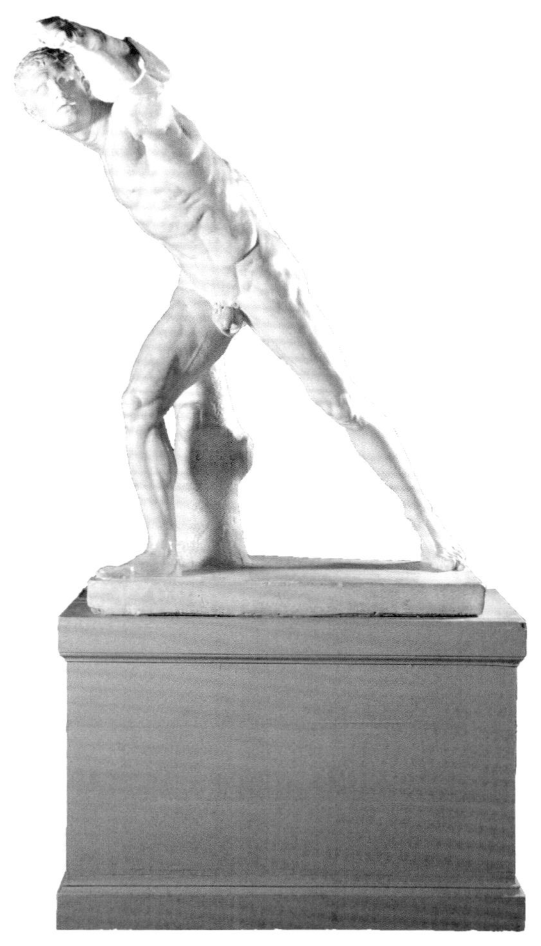

Figure 20

The Fighting Gladiator

Italian School

Plaster cast from the Roman copy in the Vatican Museum
c. 1816

From his childhood, as we have seen, Daniel Macdonald was steeped in the history, folklore and ethnography of rural unrest and regulation in Ireland. The works of Croker, the Halls and Maginn, were at the heart of his family life; indeed his father was an active player in such circles. The young Daniel would have known the rebel ballads of old, not only those adapted for drawing-room entertainment, but also the less refined originals, many of which were discovered by his father's activities as a musician and collector of traditional Irish music. Daniel's reading undoubtedly included vernacular chapbooks, with their vivid woodcuts.[121] Stories of insurgents, rebels and outlaws — legendary, true and imaginary — must have stirred his boyhood. Faction fighting peaked between 1820 and 1836, coinciding exactly with his upbringing. But as Co. Cork was riven with agrarian violence, accounts of mayhem, maiming and murder must have been sources of fear and terror as well. As Croker saw it:

> The witty servility of the Irish peasantry, mingled with occasional bursts of desperation and revenge — the devoted yet visionary patriotism — the romantic sense of honour, and improvident yet unalterable attachments, are evidences of a conquest without system, an

> irregular government, and the remains of a feudal clanship, the barbarous and arbitary
> organization of a warlike people.[122]

Although much was made of Irish violence, it was far from a one-sided problem; British efforts at subjugation were very brutal, and were in turn the cause of Irish violent retaliation. Agrarian insurgency often had clear intent and focus, but faction fighting was a more ritualistic response to appalling conditions of poverty and repression, and the erosion of a traditional moral economy. But whether of the faction variety at patterns, fairs or wakes, or the vigilantism of secret societies, rural violence called on obedience from the community.

Once the call went out for a fight, and the hunting horn sounded, families and neighbors left their hovels and hamlets and thronged to the scene where the traditional rites of combat were enacted. Faction fights were heavily ritualized since, as Croker explains:

> a man will sometimes, from a mere love of combat, and without any malice, take off his coat,
> and holding it by the collar, trail it through the assembly, challenging or beguiling any one to
> step on it; which insult he no sooner succeeds in obtaining, than he feels justified in knocking
> down the offender, and *the sport begins*.[123]

Invariably, fights kicked off in the same way, with the wheel. Wheeling involved the faction leaders storming along a strip of no-man's-land between the factions, taunting the opposing team, hurling insults until the bait was taken, then sticks were tapped and crossed, and they laid into each other. P. D. O'Donnell describes how the captains 'might advance almost to the enemy lines, and then wheel left or right, prancing up and down the lines and generally behaving in a most provocative manner … to the accompaniment of the most extraordinary exchange of language.'[124] Such a theatrical display is surely the subject of this painting. This captain is goading the enemy, getting their dander up, while also riling his own side to a frenzy. Macdonald depicts him *contraposto*, actually on the wheel, his head still to one side, his body already turned to stomp back down the line.

Charismatic faction leaders wielded massive power regionally, often controlling combined gangs (the most notorious being Captain Thomas Foley of the Knockboy gang), invariably men of the poorest class. Interestingly they tended to be highly image conscious. Many were identified by sartorial flamboyance (the red sash worn by this captain would have been an important part of his identity). And inevitably, they had a magnetic effect on young women. Notwithstanding the huge numbers, such fights — melees usually fuelled by alcohol — had their own internal logic and were to a large extent controlled by set conventions, not always obvious to the outsider. Importantly, they were pre-planned, not spontaneous events of uncontrolled violence. Macdonald's grasp of these details shows that he is knowledgeable and observant. The venue for a fight was often inaccessible or mountainous, making policing difficult (and if the authorities intervened, the opponents would immediately unite and attack the military or constabulary — always the common foe). In Macdonald's painting, the men clamber down from the mountain, waving and brandishing their sticks, rushing to the fray.

Maclise's *The Installation of Captain Rock,* as Luke Gibbons has noted, features 'the feminine' in the public space of insurgent nationalism'.[125] Macdonald also introduced several narrative elements into the scene, in a sophisticated visual manner, as vignettes rather than competing elements of the story. But the introduction of subplots, rather than competing plots, does not diminish their impact. The ardent lovers, just behind the fighter, may not be digressive, but actually provide an explanation for the significant action of the moment. If the young man does not survive the night, his sweetheart and mother may forever grieve, but there is no attempt to stop him, and her last look is one of such intensity and desire that it empowers and ennobles him for what is to come. In the Halls', *Ireland: Its Scenery, Character, &c.* (1841), the authors — family friends of Macdonald — describe the fate of one such star-crossed couple, in which a young woman, born a 'Connel' and brought up to hate the 'Lawlers', fell in love with a Lawler ...[126] It is possible that this, or the feud between the Coynes and the Caseys, or the love story between Anty Casey and John Coyne, also narrated by the Halls, provide a source for Macdonald's painting.[127]

The work of secret societies, both preventative and provocative, spilled over into all aspects of everyday life, familial, social, legal and political. As Terry Eagleton argues:

> With their carnivalesque iconography — baroque oaths, female clothing, exotic pseudonyms, mythical leaders and esoteric initiation ceremonies — these primitive rebels merged downwards into an illegal underworld of tories, rapparees, smugglers, poteen brewers and faction fighters, and shaded upwards into the daylight world of formal political activity.[128]

With Catholic Emancipation in 1829, the establishment of the Royal Irish Constabulary in 1836, and the spread of the temperance movement in the 1840s, the numbers of fights gradually diminished. Previously the authorities turned a blind eye — happy enough to shoot non-tithe payers, they were relieved that the Irish were murdering each other, rather than Protestant landlords or clergy. With the growing centralization of the Castle administration following Catholic Emancipation, the law began to exert a tighter hold on urban and rural dweller alike.

This passing of old ways applied to another more gentlemanly code of violence, that of dueling, and it is at this time that the *Portrait of General Sir Rowland Smyth KCB* **(Fig. 21)**, attributed to Macdonald, was painted. According to *The English Review:*

> Duels in Ireland … were conducted with a 'pomp and circumstance', which they certainly never attained in England. We have never heard of duels in this country in which the combatants on each side were attended to in the field by a long array of lords and gentlemen, magistrates, and county authorities, and by thousands of the lower orders, as eager and anxious witnesses of the fray.[129]

If faction fighting was the violence of the poor, dueling was the 'shameful vice of the rich'. As a way of determining affairs of honor, it reached a peak in the late eighteenth century.[130] A failure to respond 'honorably' to an insult implied cowardice, and resulted in social ostracism — hence few challenges were declined, and the survival of the practice as a method of resolution lasted well into the nineteenth century. Originally duels were fought with swords and had a high casualty rate, but replacement by the pistol reduced the number of deaths. As duels were not illegal, offenders were usually acquitted, or found guilty of manslaughter in their own defense, and released. Although banned also by the Church in the

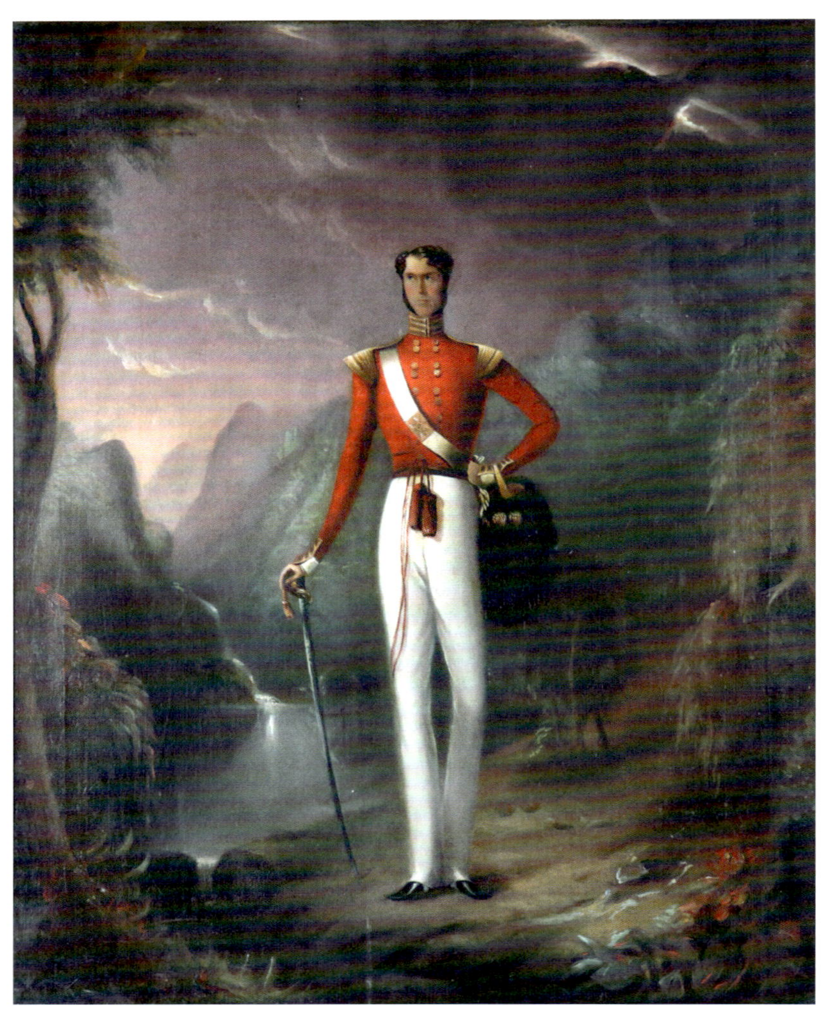

Figure 21

*Portrait of General
Sir Rowland Smyth KCB*

Daniel Macdonald

c. 1845

early nineteenth century, the permitting of Catholic gentlemen to carry arms led to a brief reprise of dueling, including a famous duel between Daniel O'Connell and John D'Esterre in 1815. O'Connell would have preferred not to fight, but he was conscious of the damage to his reputation if he refused; paradoxically, his success in killing D'Esterre affirmed his position as the non-violent champion of the people.

In 1830, the killing of Standish Stamer O'Grady in a duel in Dublin caused a sensation, and it is his killer who features in the work apparently painted by Macdonald. In this case, however, honor was notably deficient. When the handsome, wealthy and popular young barrister, Standish Stamer O'Grady, was on his way to Merrion Square in Dublin, a cabriolet hurtled towards him at speed. He mounted the footpath to avoid the vehicle, but called out: 'Damn you, sir, where the devil are you driving to!'[131] The vehicle, occupied by Captains Smyth and Markham of the 32nd Regiment, came to an abrupt halt, and Smyth alighted and proceeded to horsewhip O'Grady. O'Grady procured the services of Lieutenant MacNamara to seek an apology, but Smyth professed himself grossly insulted by O'Grady's tone, and refused, leaving O'Grady no choice but to challenge him. At 5 a.m. the next day, pistols were discharged, and O'Grady fell. Smyth now knelt by the dying O'Grady, and asked his forgiveness, which was given. Although Smyth was not found wanting in honor by the judge, the jury found him and his second, Captain Markham, guilty of manslaughter, and they were sentenced to twelve months in Kilmainham Gaol (the same court sentenced a small farmer to seven years' transportation for stealing a cow). Both Smyth and Markham were granted a year's leave of absence to serve their sentences, and went on to triumphant careers in the army, Smyth distinguishing himself while being wounded at the celebrated battle of Aliwal against the Sikhs in 1846. On their return from India, when, presumably, Macdonald's portrait was painted, Smyth's regiment was garrisoned in Ireland for several years. He was knighted in 1867, given the colonelcy of the 6th dragoon guards in 1868, promoted lieutenant-general in 1870, and died a hero in 1873.

But there is a coda to the story. One night previously, at the theatre he had found himself standing beside a veiled woman, whom he guessed was young and beautiful. He impertinently lifted her veil, whereupon her companion punched him in the face. Tempted to call his adversary out, Smyth was advised to drop it, as the young man was a marksman of note. Following a groveling apology, he was branded a coward. In a sense, Smyth had been looking for a chance to redeem his reputation, as the only way out of dishonor was to become either the victim or the perpetrator of death. O'Grady thus became Smyth's sacrificial lamb.

The portrait *General Sir Rowland Smyth KCB* features a lank, patrician officer, set in an eerie landscape. The figure is haughty, remote and cold, and the work largely uncharacteristic of Macdonald, except perhaps in that the figure has been etiolated to the point of caricature. So far, there does not seem much to go on in attributing this to Macdonald, but the signed 1847 sketch, *After the Duel* **(Fig. 22)**, shows that Macdonald did have an interest in the subject (indeed, perversely, the heavily side-burned, man, stretched out on the cart, being rushed away by his supporters, looks not unlike Smyth himself).

As it happens, this drawing ties in with two other drawings of peasants returning from funerals, but of a jauntier nature. *Returning from an Irish Funeral* (1842) **(Fig. 23)** shows much hilarity as a group of devil-may-care peasants, including the gravediggers, hitch a ride home from a funeral, in a canopied hearse, which the outlying riders are attempting to overtake, as geese scatter and pigs forage. The sketch

Figure 22
After the Duel
Daniel Macdonald
1847

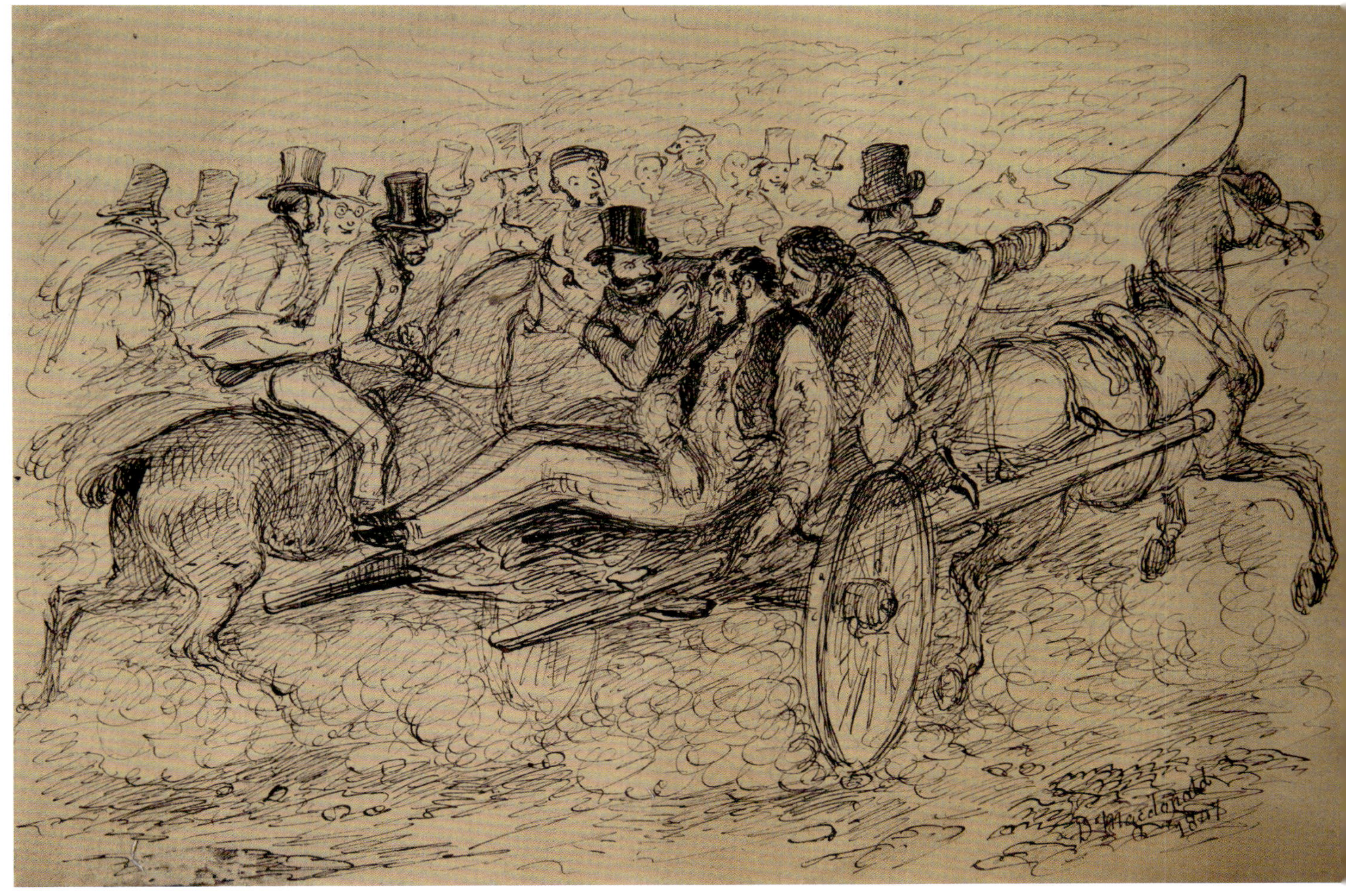

Figure 23

*Returning from an
Irish Funeral*

Daniel Macdonald

1842

Figure 24

*Going Home
After a Funeral*

Daniel Macdonald

1842

features a ruined Gothic church and round tower (a subject of much recondite but occasionally ludicrous scholarship at the time), and a deserted graveyard in the distance. The literature of the time is replete with feckless, duplicitous Irish characters taking advantage of their betters, but Macdonald's take is neither malicious nor disparaging, but demonstrative of the humor and jollity of carnivalesque aspects of everyday life. Often, when the going got heavy, Macdonald resorted to satire and humor: in *Going Home after a Funeral* (1842) (**Fig. 24**), romance is in the air. A lovely young woman rides pillion with a rather pleased looking man on his horse, and as the cock crows …

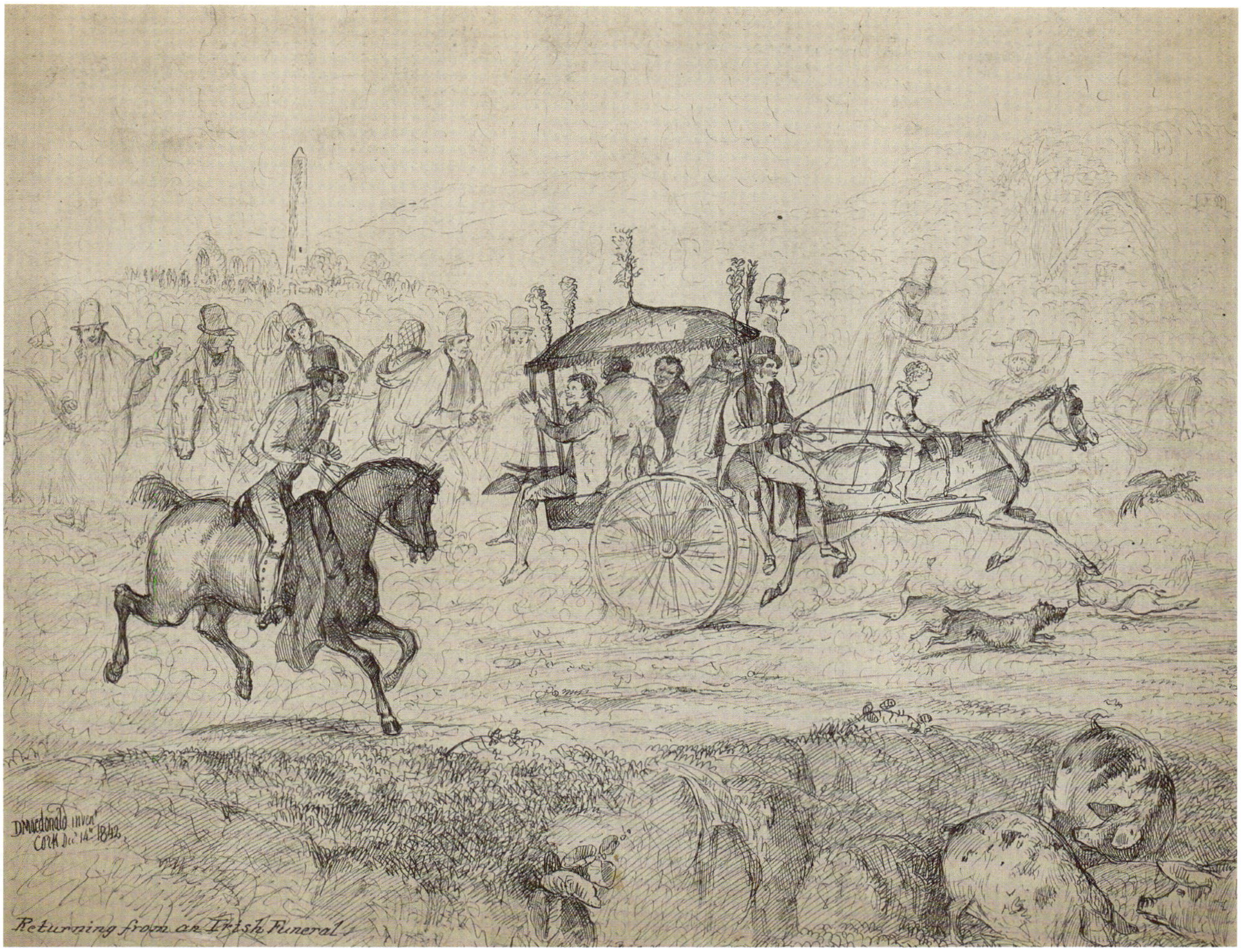

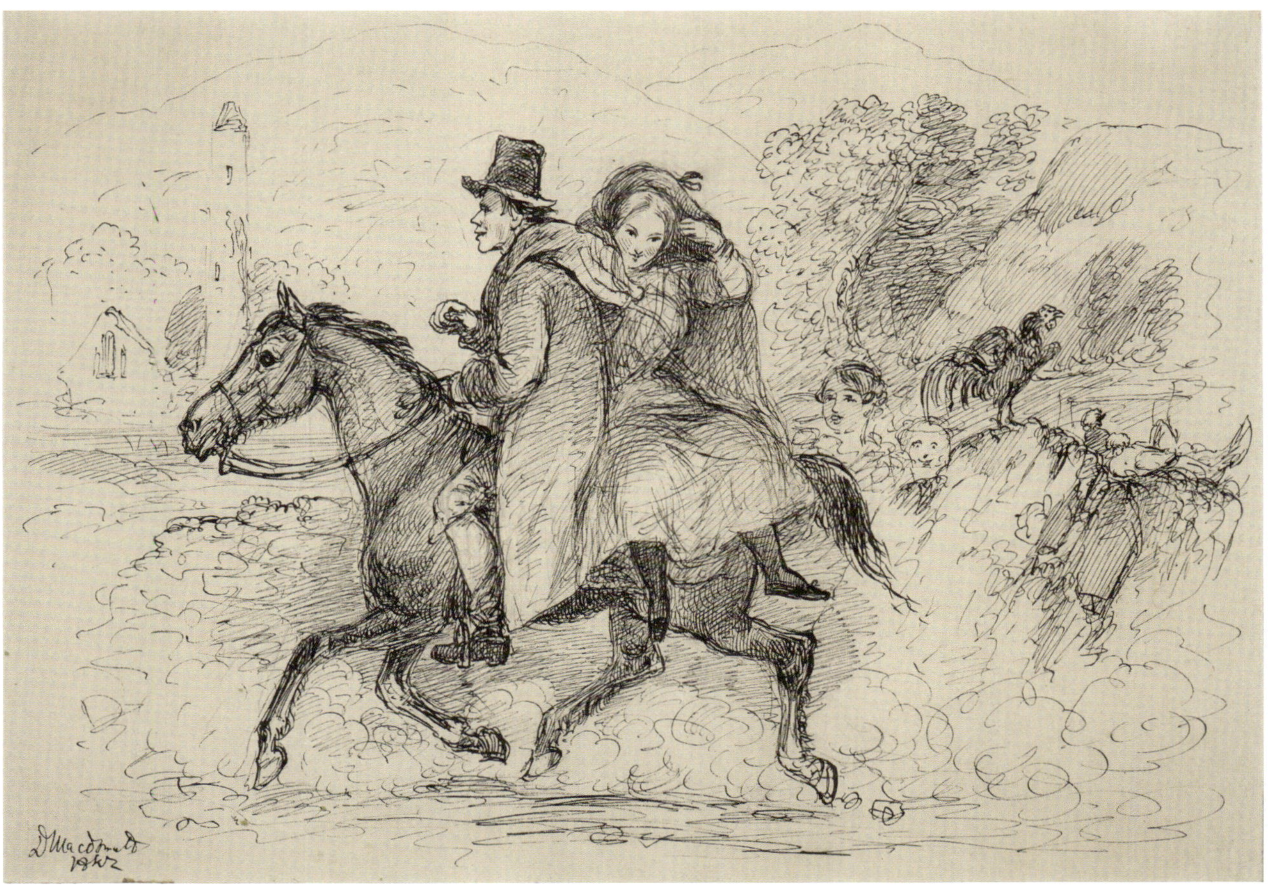

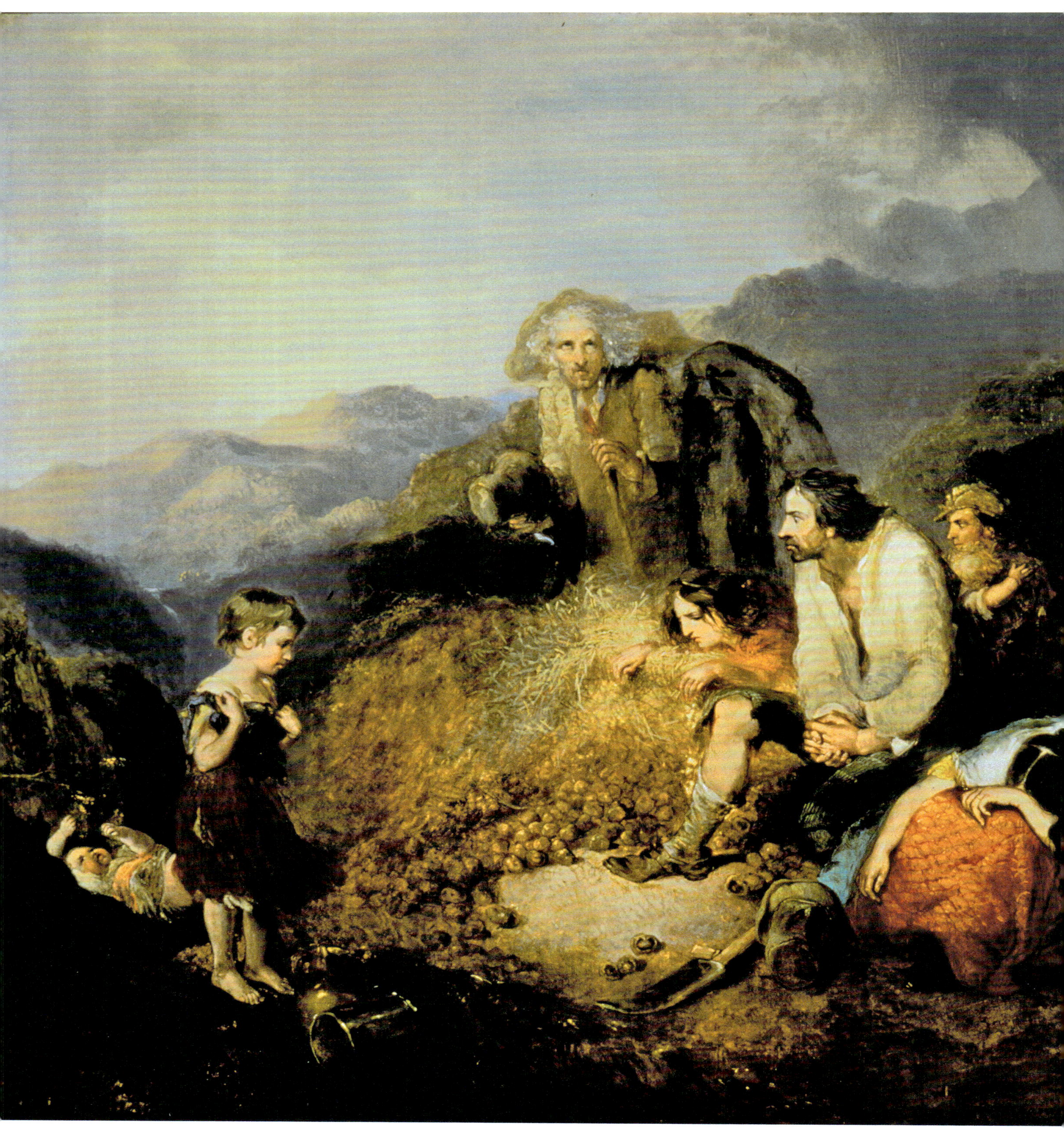

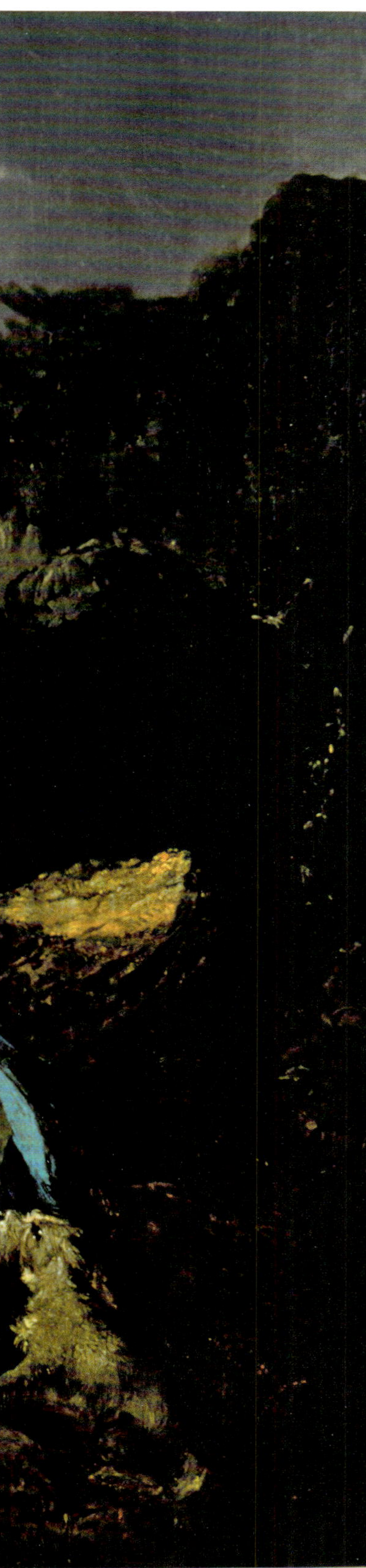

CHAPTER 3

WE ARE SCOURGED...

Macdonald's landmark painting, *An Irish Peasant Family Discovering the Blight of their Store* (**Fig. 25**) was exhibited, as noted, at the British Institution in 1847, but for all its poignancy, it went almost unremarked. From the British perspective, the less said about this painting, the better. The reason for this is not hard to see: representations of Ireland in the salons of London at the time were made to attract elite audiences, not to disturb them — keeping their desire to know what went on in Ireland in check with their own self-interests, and of course the wider interests of the Empire.

By 1845, 85 percent of the population lived on small plots of land, in unspeakable poverty. Income per head was about half of that in England. Isaac Weld described hovels constructed from

> backs of fences; the floors sunk in the ditches; the height scarcely enough for a man to stand upright; poles not thicker than a broomstick for couples; a few pieces of grass sods the only covering; and these extending only partially over the thing called a roof; the elderly people miserably clothed; the children all but naked.[132]

One reporter came across a bedstead 'literally propped on stones, around which was collected a filthy pool.' The hovel scarcely exceeded the length of its occupier who had a wife and three children, leading the reporter to conclude: '[h]e will have almost as much space when laid in his grave.' (*Pictorial Times*, February 7, 1846) Indeed, noted the *Illustrated London News*, 'a bed or a blanket is a rare luxury, and nearly in all, their pig and manure-heap constitute their only property.' (January 10, 1846)

Figure 25

An Irish Peasant Family Discovering the Blight of their Store

Daniel Macdonald

1847

THE ILLUSTRATED LONDON NEWS.   [Jan. 5, 1850.

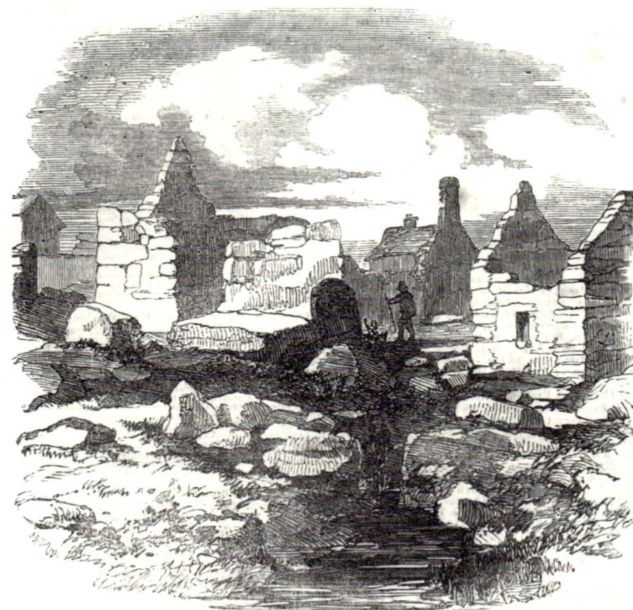

RUINS IN THE VILLAGE OF CARIHAKEN, COUNTY OF GALWAY.

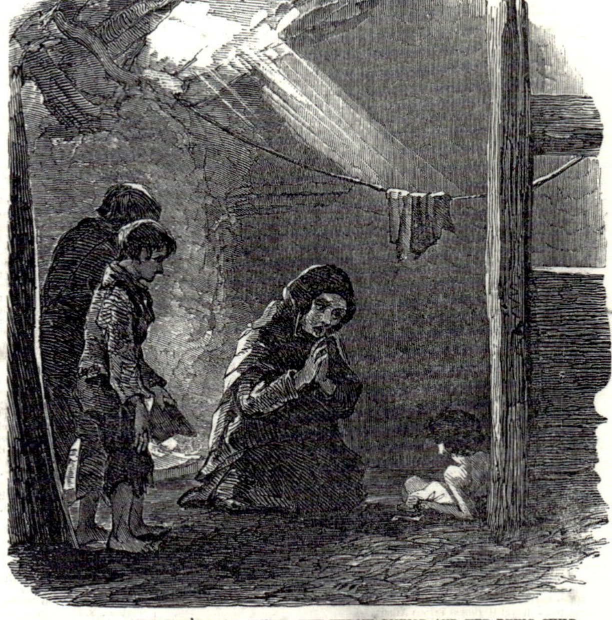

SKETCH IN A HOUSE AT FAHEY'S QUAY, ENNIS.—THE WIDOW CONNOR AND HER DYING CHILD.

only another evidence of the impropriety of establishing such a law for a people in such a condition.

I crossed the Bay to Galway, and proceeded towards Clifden by a route devoid of interest, exhibiting, in a less degree than in Clare, the usual signs of devastation in progress. Mr. Martin's property extends almost the whole way from Ouchterade to Clifden, and is a mixture of mountain, moor, and fertile land, capable of indefinite improvement, with great facility of water carriage, but most sadly neglected. It is a bad sign for the next harvest, and for the people of this country, that in my whole journey from Galway I did not see more than from thirty to forty persons, including all ages and sexes; and, with the exception of ten men working under a road contractor, few or none of them were at work.

At Carihaken the levellers have been at work, and tumbled down eighteen houses. In one of them dwelt John Killian, who stood by me while I made the accompanying Sketch of the remains of his dwelling. He told me that he and his fathers before him had owned this now ruined cabin for ages, and that he had paid £4 a year for four acres of ground. He owed no rent: before it was due, the landlord's drivers cut down his crops, carried them off, gave him no account of the proceeds, and then tumbled his house. The hut made against the end wall of a former habitation was not likely to remain, as a decree had gone forth entirely to clear the place. The old man also told me that his son having cut down, on the spot that was once his own garden, a few sticks to make him a shelter, was taken up, prosecuted, and sentenced to two months' confinement for destroying trees and making waste of the property.

I must supply you with another Sketch of a similar subject on the road between Maam and Clifden, in Joyce's County, once famous for the Patagonian stature of the inhabitants, who are now starved down to ordinary dimensions. High up on the mountain, but on the road-side, stands the scalpeen of Keillines. It is near General Thompson's property. Conceive five human beings living in such a hole: the father was out, at work; the mother was getting fuel on the hills, and the children left in the hut could only say they were hungry. Their appearance confirmed their words—want was deeply engraved in their faces, and their lank bodies were almost unprotected by clothing.

At Kylemore my companion bought a turbot, weighing from 18lb. to 20lb., for 1s. 6d., and might have had it for 1s. had he driven a hard bargain. The fact indicates that the sea would supply plenty of food if man would take the trouble to procure it. A similar proof of the equal capacity of the soil is found at a short distance from Kylemore. Two enterprising Englishmen, of the name of Eastwood, planted themselves there about four years ago, and all around them the bleak and barren moor has been changed into well laid-out fields—some green with herbage, and others brown and dingy with the stubble of the carried corn. There is a comfortable lodge, in the Elizabethan style, and around it suitable farm buildings. The whole indicates skill, industry, and good taste; it indicates, too, great courage in overcoming a moral as well as a physical opposition. The Messrs. Eastwood have, in some measure, conquered the habits of the people, which was a more difficult task than subduing the neglected and deserted heath. They will be pioneers to others, who will select, let us hope, this fertile and promising wilderness for the scene of their exertions, instead of wrestling against the arid sands of Australasia, or engaging in competition for the plains of the Mississippi with emigrants from all the countries of Europe. Their example has in fact been followed; and between their abode and Clifden two or three beginnings have been made—so that the country adjoining that town exhibits several signs of improvement.

This neighbourhood, before the potato rot came, was not so entirely occupied by the cultivation of the root as some other parts of the country. In the Union of Kilrush, for example, in 1848, there were 11,569 acres under potatoes, out of an area of 178,935 acres; in the Union of Clifden there were only 3714 acres, out of an area of 189,504 acres, under potatoes. The fact is of some importance, in explaining the compa-

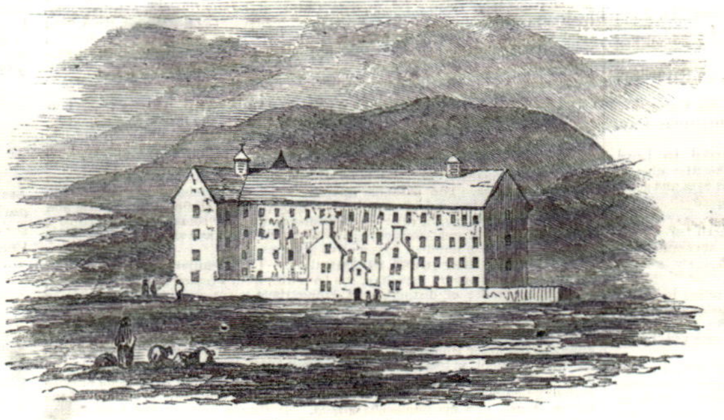

THE WORKHOUSE, CLIFDEN.

rative ease with which the poor in Clifden have been disposed of. Clifden itself is an exotic in an unfavourable climate. It was reared by the patronage of the late Viscount; and since that ceased, it began to decline: the Poor-law has almost finished it. Before we reached, we learned that the *guardians* of the union were out of money, and obliged to pay for what they wanted by cheques, which they are to receive in payment of the rates. Extreme poverty exists in the neighbourhood—the soil around is poor—great numbers of houses have been levelled—but the poor, unlike those of Kilrush, have in great part disappeared with the houses. They have not found refuge in the workhouse—they have not been carried away as emigrants; they have either wandered away or have died, or both may have contributed to cause their disappearance. I have a list of 111 houses levelled within a few months in the immediate neighbourhood of Clifden, which is very considerable, considering that the whole population of the Union was only 33,465 in 1841. Assuming five inmates to a house, the sixtieth part of the population has been dispossessed. Here, too, there is little more than one person to every six acres; or, scanty as is the population of Clare, the population of the Union of Clifden is not, in relation to acres, half so abundant. I have taken a Sketch of the workhouse, which I send as a memorial of this pet place of the late Viscount Clifden.

From Clifden to Ouchterade, twenty-one miles, is a dreary drive over a moor, unrelieved except by a glimpse of Mr. Martin's house at Ballynahinch, and of the residence of Dean Mahon. Destitute as this tract is of inhabitants, about Ouchterade some thirty houses have been recently demolished. A gentleman who witnessed the scene told me nothing could exceed the heartlessness of the levellers, if it were not the patient submission of the sufferers. They wept, indeed; and the children screamed with agony at seeing their homes destroyed and their parents in tears; but the latter allowed themselves unresistingly to be deprived of what is to most people the dearest thing on earth next to their lives—their only home.

I returned to Galway, where the Poor-law officials are not communicative, nor is there in the Union any extraordinary fact to communicate. The old town is a jumble of thatched mud cabins, stone-built houses, and the remains of a former splendour, old sculptures and carvings, putting to shame the homely and even rude houses of a modern date. The people are remarkable for the vivid colours of their dresses, amongst which red predominates, and some lingering traces of a foreign origin may yet be discovered in their countenances. Here, as in most other sea-ports and fishing towns, particularly of Ireland, hulking men lounging about were numerous, and appeared to have every other capacity to work but the will. You are not annoyed, however, by mendicants in Galway, as in other Irish towns, though there is a universal complaint of distress finished by the exclamation, "That last five-shilling rate is a death-blow to all."

From Galway I proceeded to Ennis, and in the neighbourhood inspected the village of Clear, which had been destroyed within a few weeks, and some part of it within a few days. The *Sketch of Pat Macnamara's Cabin* shews the condition of the village. In Ennis I went through the lanes and alleys, and amongst the most distressed part of the population. In one small room, not 20 feet square, I found congregated fifteen people, young and old, exhibiting nearly all the phases of want and squalor. From the smoke which filled the place, it was a Rembrandt scene, and it was with difficulty I could make out the forms of the wretched groups, or of the squalid and dying child on the floor. In the union workhouse of Ennis there is order, decency, and regularity. With it is conjoined a farm of eighteen acres, which is well cultivated by the labour of the paupers. It is wisely placed under the superintendence of one of Lord Clarendon's practical agricultural instructors; and probably he is as well employed in displaying his skill at the farm as in any other mode of teaching his art.

At Ennis, I consider my tour terminated; and I shall only send you further some general observations on the Poor-law, and some suggestions as to what might reasonably be done for Ireland.

(To be continued next week.)

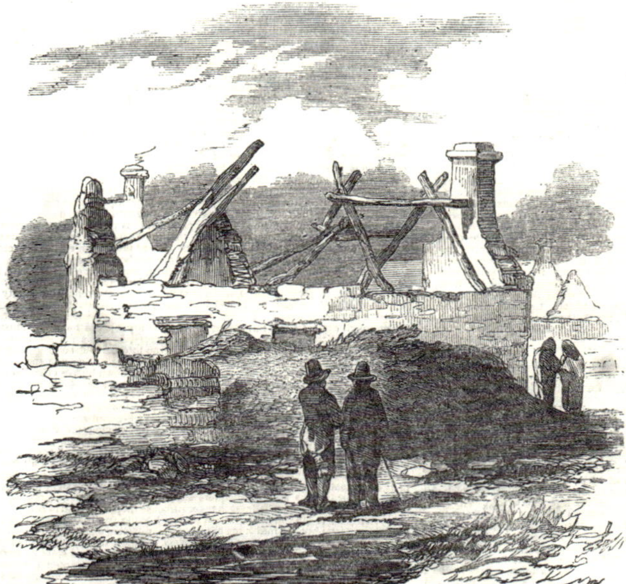

CABIN OF PAT. MACNAMARA, VILLAGE OF CLEAR.

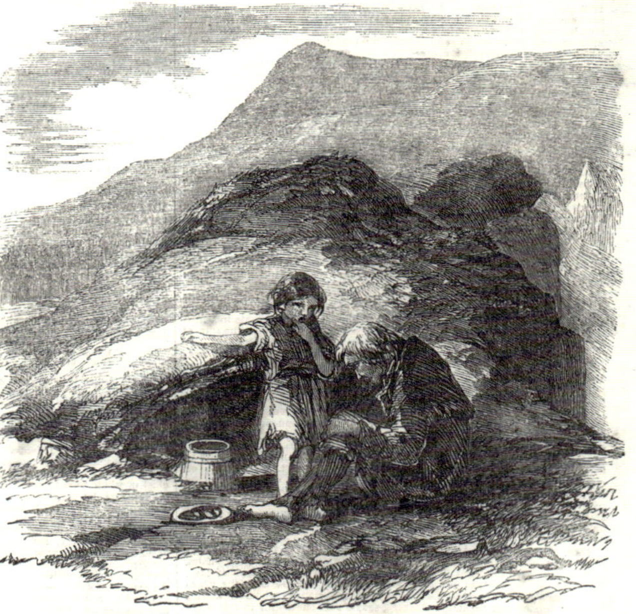

KEILLINES, NEAR GENERAL THOMPSON'S PROPERTY.

Cyclical famines in Ireland were devastating to their victims, but before the Great Famine, they rarely outlasted a single year, allowing for some recovery before the next. The 1845–52 Great Hunger, however, is best understood as an outcome of systematic neglect by the British government over a hundred-year period, rather than a series of unconnected single events. In 1846, as the Great Famine entered its second year, Father Theobald Mathew wrote to the Assistant Secretary of the Treasury, Charles Trevelyan:

> A blast ... has passed over the land, and the hopes of the poor potato cultivators are totally blighted, and the food of a whole nation has perished ... the wretched people were seated on the fences of their decaying gardens, wringing their hands and wailing bitterly the destruction that had left them foodless. (August 7, 1846)

A week later *The Nation* lamented:

> a cry of FAMINE, wilder and more fearful than ever, is rising from every parish and county in the land … there is a loathsome mass of putrefaction: the sole food on which millions of men, women and children are to be fed is stricken by a deadly blight before their eyes; and probably within one month those millions will be hungry and have nothing to eat. (August 15, 1846)

There were complete failures in 1846 and 1848, and extensive failures in the other five years, and the effects were cumulative. Prior to 1845, the Irish peasant was among the healthiest in Europe; after 1852, the rural survivor was a shadow of him or herself.

Death from starvation vied with death from famine disease, both emanating from, as Laurence Geary describes it, 'the wretched housing of the poor, the paucity and inferior quality of their diet, their lack of clothing and fuel, dirt, depression, and intoxication, not to mention the pig in the kitchen and the middens that disgraced the frontage of every cabin in the country.'[133] **(Fig. 26)** Relapsing fever was pernicious; extreme toxemia led to internal hemorrhaging as the body disintegrated, emitting the foulest stench as it discharged and decomposed while the poor person was still alive. Lice feasted on filthy, unfed bodies and spread like wildfire. People were terrified of contagion. Valued neither in life, nor death, their bodies were disposed of without shroud or coffin, wake or prayer. And yet the *Times* wrote of 'ingredients in the Irish character which must be modified and corrected', and declared the blight 'a blessing' (September 22, 1846). But there was method in the indifference of the landlords, and the inaction of Government. The blight culled the population, and cleared the land ruthlessly and efficiently. As Charles Trevelyan at the Treasury saw it: '[t]he judgment of God sent the calamity to teach the Irish a lesson, that calamity must not be too much mitigated. … The real evil with which we have to contend is not the physical evil of the Famine, but the moral evil of the selfish, perverse and turbulent character of the people'.[134] It was such chilling sentiments that occasioned John Mitchel's famous riposte: '[t]he Almighty, indeed, sent the blight but the British government sent the Famine.'[135]

At this time, artists were classically trained in academies where the emphasis was on the human figure, learned from Greek and Roman casts. Consequently, they had little or no experience of looking at

Figure 26

The *Illustrated London News*

January 5, 1850

unfiltered images of real-life trauma or poverty. The diluted images of Irish distress in the illustrated press were considered frightful, and were certainly not a subject Victorians would have chosen to adorn their homes in the more elevated medium of painting. The representation of peasants even in the whole of their health was unpalatable enough, but for painters, the task of representing the Famine was morally, technically and aesthetically almost insurmountable. Historical precedents of the depiction of atrocity — intended to glorify, exhort or commemorate — were executed at a remove in time and place. Paintings of wars and plagues were not intended as documentary accounts of events, but the opportunity to reflect on the values they stood for. Atrocity art — intended for consumption by those contemporaneous with a calamitous event — is largely unprecedented before the Great Famine, except for artists such as Francisco Goya and select others.

The protocols of history painting, the dominant genre, required that important ideas be accorded commensurate size and scale. The difficulty in finding an appropriate form for the visualization of violent death is evident throughout the history of art, until extending the boundaries of Realism provided new opportunities in representation. At the turn of the nineteenth century, Jacques-Louis David's *Death of Marat* (1793) (Musées Royaux des Beaux-Arts at Brussels), the first convincing image of death, Antoine-Jean Gros' *Napoleon Bonaparte Visiting the Plague-Stricken in Jaffa* (1804) (Musée du Louvre), showing Napoleon touching a bubonic plague victim — as Christ a leper — and Théodore Géricault's *Raft of the Medusa* (1818–19) (Musée du Louvre) with its whiff of scandal (and cannibalism), were the first images to demonstrate the power of art to communicate shocking contemporary events.[136] But there is nothing comparable in Britain at this time, and Macdonald's painting marks a notable shift in the Victorian portrayal, not only of poverty, but people in a state of disintegration.

Whether from protectiveness or shame, lack of courage or skill, few Irish artists attempted to capture the appalling conditions presented to them by the Great famine.[137] Surprisingly, English artists Frederick Goodall, Francis Topham and Alfred Fripp visited Galway in 1844, where they painted homely scenes of domesticity, set in desperately poor cabins, made of mud or driftwood. The bare dresser and the absence of a pot over the fire tell of the poverty of the people, but the scenes are sweetened and sentimentalized for British audiences. It was not simply that artists could not bear to represent the suffering, but that the art market simply would not have stood for it. Exceptionally, a small number of allegorical works appeared. By selecting a subject that had no apparent connection with a real-life contemporary event, artists felt able to comment allegorically. Daniel Maclise's post-Famine *Marriage of Strongbow and Aoife* (1854) (National Gallery of Ireland) depicts the arranged marriage between Richard de Clare, Earl of Pembroke, and Aoife, daughter of the King of Leinster, that heralded the invasion of Ireland by the Normans. But the meaning also extends to the Act of Union in 1800, and to the Famine. The destruction of Irish culture is displayed in the abundance of archaeological detail (the torcs and armlets from the Bronze Age); Strongbow's foot and sword against the shattered High Cross, and the ruined church and round tower, signal the death of monastic spirituality; and the burning of Waterford in the background, and the fallen heroes in the foreground, symbolize the end of Irish right and might. Above all, the massacred bodies, in the wake of the Famine, speak of the death, not only

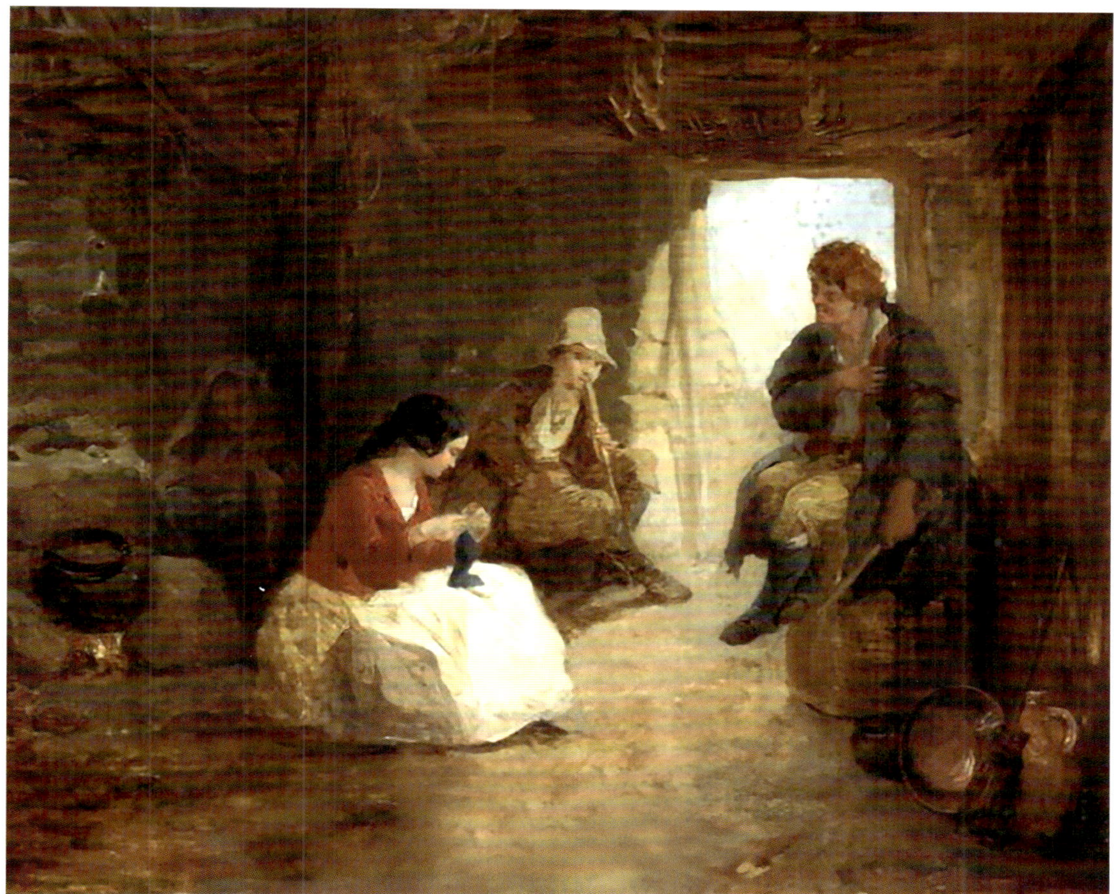

of one million people, but of an ancient culture, confirming that the storm clouds in the painting are as much about recent history, as events in the past.[138]

Moreover, aesthetic conventions did not allow ordinary people serious treatment in art, a significant exception being Frederic Burton's *Aran Fisherman's Drowned Child* (1841). It was not just that the depiction of famine-ravaged bodies challenged the skills of artists, but the conceptual frames of reference of the time ensured that artists brushed over the worst aspects, allowing shorthand features, such as tattered rags, spiky hairs and dirt, to imply the rest. The few attempts to breach the barrier in illustration did not cross over into painting.[139] For these reasons, the Macdonald image is extraordinary for its time. It was an important subject, and he gave it size, scale and solemnity, but its strangeness was such that it was greeted with but one comment. *The Art Union* declared that '[t]here is much power manifested in the conception of this picture; the subject is not exaggerated', but the commentator went on to add the non sequitur: 'the female figure is not in an Irish dress'.[140]

Some 561 pictures were shown that year (and 400 rejected), and the opening was attended by 'the great and celebrated of the land.'[141] While the reviewers enthused about James Inskipp's inconsequential *The Venetian Letter Writer,* it was another 'Irish' picture that stole the show, Frederick Goodall's *Irish Courtship* **(Fig. 27).** The *Daily News* described the exhibition as one 'of stupefying mediocrity'. (February 8, 1847) The *Morning Post* concurred: 'To call the exhibition bad is to use a term so far above its merits.' Nevertheless, of *Irish Courtship,* the latter spoke ecstatically:

> The works of Goodall are of such even beauty that we long to speak of them … we have rarely looked upon a work of art which afforded more unmixed pleasure … This is one of those paintings which please at first sight and grow upon acquaintance. The colouring is vivid, and all the details carefully elaborated. The style is minute, but the handling free. The result is a picture perfect of its kind … . A homely picture is the medium of depicting the character of a nation, and a history is told which inculcates a moral lesson. In the cabin of an Irish farmer of the better class five figures occupy the foreground.

It went on to describe the painting as 'deliciously charming', but conceded that 'its deepened shadows foretells events to come'. Even in this comment, the portentousness was not about the Famine killing hundreds of thousands, but time running out for the old woman in the painting (February 8, 1847). *The Spectator* also missed its chance, denouncing as 'ludicrous' the significant glances passing between the *dramatis personae*, insisting that neither one is really looking at the other; 'most or all of them are looking out of the picture; many, with pupils unconverged, are gazing at nothing in particular, but slyly looking at vacancy' (February 13, 1847). But instead of attributing this dissociation to the trauma of the Famine, the reviewer simply perceived a flaw in the ability of the artist to convincingly portray romantic love. Given the grim subject matter of Macdonald's painting, it is extraordinary that in the many lengthy reviews of the 1847 exhibition, none mentioned the cataclysm that had befallen Ireland, other than one brief mention in *The Art-Union*.

As this painting was on view, the *Southern Reporter* lamented:

> We are overwhelmed with distress; we are crushed with taxation; we are scourged by famine; and visited by pestilence. Our jails are full; our poor houses choked; our public edifices turned into lazar houses; our cities mendicities; our streets *morgues*; our churchyards fields of carnage. Our ordinary trade is gone; our people are partially demoralised. Society itself is breaking up; selfishness seizes upon all; class repudiates class; the very ties of closest kindred are snapt asunder. Sire and son, landlord and occupier, town and country repudiate each other, ceasing to co-operate — Terror and hunger, disease and death afflict us … horrible suffering, utter penury … (May 1, 1847)

First brought to Europe from America in 1573, the potato had reached Ireland before the turn of the sixteenth century. Grown on marginal lands, by 1800 it had become the staple food of poorer people.[142] A tiny patch of even the most inhospitable land, and a few weeks' work, produced enough to see a family through at least nine months of the year (the lean months in the summer, until the new crop was ready, were generally hard). Potatoes were grown in 'lazy beds', low trenches at about three-foot intervals, enriched with manure and sea weed. Harvested twice a year, for winter and spring consumption, they were stored in pits, outside the house, covered with straw and earth, to preserve them as long as possible. As needed, they were retrieved with a *slane / sleaghdn* or turf spade.[143] The proximate cause of the Famine, the fungus, *Phytophthora infestans,* struck in August 1845.

Macdonald's painting shows a family of four generations as they discover to their horror that blight has hit their food store. That they will now starve to death is virtually certain. The three figures in the middle (or close versions thereof) have migrated from *The Fighter* and *Irish Peasant Children*, but there is no fight left in this family. The figures at the top of the painting, an elderly man, the family patriarch, and his already shrouded wife, look down on the fateful scene, their children and their children's children. Each stricken, they are beyond communicating. Each knows what lies ahead. The diseased potatoes are strewn, the now useless *slane* cast down, the setting sun dims the light, and the gathering storm closes in. We can almost hear the Banshee or White Fairy on the wind. The banshee was no evil spirit, but 'a respected messenger of death', described by Thomas Crofton Croker as 'a small and shrivelled old woman with long white hair, supposed to be peculiarly attached to old houses or families, and to announce the approaching dissolution of any members by mournful lamentations. This fairy attendant is considered as highly honourable', and only associated with those of 'illustrious descent.'[144] The scene may seem melodramatic, but it does not resort to stereotype, and although frozen with fright by the sight before their eyes, this family remains dignified in the face of disaster.

The two incongruous presences in the picture are the rather strange looking baby on the left, and the dwarf-like figure on the right. The painting was made two years into the Famine. Notwithstanding the constraints inherent in fine art training, it is striking that the family is not already showing signs of emaciation. The younger generations look fit, and young woman on the right is relatively well dressed and groomed, indicating that this family was, until now, relatively prosperous. But the pail is empty. The young father, although shod, is in tatters, as is his barefooted daughter. Their impoverishment is taking place before our eyes.

An Irish Peasant Family Discovering the Blight of their Store has its own interesting provenance, having been donated by Cecil Woodham-Smith, Ireland's first modern Famine historian, in gratitude to the National Folklore Commission for help in researching her seminal book, *The Great Hunger: Ireland 1845–1849* (1962).

OUT, OUT, OUT

British newspapers also filtered out many aspects of the Famine that might cast a critical eye on British handling of the catastrophe.[145] And middle class prudery would have discouraged the sharing of the overly graphic effects of famine on the human body and spirit. For most English readers, therefore, hunger remained a poorly understood phenomenon. Whether one believed the Famine to be the fault of the victims, or the will of God, as many did, accurate descriptions of the pathology of starvation and disease — documented for the first time during the Great Hunger — were initially circulated amongst the medical confraternity, and would not have made it to the breakfast table of average readers in expanded form.

Dr. Daniel Donovan of Skibbereen was one of the first study famine disease: 'the face and limbs become frightfully emaciated; the eyes acquire a most peculiar stare; the skin exhaled a peculiar and offensive foetor, and was covered with a brownish filthy-looking coating, almost as indelible as varnish'.

At first Dr. Donovan believed the 'coating' was encrusted dirt, but soon realized that this was 'a secretion poured out from the exhalants on the surface of the body.' His descriptions of the tooth loss, swollen joints, distended stomachs and bursting blood vessels, leading to painful and distressing diseases, and ultimately death, were unprecedented. He was also one of the few to consider the psychological trauma, and the breakdown of normal human behavior, describing the insensibility wrought by Famine to the extent that he had observed 'parents look on the putrid bodies of their offspring without evincing a symptom of sorrow'.[146] In extracts from his 'Diary of a Dispensary Doctor' in the *Southern Reporter* throughout 1847 and 1848, he described life and death in homes, workhouses and by the roadside. But his contributions to the medical journals, the *Lancet*, the *Dublin Journal of Medical Science* and the *Dublin Medical Press*, notably his distinctions between death from disease and from famine, were largely disseminated after the fact, the pathology of starvation being poorly understood or known at the time.[147]

Doctors and clergy were of course joined by courageous and generous members of the public who risked their own lives to help the hungry and diseased. Macdonald, now living in London, expressed his concern in an unexpected way, and probably more frequently that we now know. In 1847, he was asked to mark the work of Daniel Welply, a wealthy Catholic merchant and landowner who lived in Skibbereen, in thanks for the 'exceedingly generous and humane conduct pursued by Mr. Welply, in mitigating, both by subscriptions and personal exertions, the calamitous condition of the population of Skibereen.'[148] The *Welply Tribute* was framed and embossed, and decorated 'by the most competent person that could be selected', namely Macdonald. The chairman of the committee then read an extract from a letter by Macdonald 'an artist of very considerable celebrity, who is a native of Cork, and resided for a long time in that city' who said,

> Your directions shall be strictly attended to respecting this matter. Under the distressing circumstances of our unfortunate country, we could not make any charge where demands of a public and private nature press so heavily on all classes. You may calculate on receiving it to your directions this week, or early next, which I hope will be in sufficient time to carry out the intentions of the gentlemen concerned in conferring this mark of their respect and esteem upon a worthy man. (December 18, 1846)

The *Cork Examiner* reported Welply saying 'There must be something wrong in the state of Denmark — there must something radically bad in the constitutional government of this country, or the loss of the potato crop would not have destroyed its limited prosperity and completely annihilated its population.' (January 11, 1847)

Between 1728 and 1845, there were twenty-eight famines in which millions of Irish men, women and children died, while food continued to be exported to England. In 1790, the population of Ireland was approximately 4 million. Fifty years later, it had exploded to over 8.1 million. Between 1841 and 1891, it dropped to 4.7 million. One million died, during, and in the immediate aftermath of the Great Hunger, 1.25 million emigrated during the Famine years (two-thirds of these to the US alone), followed by up to 2 million further emigrations to the end of the nineteenth century. Over a fifty-year period, the population of an entire country was halved.[149]

Wholesale evictions swept through the country, as entire villages were emptied in systematic efforts to clear out what were considered surplus people. Evictions were the evidential scandal of the time. Landlords knew that evictions that were often death sentences. If the biology of hunger was difficult to imagine, the social consequences of homelessness were immediately evident.[150] Other than for those who had the means to emigrate, eviction meant certain and awful death.

A small number of paintings and a larger number of illustrations exist, including a number of British paintings, such as Goodall's *An Irish Eviction* (1850) (New Walk Museum and Gallery, Leicester Arts and Museum Services), a wooden rendition, lacking any conviction. George Frederic Watts (1817–1904), on the other hand, did not even visit Ireland until after he painted his eviction scene, *The Irish Famine* (c. 1848–50) **(Fig. 28)**. His interest was derived from reading newspaper reports at the time, and the

Figure 28
The Irish Famine
George Frederic Watts
1850

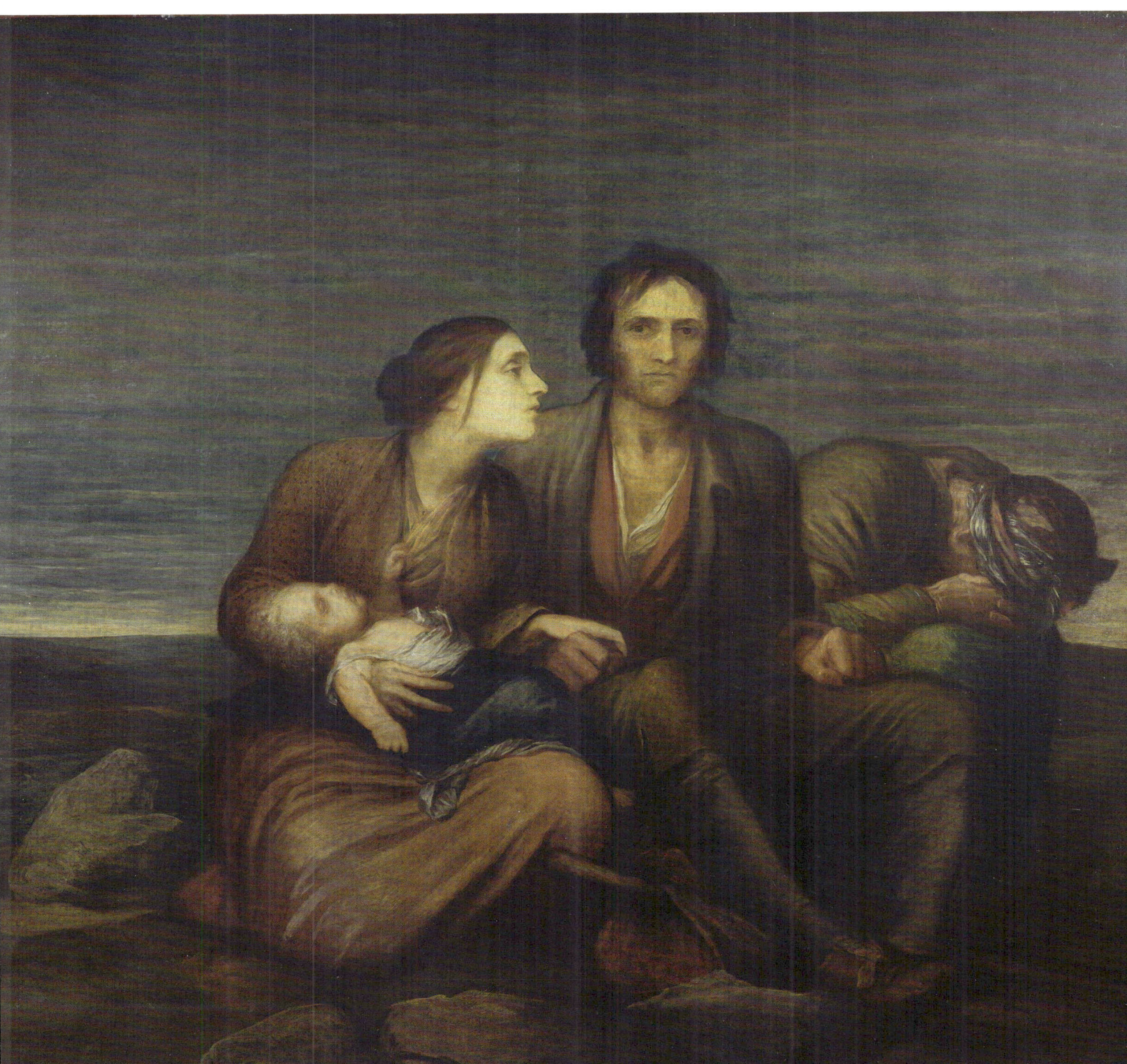

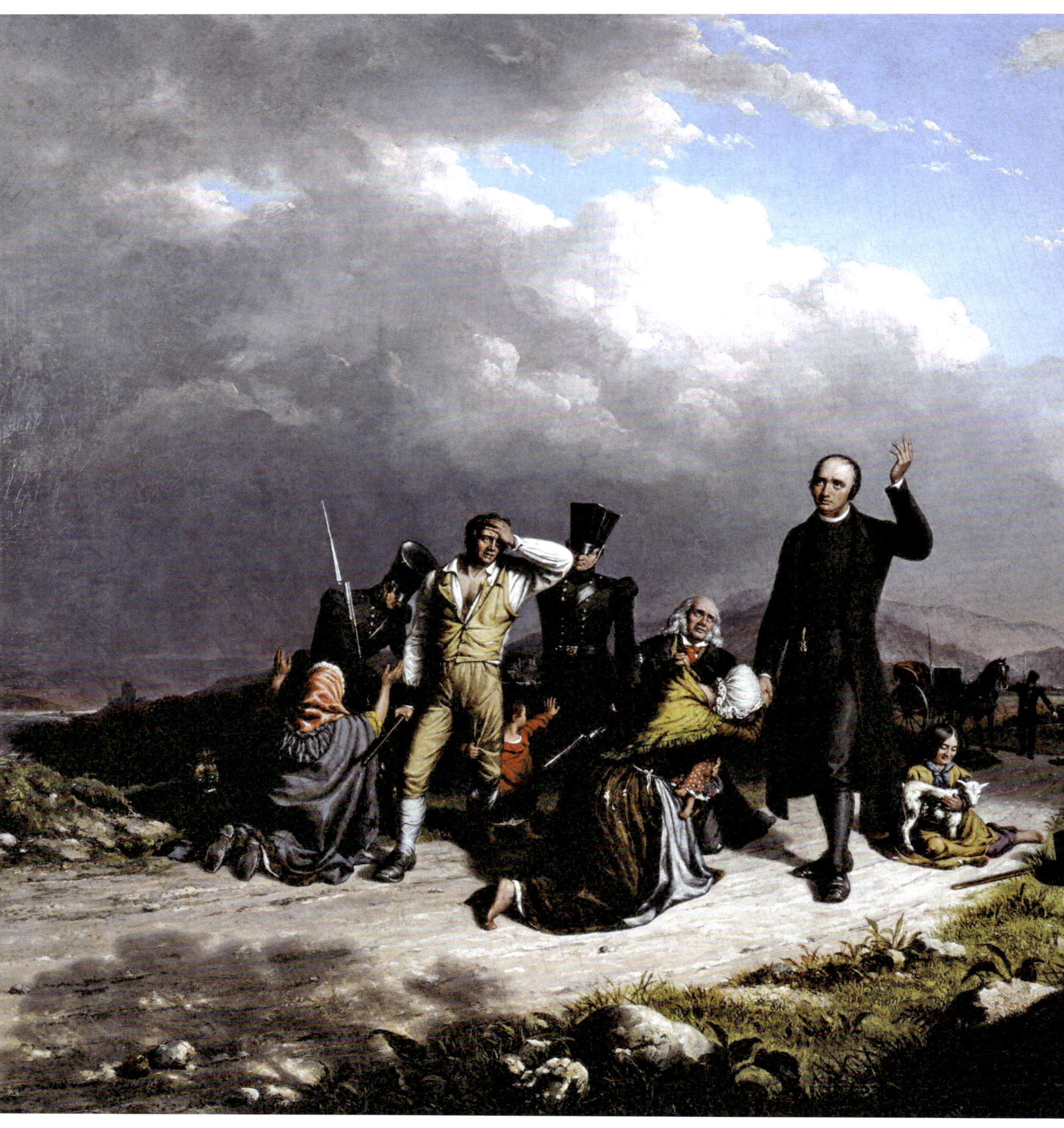

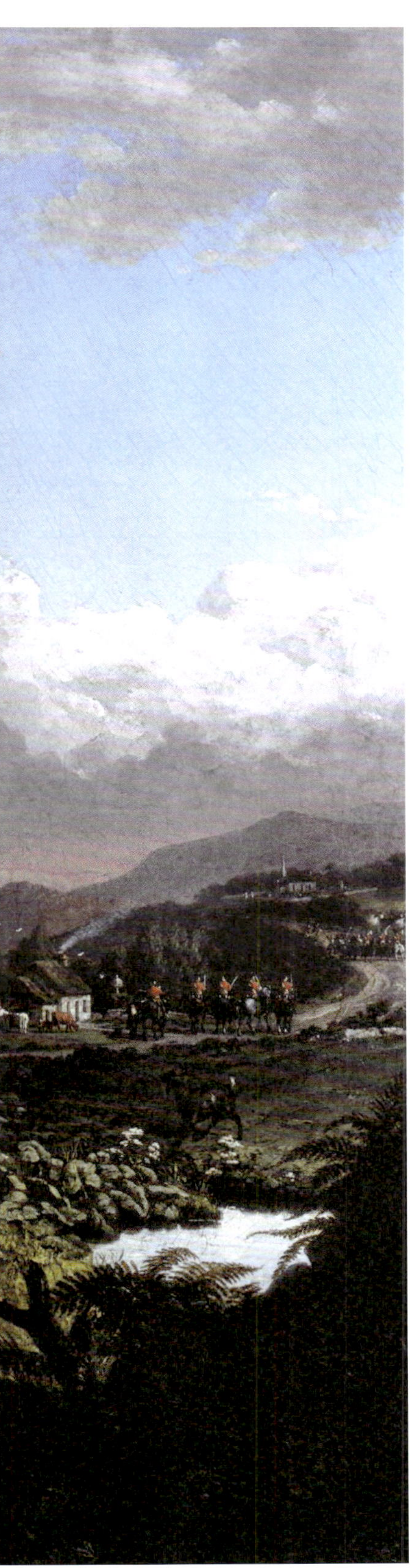

anatomical sturdiness of the figures shows just how little Watts knew of famine. But still, the painting — dying baby, angry father, terrified mother, and grandparent already abandoned to grief — has a deep emotional charge. In the compositional tradition of a Renaissance Holy Family, the mother's face is marble smooth, the bodies are robust, and they are decently shod and clad. However, although considered radical, the Watts depiction was likely to have confirmed the views of many that the Irish peasant — nourished, fit and healthy — was once again looking for undeserved English charity.

'Rack renting', whereby rents were raised so the tenant could not afford to pay, was the prelude to eviction. As the crops failed over successive years, and the poor were unable to pay their rents, many landlords seized their chance to clear their land of undesirable tenants, and turn it to pasture. In some instances, they did not even wait for the tenant to default. Evictions involved considerable brute force, and were supported by armed soldiers and constabulary, aided by battering rams and crowbars, wielded by gangs known as 'wreckers'. In March 1846, in a concerted exercise, more that 300 men women and children (some reports say 447), who *had* paid their rent, were evicted by Marcella Gerrard from her estate at Ballinlass, Co. Galway. To ensure that the poor 'wretches' could not return to take shelter in what remained of their tumbled cabins, she had the foundations dug up.

The high road to the poorhouse, or the low road to the ditches, both led to death. Captain Arthur Edward Kennedy, Poor Law Inspector of the Kilrush Union, described how

> As soon as one horde of houseless and all but naked paupers are dead, or provided for in the workhouse, another wholesale eviction doubles the number, who in their turn pass through the same ordeal of wandering from house to house, or burrowing in bogs or behind ditches, till broken down by privation and exposure to the elements, they seek the workhouse, or die by the roadside. (*Report and Returns Relating to Evictions in the Kilrush Union*, May 7, 1849)

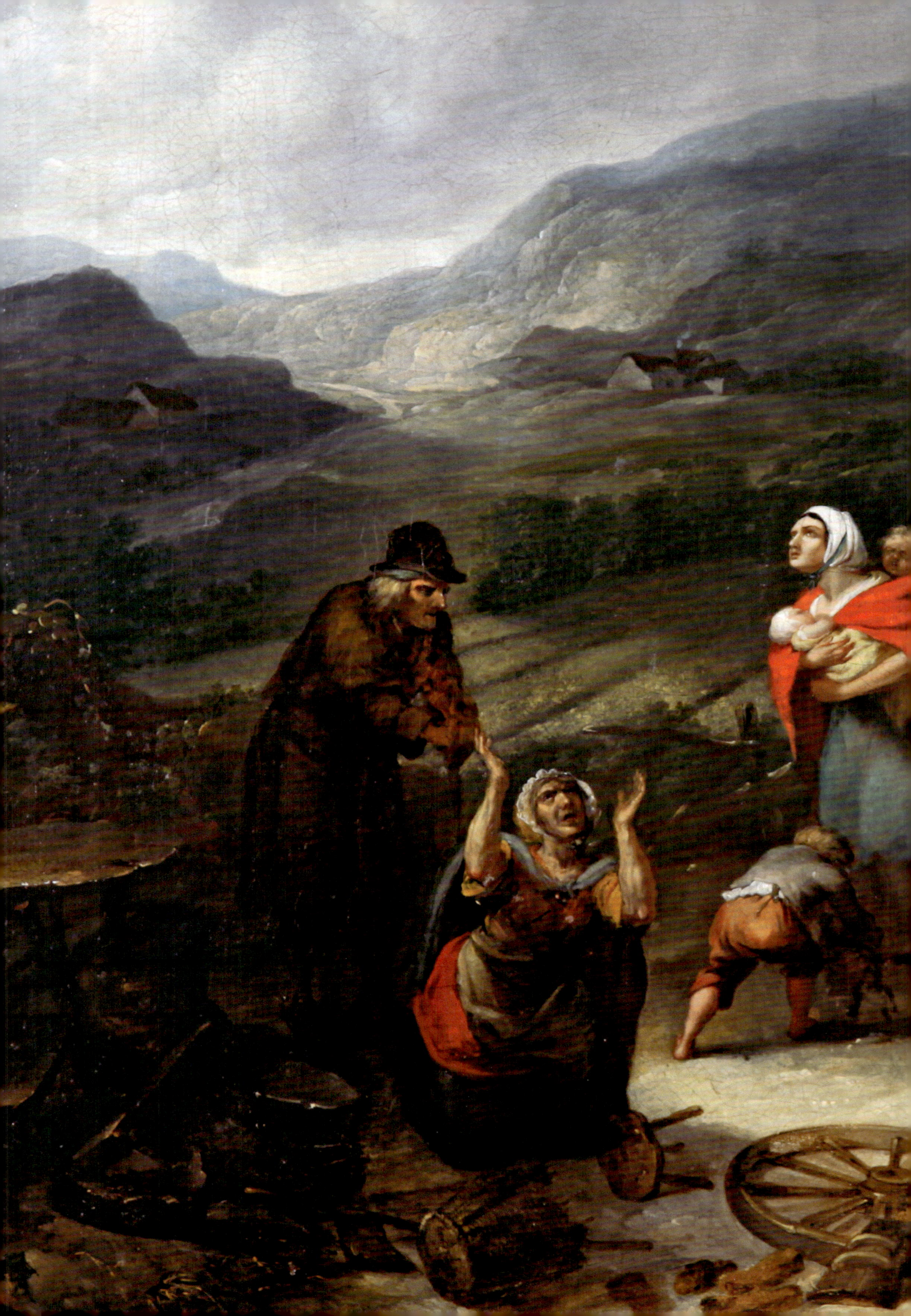

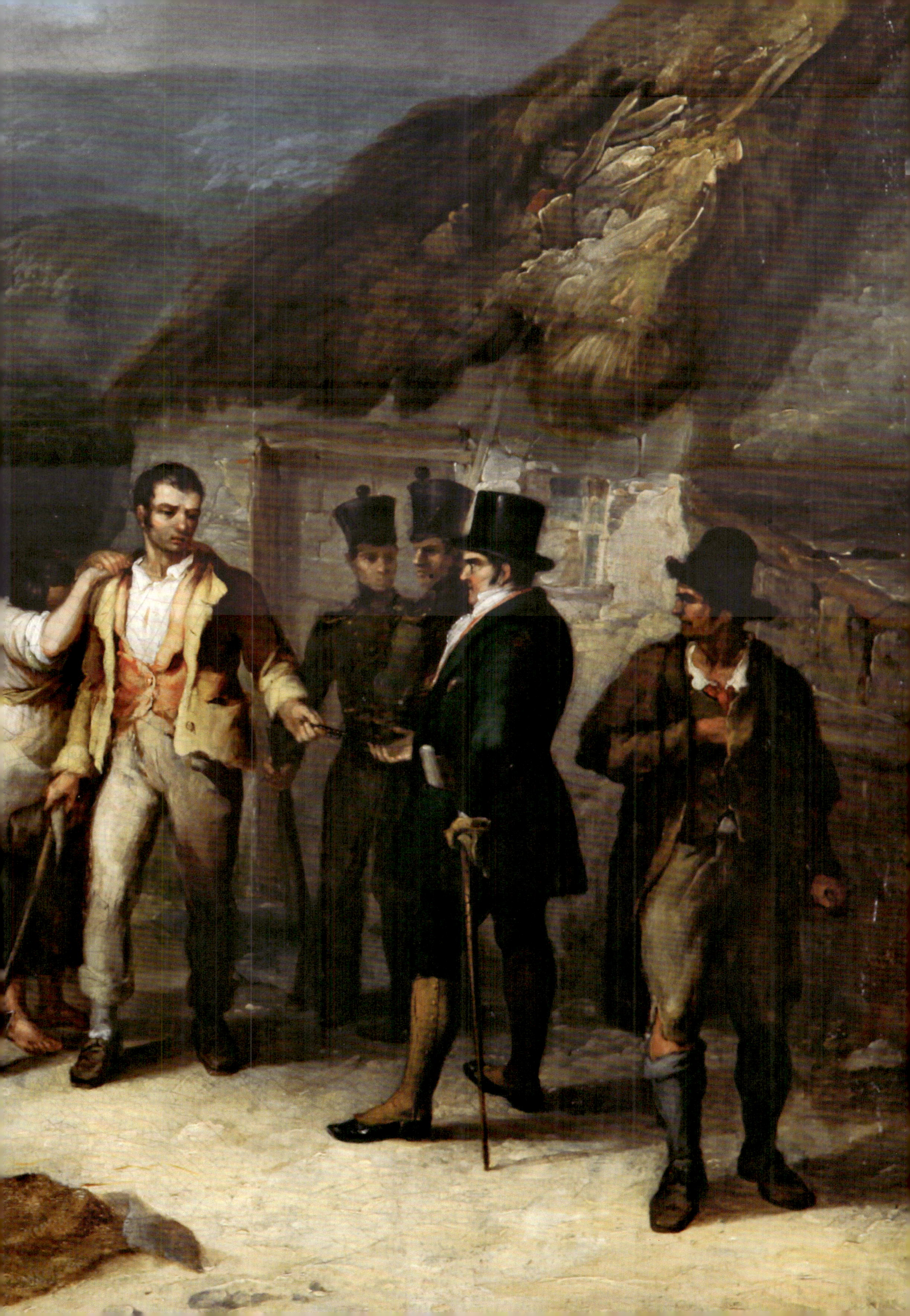

The destitute who resorted to living in 'scalpeens' — makeshift dwellings erected between what walls remained — were not left to die in peace; even from here, they were hunted. But there was worse again, 'scalps', in effect human burrows, troughs dug in the earth, two- or three-feet deep, into which whole families crawled. Unbelievably, there were cases of people being burnt out of these holes, including one of a child whose charred remains were brought out on a shovel. Estimates vary, but eviction was probably endured by up to 750,000 people between 1845 and 1855.

Erskine Nicol, the Scottish artist, also addressed the subject in *An Ejected Family* (1853) (National Gallery of Ireland), showing three generations of one family, in a state of utter bewilderment, following their ejection to the side of the road. But the Irish artist, Robert George Kelly, attempted a much more complex narrative in *An Ejectment in Ireland* (*A Tear and a Prayer for Erin*) (1848, reworked and re-titled 1851) **(Fig. 29)**. According to most accounts, the shock of eviction was such that an already debilitated people generally remained passive when the worst came to pass. But Kelly's tenant took matters into his own hands, and murdered the bailiff. This painting is one of the rare depictions of violent response to eviction. Upon his father's arrest, his little boy tries to push one constable away, his wife and mother beg for mercy, as the priest raises his arm toward heaven, holding the hand of the woman cradling her baby. In the distance, the sheriff's party and cavalrymen march down the road, on to the next job … Although full of informative detail, the painting was considered inferior and vulgar, as much for its subject as its treatment, no doubt.

Daniel Macdonald's unsigned *Eviction* (c. 1850) **(Fig. 30)** — attributed to him on stylistic grounds and features common to his works — was more nuanced. Set in a west Cork–type landscape, with lazy beds in the background, it displays similarities with *An Irish Peasant Family Discovering the Blight of their Store.* The landscape is almost identical, but more foregrounded in the latter. And, as Tom Dunne has pointed out, there are many likenesses in the figures.[151] Again, it shows generations of one family, in this instance already evicted. Here, the dwelling is comparatively substantial, with window, door and chimney, features not to be taken as the norm. The family is relatively well dressed; their possessions, flung out by the bailiffs, now strewn and broken, were more extensive than most.

The image of the impish little boy trying to catch the dog, is stiffened by the man on the right, putting his hand to his inner pocket where lies his pistol, signaling reprisals to come, a trope that recurs in the illustrations of the period, such as Edmund Fitzpatrick's, *The Ejectment* **(Fig. 31)** in the *Illustrated London News* (December 16, 1848) and in other work by Macdonald.

Eviction meant the poorhouse, and the poorhouse was, in effect, a slower form of death than starvation. Despite their relatively prosperous circumstances, things cannot now end well for this family, although the young man in the center, handing over the key to the house, is holding on to his spade and will, for a time, try to earn his living as a *spailpín*, or wandering laborer. Eviction led to not just the breaking up of families but the destruction of communities. An enduring way of life was brought to an abrupt end.

Although the wreckers have already begun to tumble the roof, the door has been bricked up, indicating that this landlord intends to find a higher rent for this dwelling. Taking over the cabin of an evicted family, however, was considered the ultimate betrayal, and brought down the wrath of the community.

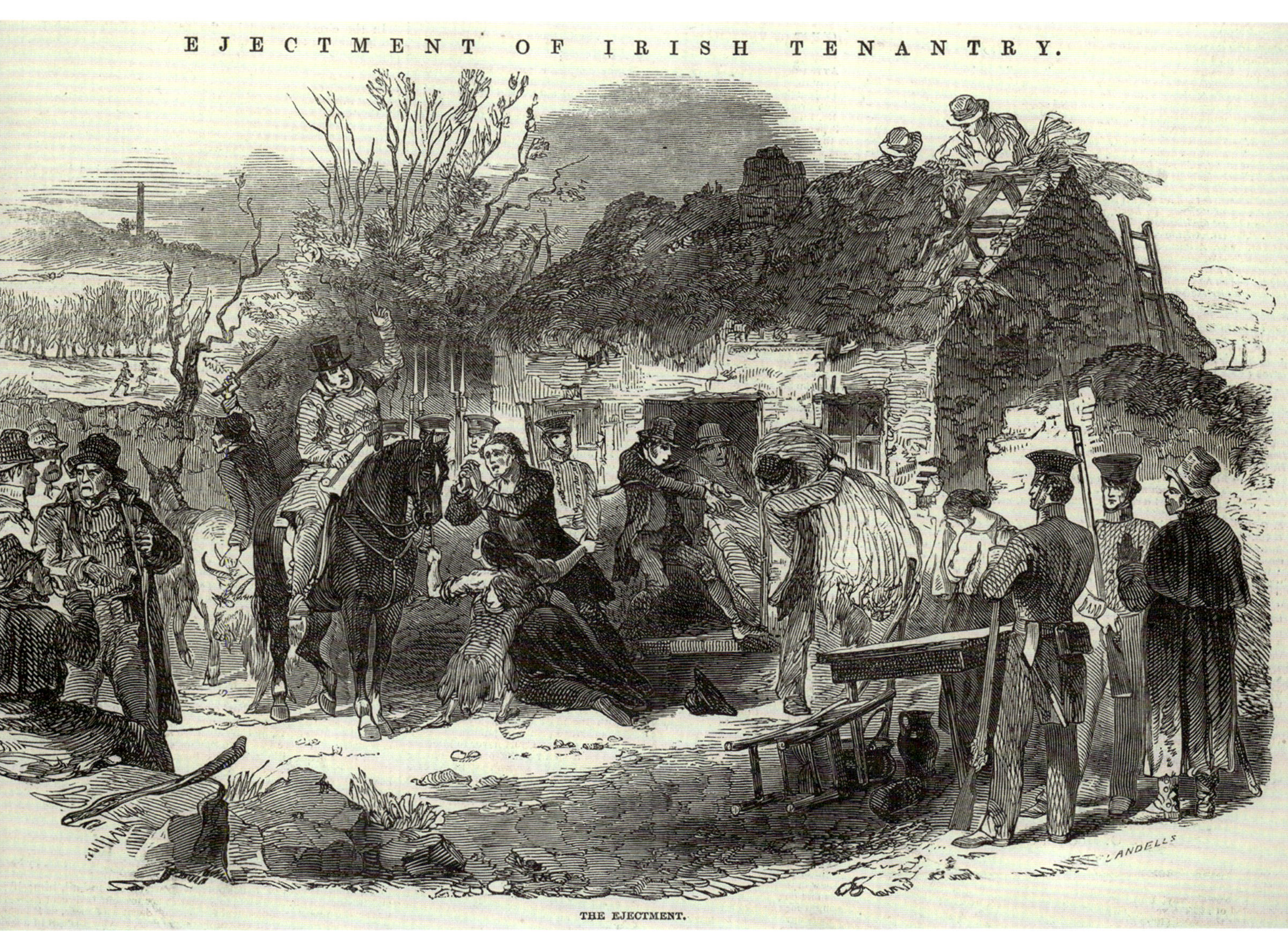

The evictions were relentless, as *The Tipperary Vindicator* reported in December 1848:

> The work of undermining the population is going on stealthily, but steadily … more deadly than the plague. We do not say that there exists a conspiracy to uproot the 'mere Irish'; but we do aver, that the fearful system of wholesale ejectment, of which we daily hear, and which we daily behold, is a mockery of the eternal laws of God. Whole districts are cleared … The ditch side, the dripping rain, the cold sleet are the covering of the wretched outcast the moment the cabin is tumbled over him; for who dare give shelter of protection from 'the pelting or the pitiless storm?' Who has the temerity to afford him the ordinary rites of hospitality, when the warrant has been signed for his extinction? … [The evicted] are hunted like wolves, or they perish without a murmur.

The newspaper went on to comment on the timing of many of these 'revolting' deeds. The number of evictions that took place in the dead of winter, and around Christmas, was particularly sadistic. In sympathizing with readers on the relentlessness of Famine news at the British breakfast table, the *Times* noted sardonically that further deaths by starvation are 'rather like a wet blanket on the warm curiosity of the gentleman in a dressing-gown, with a devilled drumstick on his plate, and a game pie in reserve'

Figure 31

The Ejectment

The *Illustrated London News*

Edmund Fitzpatrick

December 16, 1848

(December 1, 1846). Weeks later, Nicholas Cummins, a Cork Justice of the Peace, wrote to the Duke of Wellington of a different Christmas scene. In west Cork, 'six famished and ghastly skeletons, to all appearance dead, huddled in a corner on some filthy straw, their sole covering what seemed a ragged horse-cloth, naked above the knees.' When he approached the children and their mother (and what had once been their father), he found 'by a low moaning they were alive.' Suddenly he found himself 'surrounded by at least 200 of such phantoms … . By far the greater number were delirious, either from famine or fever. Their demonic yells are still yelling in my ears, and their horrible images are fixed upon my brain.' His clothes were nearly torn off by 'the throng of pestilence', and when he tried to leave, he found himself

> grasped by a woman with an infant, just born, in her arms, and the remains of a filthy sack across her loins — the sole covering of herself and babe. The same morning the police opening a house on the adjoining lands, which was observed shut for many days, and two frozen corpses were found lying upon the mud floor half devoured by the rats. A mother, herself in fever, was seen the same day to drag out the corpse of her child, a girl about twelve, perfectly naked, and leave it half covered with stones. In another house, within 500 yards of the cavalry station at Skibbereen, the dispensary doctor found seven wretches lying, unable to move under the same cloak, one had been dead for many hours, but the others were unable to move themselves or the corpse. If these be not sufficient … . let them, however, believe and tremble that they shall one day hear the Judge of all the Earth pronounce their tremendous doom, with the addition, 'I was hungered and ye gave Me no meat; thirsty and ye gave Me no drink; naked, and ye clothed Me not.' … . I implore you, break the frigid and flimsy chain of official etiquette, and save the land of your birth – the kindred of the gallant Irish blood which you have so often seen lavished to support the honour of the British name — and let there be inscribed upon your tomb, *Servata Hibernia*. (December 17, 1846)

Three days before Christmas, the *Illustrated London News* described whole villages — where the ties of family and community stretched back decades — returned to a state of nature, to the extent that the artist professed relief 'at seeing one or two half-clad spectres gliding about, as an evidence that I was not in the land of the dead'. The artist went to say that the deserted villages 'look like the tombs of a departed race, rather than the recent abodes of a yet living people'. The savage inhumanity of eviction — knowingly forcing people to 'burrow in holes, and share, till they are discovered, the ditches and the bogs with otters and snipes' — was made public by these and other reports, and yet evictions continued, then and after, as a legal way of culling the population (December 22, 1849).

History painters conceptualized narrative complexity, not by representing the climax of a story, but by identifying what was known as the 'pregnant moment'. The painter, according to Gotthold Ephraim Lessing in 1766, must select 'one single moment of the action, and must therefore choose the most pregnant, from which what precedes and follows will be the most easily apprehended'. Thus, the artist must represent the moment that best encapsulates what has already happened in the past, and what is about to happen in the future.[152]

The Macdonald *Eviction* contains the extended narrative of an eviction, the before, during and aftermath. The device of three generations, as well as reflecting familial living patterns, allows for narrative expansion. In the mid ground, lazy beds, once abundant with potatoes — the staff of life — slope gently upwards. Several prosperous-looking cottages, nestle in the foothills. Come the day, this hardworking family, through no fault of their own, are unable to pay their rent and are forced out into the elements. Their kitchen and farming implements are dashed about, broken and useless. The elderly parents are already in despair, they have no future, and their children and children's children are doomed.

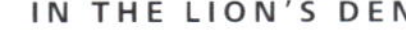

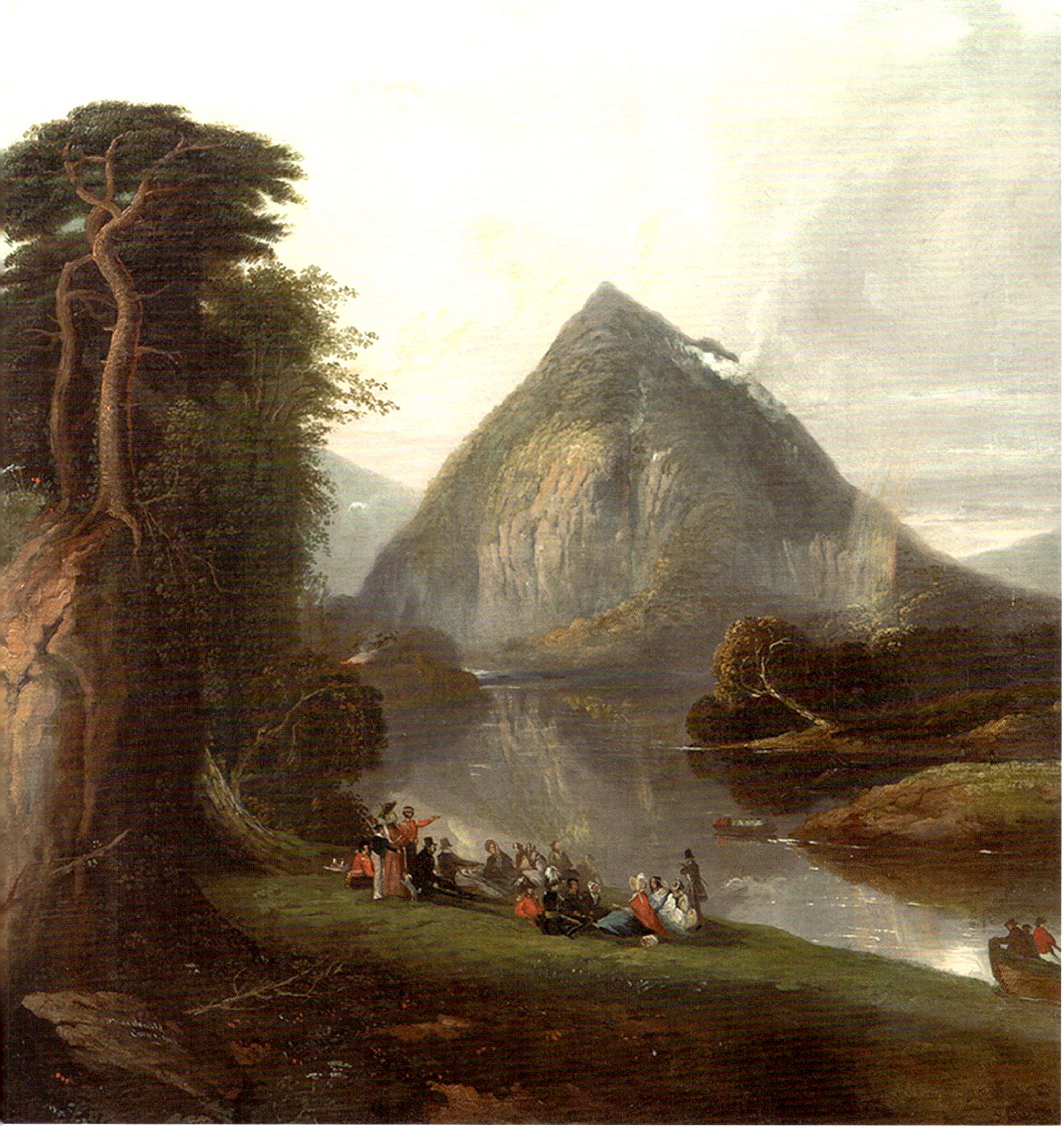

CHAPTER 4

TALES OF RURAL IRELAND

In 1842, Macdonald burst upon the exhibition circuit, showing eight works at the Cork Art Union, a mixture of still lifes and portraits, and two subject pictures, *Bowl Playing* and *A Sídhe Gaoithe / Fairy Blast*. In the same year, he had four paintings accepted by the Royal Hibernian Academy in Dublin, including the still life *Dead Widgeon and Cork Harbour Oysters*, '*Royalty*' — *A Stag Hound from Nature*, *Preparing for Bed in an Irish Cabin*, and *Falstaff, Bardolph and the Page* (*Henry IV*) — an eclectic mix of subjects designed to show his wide range of skills.[153]

If the perception of an Irish peasantry 'until then seen as the pauperized, brutish and sullen dregs of a dead old culture, full of disaffection and hatred for their new rulers' shifts towards a peasantry of 'cultural interest', Macdonald's contribution to that change should be credited; Joep Leerssen argues that the peasantry had by his time 'come to be seen, in Romantic, Grimm-like fashion, as the repository of quaint superstition and primordial folk and fairy tales.'[154] Macdonald's *Sídhe Gaoithe / Fairy Blast* (1842) displays this populist Romanticism, but it was an early work, and before long, he evolved his own robust form of realism that, in effect, humanized and normalized Irish country people, in all their guises.

Working across the genres — history painting, portraiture, still life, landscape and genre painting — in each, Macdonald shows himself to have been an acute observer of everyday life. His focus was on rural Ireland and its people — not stereotyped, aggrandized, or romanticized — his achievements reaching an apogee with *An Irish Peasant Family Discovering the Blight of their Store* in 1847.

THE LIE OF THE LAND

Macdonald's first known landscape painting, *Eagle's Nest, Killarney* (1841) **(Fig. 32)**, demonstrates his recognition of the inherent capacity of each genre to yield rich social, cultural, political and economic details of life in Ireland. Killarney was a small market town until 1750 when Viscount Kenmare thought to develop it as a tourist destination. He built roads, boat facilities and inns. In the Lakes, he had a spectacular beauty spot. And by the Eagle's Nest — mid way between the Upper and Middle Lakes — an extraordinary natural phenomenon, a pyramidal 1,700-foot high mountain that also housed an eyrie of royal birds. Kenmare positioned cannons at strategic spots on the shore, installed small guns on the boats, and engaged locals as bugle and horn players, all to play out the remarkable echoes that reverberated from the mountain, but it was an expensive business. Soon the paradoxes of tourism became all too obvious.[155]

Guides and horses and boats and musicians all had to be paid for, and many complained about the costs involved. A trip to Killarney, therefore, could not be embarked upon casually; it had to be meticulously organized. The commodification of Ireland as a tourist destination fed both the prejudices of critics and the expectations of reforming thinkers. Actual encounters with the natives both reinforced stereotypes about the Irish and dispelled them.

The Killarney mountains were sublime, the lakes picturesque, and, although just twenty-one years old, when he painted this scene, Macdonald shows himself to have been aware of the artistic potential of both modes of representation. Subject-wise, it was the orchestrated combination of the scenery, cannon fire and music that drew the tourists. A variation of the cannon discharge, the bugle call, was later immortalized by Alfred Lord Tennyson in *The Splendour Falls on Castle Walls*:

> *Blow, bugle, blow, set the wild echoes flying*
> *Blow, bugle: answer, echoes, dying, dying, dying!*

The optimal position was just opposite the Eagle's Nest, high on the promontory, soaring above the Long Range River. William Ockenden (1760) described how ' … suddenly, to our inexpressible amazement, we were surprised with music sweeter than any I had ever heard before, which seemed to arise from the rock, at which we gazed; and breaking upon us in short melodious strains, filled the very soul with transport.' Serenaded thus for 15 minutes, a explosion 'rent the mountain with its roar and filled us with the apprehension of being instantly buried in a chaos of hill, wood, and water; but the horror was suddenly dissipated by the return of the same soothing strains which had before enchanted us.'[156] Cannon and musicians had been secretly placed on the shore, where they could be heard but not seen, and continued to bounce 'sound and fury off the Eagle's Nest' to the utter delight of the spectators. John Bush also recognized the inherent sublime in the 'supereminent landscape, which will carry imagination to the highest pitch of frantic enthusiasm, i[n] the melodious echoing of the horn … . If any scene in the world can elevate conceptions of the sublime of nature, it must be a situation like this.'[157]

Visitors were enthralled. Arthur Young explained that 'the report does not consist of direct reverberation from one rock to another with a pause between, but has an exact resemblance to a peal of thunder rattling behind the rock as if travelling the whole scenery we had viewed, and lost in the immensity of MacGillicuddy's Reeks'.[158] John Wilkes, in 1812, described how 'Twelve reverberations, and sometimes more, may be distinctly counted; and what appears extraordinary, after the sound has been totally lost, it occasionally revives, becomes louder and louder for a few seconds and then again dies away'. [159] In time, rousing the echoes became more calibrated. James Johnson suggested that the musicians should direct their notes, not at the visitors but at the 'grand reverberator', the hill itself. By this means, the visitors did not hear the notes themselves, but their echoes, rendering the sound 'so mellowed as to be hardly earthly, but rather the emanation of some celestial organ.' [160]

William Williams's discussion of John Urry's concept of 'sacralization' — a process that transforms an object or place of tourist interest to a level of sacredness — is apposite here. As well as 'naming, framing, enshrinement' the 'mechanical reproduction of the sacred object' became an essential part of the process.[161] While the experience was primarily aural, numerous artists gave the scenario visual form. From the eighteenth century, artists such as George Barrett in his *Powerscourt Waterfall* (1760), for example, visualized the sublime. For over a century and a half, artists continued to paint the Eagle's Nest, attempting a visual articulation of the experience. In 1770, Jonathan Fisher published a series of etchings, *Views of Killarney,* including one of *The Eagle's Nest*, and a painting, c. 1769, now in the National Gallery of Ireland. This was followed by William Sadler, Thomas Walmsley, George Petrie, Henry John Noblett, Thomas Francis Mulvany (*The Eagle's Nest* in Ireland's Great Hunger Museum is attributed to Mulvany) and, as a subject, it endured into the late nineteenth century, as evidenced by Bartholomew Colles Watkins.

Macdonald's contribution to the iconography is noteworthy. Agostino Aglio's version, produced the year after the Macdonald, is clearly based on it. He asserts the primacy of the landscape, soaring mountain, trees clinging to rocky outcrop, light on lake. The tourists — ladies, gentlemen and officers — gaily boat out into the sound, or picnic on shore, performing staffage to the grandeur of the landscape.

Sometimes a military band could be had. And while there were plenty of poor musicians who marred the experience, there were also some wonderful ones, such as Spillane, who produced spellbinding melodies. Mr. and Mrs. Samuel Carter Hall, inveterate travelers, produced the first of the three volumes of their influential guide, *Ireland: its Scenery, Character, etc.,* in 1841. Here they described the bugle playing of Spillane:

> First he played a single note — it was caught up and repeated, loudly, softly, again loudly, again softly, and then as if by a hundred instruments, each a thousand times more musical than that which gave its rivals both twirling and twisting around the mountain, running up from its foot to its summit, then rolling over it, and at length dying away in the distance until it was heard as a mere whisper, barely audible, far away. Then he blew a few notes — ti-ra-la-ti-ra-la: a multitude of choices, seemingly from a multitude of hills, at once sent forth a reply; sometimes pausing for a second, as if waiting for some tardy comrade to join in the marvelous chorus, then mingling together in a strain of sublime grandeur, and delicate sweetness, utterly indescribable. Again Spillane sent forth his summons to the mountains, and blew, for perhaps a minute a variety of sounds; the effect was indeed that of 'enchanting ravishment'.

The Halls went on to describe the firing of the cannon:

> The match was applied. In an instant every mountain for miles around seemed instinct with angry life, and replied in voices of thunder to the insignificant and miserable sound that had roused them from the slumbers. The imagination was excited to absolute terror … the sound was multiplied a thousand-fold, and with infinite variety; at first it was repeated with a terrific growl, then a fearful crash, both were caught up and returned by the surrounding hills; mingling together, now in perfect harmony, now in utter discordance; awhile those that were nearest became silent, awaiting the on coming of those that were distant; then joining together in one mighty sound, louder and louder, then dropping to a gentle lull, as if the winds only created them; then breaking forth again into a combined roar that would seem to have been heard hundreds of miles away. [162]

Figure 33

Irish Peasant Children

Daniel Macdonald

1846

Macdonald travelled around Co. Cork regularly, and visited Kerry in 1841, 1844 and 1845, and probably before and after too. *The Eagle's Nest* was painted in the same year as the publication of the first volume of Mr. and Mrs. Hall's book in which the lakes of Killarney and the echoes are described in such evocative detail. Although the painting would have been executed before the book appeared, it was likely a subject of discussion between them. *Ireland: its Scenery, Character etc.,* does not contain illustrations by Macdonald, but Anna Hall's album, which contains the original sketches for the book, does include a sketch by Macdonald, *Irish Peasant Travelling in Summer Trim* (1841), of a jaunty youth returning from work, holding his shoes in his hand so that they'll last the winter. [163]

Engulfed by nature, the lingering cadences of both the man made and natural sounds led Lord Manners to describe how he 'listened in a sort of dreamy ecstasy to the wild and mournful notes as they lingered in the air' before coming to his senses and realizing that the whole thing was really a form of social contamination and more suited to the 'lower' sort. And of course, enterprising peasants became, if not adept at guiding, adept at importuning — as many as six or eight might attach themselves to a group, causing much annoyance to tourists in search of a 'pure' experience.

Negotiating the Gap of Dunloe was an assault course as the natives tripped over each other to sell 'mountain dew', goat's milk, bog oak or even homespun stockings. And of course, these tourist traps lent themselves to much 'fakelore'. Peasants loved to spin yarns and, to add to the authenticity, would tell tourists that *he* was the one in Croker's famous book who did this and that But Macdonald's sketches of the *Torc Waterfall* and the *Gap of Dunloe* (1845) (British Museum) eschew the tawdriness of the tourist industry and the fad for sensational landscapes, and focus instead on the simplicity of a people and their way of life.

Five years later, it would seem, he painted the same scenery in his beguiling painting, *Irish Peasant Children* (**Fig. 33**). Three children sit on a rocky outcrop, high above the lakes, with the mountains in the background. If *Eagle's Nest* gave us a glimpse into the world of the moneyed classes, *Irish Peasant Children* shows a different Ireland. The children are beautiful and winsome; mischievous and dangerous; and resentful and remote. The boy behind the rock is quick and wily, already a handful and may grow to become menacing; the girl on the left has a desperate demeanor, indeed the bottle in her right is cocked like a missile, she has seen terrible things, and there is worse to come; the girl in front (in the vibrant madder skirt and plaid shawl) is very beautiful, with that dark Spanish look sometimes found in Ireland, she is captivating and biddable — the acceptable face of Ireland.

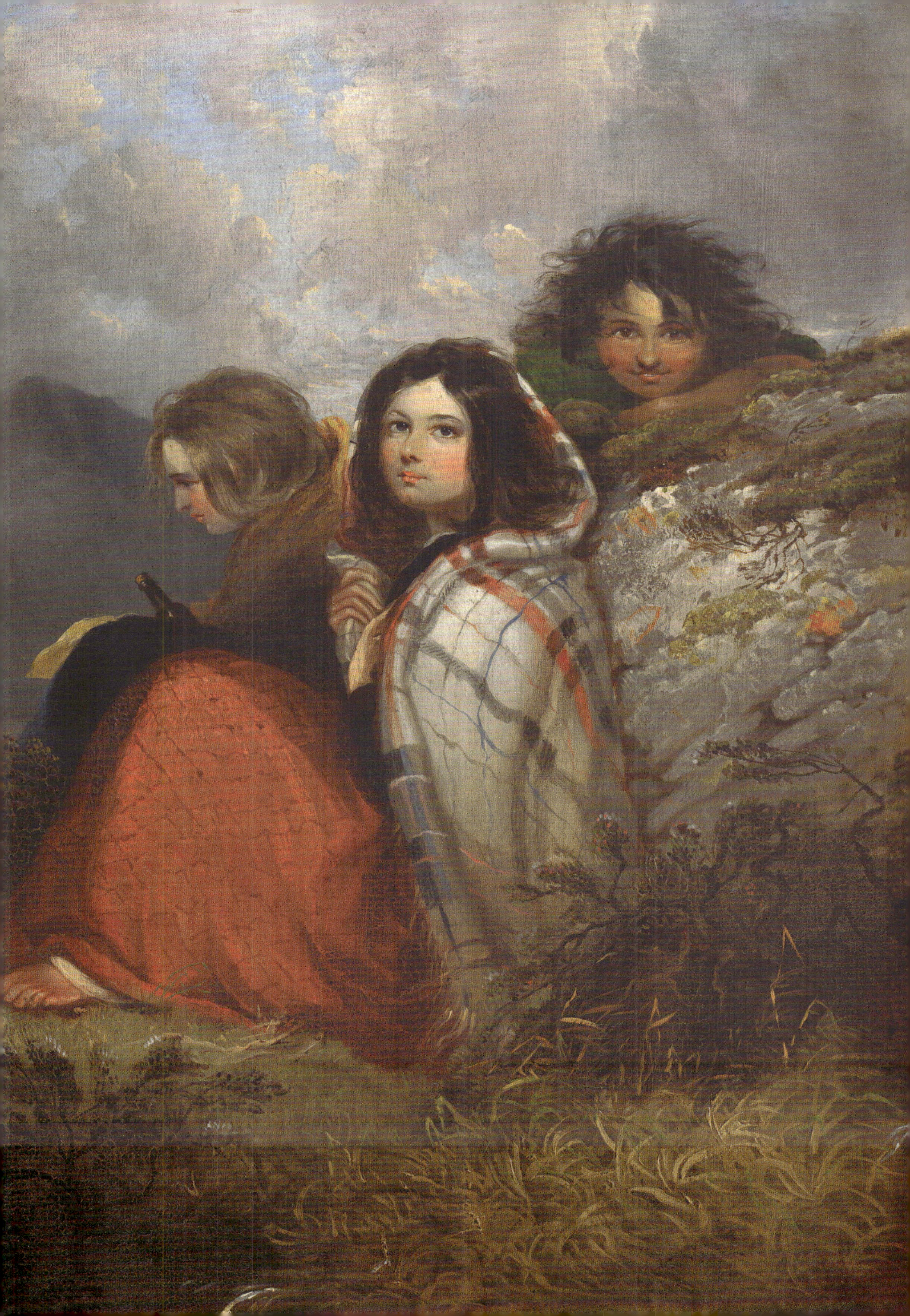

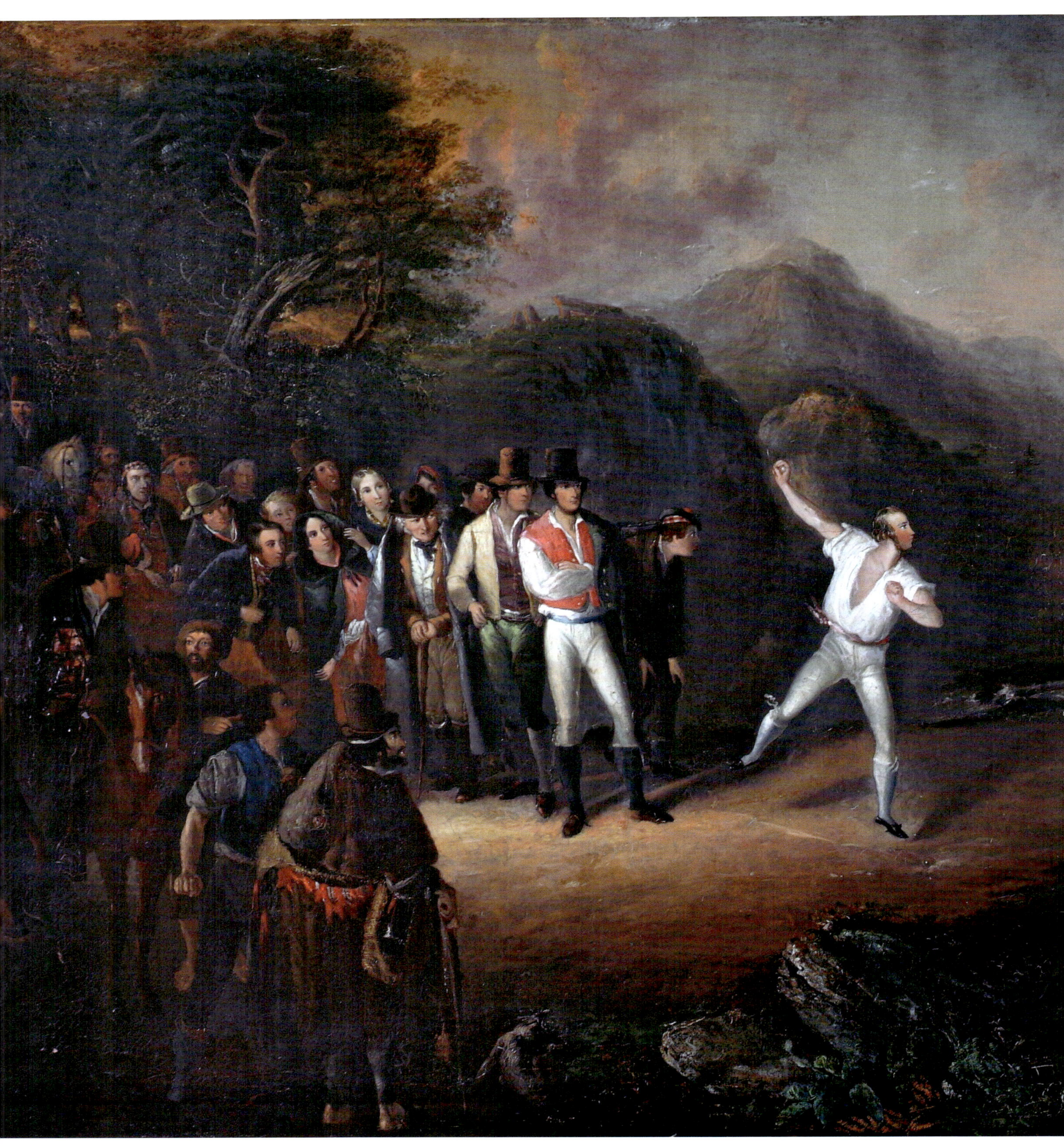

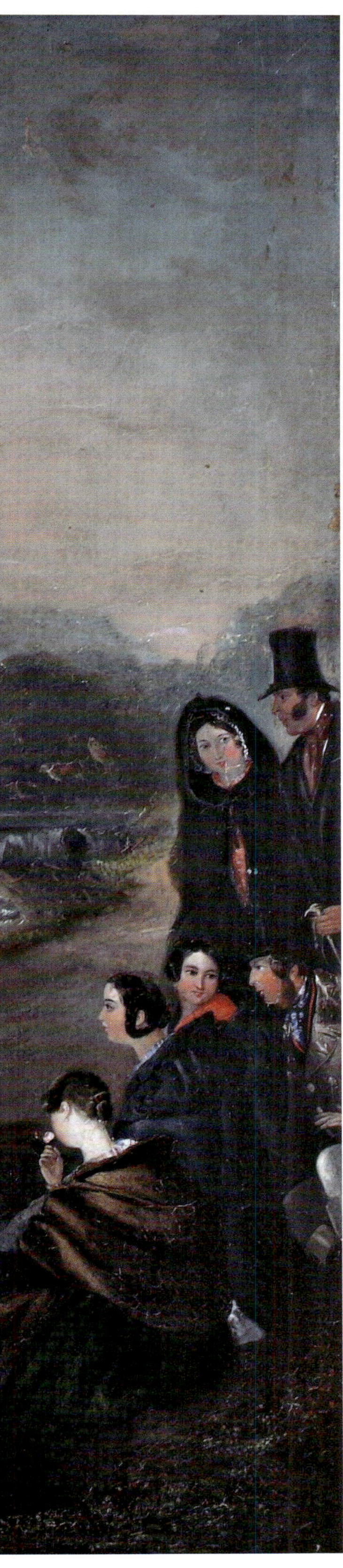

Macdonald's eclectic range of pictorial references signals his knowledge of European art styles. On the one hand, *Irish Peasant Children* remains close to the conventions of Victorian narrative painting, albeit with a disturbing slant. All does not bode well for these children. There are no parents or guardians to look out for them. Their different characteristics, personalities and moods hint at social disintegration — their future is uncertain, to say the least. Anne Crookshank and the Knight of Glin describe Macdonald as 'a landscape and genre painter of naïve quality', but that is a simplistic reading of a complex Irish artist making his way through a metropolitan audience, insinuating Irish subject matter into salons hostile to contemplating poverty and hunger.[164]

What at first glance may seem a mild blend of landscape and genre painting is far from it. The scale of the figures is significant. They are not shrunk into the landscape, as convention dictated — as Thomas Gainsborough's peasants were, for example — but foregrounded and painted in a dominant position, indicating an awareness of and sympathy with contemporary work by a Gustave Courbet or Jean-François Millet.

Macdonald grapples with, and often succeeds in making the local epic. The idyllic landscape, set deep in the valley, presents itself with the classical serenity of a Claude Lorrain, but the swirling mist and gathering storm represent the national tragedy that is already in train. This was painted in 1846, the second year of the Famine. The climatic conditions and brooding girl hint at social and political reprisals to come, while the seductive beauty of her sister, and the lovely landscape, make the painting palatable to British audiences. To paint a subject as vexing as the Great Irish Famine for British audiences was audacious. It must have been painted to make a political point. A fact not lost on its later owners, the family of the revolutionary republican heroine, Constance Gore-Booth (later Countess Markievicz) Macdonald's acceptance among the British elite, actually merits his re-evaluation as an Irish painter of considerable nuance.

FUN AND GAMES

Bowl Playing (**Fig. 34**) shows two prominent Corkmen playing a game of road bowls, followed by an enthusiastic group of supporters. Although the painting is unsigned, the *Cork Examiner* review confirmed it as the work of Macdonald (as does his signature puppy scampering about the canvas). But what the reviewer gave with one hand, he took away with the other:

Figure 34

Bowl Playing

Daniel Macdonald

1842

> No. 41 Demands our attention … Its characteristic is floridness. It seems, in scenery and colouring, too fine for its subject. But when the artist's judgement shall have been sobered down, somewhat, to the forcible simplicity of things as they are, we think he will be capable of a great deal. His figures on the left are well disposed, though rather too crowded, and too freshly tinted. Those on the right are very expressive and very good. The squire, or well-dressed young farmer, leaning forward, less to mark the chances of the bowl, than to put his 'commether' on the coquettish little peasant girls before him, is very well imagined and executed. The principal figure — yes, really, we should be much better pleased if that principal figure was left out altogether, by particular desire. The head seems arranged for an appearance on the stage, and it wears pumps — the figure, we mean. Moreover, the face is the very facsimile of a portrait in the room by the same artist. Mr. MacDonald has much to unlearn. (*Cork Examiner*, October 3, 1842)

However, the other three portraits in the room by Macdonald were an oil and a pen sketch of *The Late Arthur Crawford of Cork* and an oil *Mr. Caughy of America*. In fact the central figure, the bowler, was Abraham Morris, a wealthy landowner, merchant and yachtsman of Dunkettle/Dunkathel. The Morris family had built their fine Palladian House at Glanmire in the late eighteenth century, and they remained there a family of standing. (Infamously, Morris was related to the Cork sheriff who shot the patriot, Art O'Laoghaire, in 1772). His opponent was Mountiford Longfield, of Castlemary, Cloyne, both Orangemen and Tories. The match takes place at Castle Mary, eighteen miles from Cork city, the seat of the Anglo-Irish Longfield family since the seventeenth century. Longfield, a graduate of Trinity College Dublin, had a brutish reputation (according to one story, he callously rode over a child who was in his way). As a landlord, he was an exterminator, evicting 378 tenants unable to pay rent, and he had 35 homes demolished. The landscape, however, is more composite than specific (the remains of a dolmen on the Castle Mary estate, sometimes described erroneously as a druid altar, has been relocated in the painting).

In the painting all, or almost all, appears civil and social. Morris wears the silk stockings and pump shoes of a gentleman. Both wear silk ribbons at the knees. Longfield wears a red waistcoat, green wool jacket with brass buttons, and fine linen shirt. Both wear half-fall front breeches (then rather out of fashion). Although rather effete and stylized, and far from the virility of *The Fighter*, the Morris figure is derived in pose from *The Discobolus*, sculpted by Myron of Eleutherai in the 5th century BC and, as a model, available to Macdonald as one of the Canova casts in Cork city, albeit here dandified beyond recognition. Some of the gentlemen wear silk top hats, others hard wearing felt ones. The men behind the waiting bowler wear brogues, linen shirts, and waist-length swallow-tailed coats, but here and there a fashionable satin waistcoat can be seen, and the sheen on the old man's coat, worn over his shoulders, looks silken. There is solid evidence of wealth and displays of class confidence at play here. The fashionably coiffed women on the left wear Kinsale cloaks, with satin-lined hoods, while those on the right wear more up-to-date carriage cloaks.

The painting includes a distinguishable cross-section of Cork society — a mixture of aristocrats and veterans (the two landed families had associations with military settlers), peasants and beggars. The figures on the lower left are obviously less well-off, less well-dressed: these are Longfield tenants and laborers. The man beside the boccaugh on the front left shows a clenched fist, ostensibly anxious about the bet he has placed perhaps, but the subtext, given Longfield's reputation, is class resentment. Dunlevy and Ó Gráda suggest that the boccaugh is reminiscent of Sampson Towgood Roche's sketches of rural life around Youghal, Co. Cork, in the 1830s.[165]

 Like *Sídhe Gaoithe / The Fairy Blast*, *Bowl Playing* shows an intermingling of the social classes. Originally enjoyed by the gentry, by the mid century bowls were played by the poor, accounting here perhaps for the attendance of people from both classes. And, as so often the case with Macdonald, individuals flit from one painting to another. The boccaugh on the left migrates the following year to the left of the sketch, *Public Characters* (1843), where he is described as a 'Rag-ut': The man on the extreme right has also stepped out of Public Characters: 'No. 14. Kill the Ladies, a fascinator of the first order who must ere now have a gold chain strung with the hearts of young ladies.'* With his long sideburns and supercilious expression, he is dressed in the coat and top hat of a Regency dandy. 'The coquettish little peasant girl', as the *Cork Examiner* described her, holding the bowler's coat and hat, is more intent on smelling the rose he has given her than watching the match.

Although localized to Cork, the origins of the sport are unclear, it may have been introduced by weavers from Yorkshire and West Lancashire, who worked in the linen industry, especially in Cork and Armagh.[166] Bowling was also known as 'bullets' or 'road bowls'. It involved throwing a 28-ounce solid iron ball or bullet (originally perhaps a cannonball). The winner was he who could complete the three- or four-mile course in the fewest throws. The game required great skill in spinning the bowls around corners and over bumps in the road. The Cork technique involved rotating the arm 360 degrees before releasing the bowl. The balletic pose of the bowler is typical, as he establishes the best position to generate momentum. The crowd have divided to facilitate the throw, they will regroup and follow the bowlers along the course.

Less than ten years later, in his *Popular Irish Superstitions*, Sir William Wilde lamented:

> The old forms, and customs too, are becoming obliterated. The festivals are unobserved and the rustic festivities neglected or forgotten — the bowlings, the cakes, the prinkums, do not often take place when starvation and pestilence stalk over a country, many parts of which appear as if a destroying army had but recently passed through it. Such is the desolation which whole districts, of Connaught at least, at this moment presents. Entire villages being levelled to the ground; fences broken; the land untilled and often unstocked, and miles of country lying idle and unproductive, without the face of a human being to be seen upon it.[167]

But in this pre-Famine painting, times were good enough. Macdonald's interest in the leisures of Cork also manifested itself in a series of frisky sketches of the red-coated riders of the South Union Hunt on horseback — typically gentle caricatures of the country gentry of Cork at play (several of which were in the collection of the Cork and County Club, alongside *Bowl Playing*).

RURAL ROMANCING

Despite poverty, the joyful side of Irish life was irrepressible. Festivals and fairs were celebrated with gusto (even if they ended in mayhem). From Gaelic times, each of the four seasons was marked with a festival. The Church commandeered February for St. Bridget and November for All Saints, but the pagan and Christian co-existed, as the festivals corresponded with the agricultural cycles and labors of the year. As well as allowing social opportunities, they facilitated business: livestock was sold, news was exchanged, and bardic and folk traditions were kept alive — the *aonach* for pleasure, and the *aireacht* for business.[168] Whatever the occasion, there was always music and dancing. According to Thomas Crofton Croker, the lower orders were 'immoderately attached' to dancing.[169]

Dancing was serious business. The dancing master, usually itinerant, would be accompanied by a fiddler or piper (often blind). The *Cork Examiner* declared Macdonald's unlocated *Blind Fiddler* (1844) (exhibited at the Cork Art Union) 'one of the best pictures' in the Cork Art Union, displaying 'an advance in all the great elements that constitute good painting':

> The face is delicately handled; and though there are too many naked grays, still the painting
> is really excellent. We much like the meek, patient expression of the Blind Man, so helpless,
> so subdued. It harmonises well with the timid outstretching of the cautious hand, and the
> faltering indecision of the step forward. The detail is altogether very careful, the whole picture
> doing infinite credit to a young and evidently progressing artist (December 11, 1844).[170]

The dancing master would stay about six weeks in an area, lodge in a farmhouse (teaching the farmer's children free of charge). In parts of the country, he would teach in the same room with the schoolmaster. The dances taught were mostly jigs and reels: the rising step of the jig and the sidestep of the reel. Young, tells us that the dancing master was paid 6d. per pupil — 3d. for himself and 3d. for the musician, with the result that country people were adept and enthusiastic dancers.[171]

That music and dancing permeated Irish social life is evident from *A Country Dance / A Wedding Dance* (**Fig. 35**). Dancers achieved greater syncopation by dancing on a door, unhinged and laid on the earthen floor, as we see in this painting. Once known as *A Country Dance*, it was redesignated *A Wedding Dance* (1848) by the Crawford, although, that it is actually a wedding is far from certain if we consider contemporary descriptions of weddings. As so often, Croker's account of rural wedding customs and social stratifications came straight from the pen of James McDaniel:

> A house with three contiguous apartments is selected for a wedding; the reason of this is
> to preserve a distinction between the classes of company expected. The best apartment
> is reserved for the bride and bridegroom, the priest, the piper, and the more opulent
> and respectable guests, as the landlord, his family and the neighbouring gentry, who are

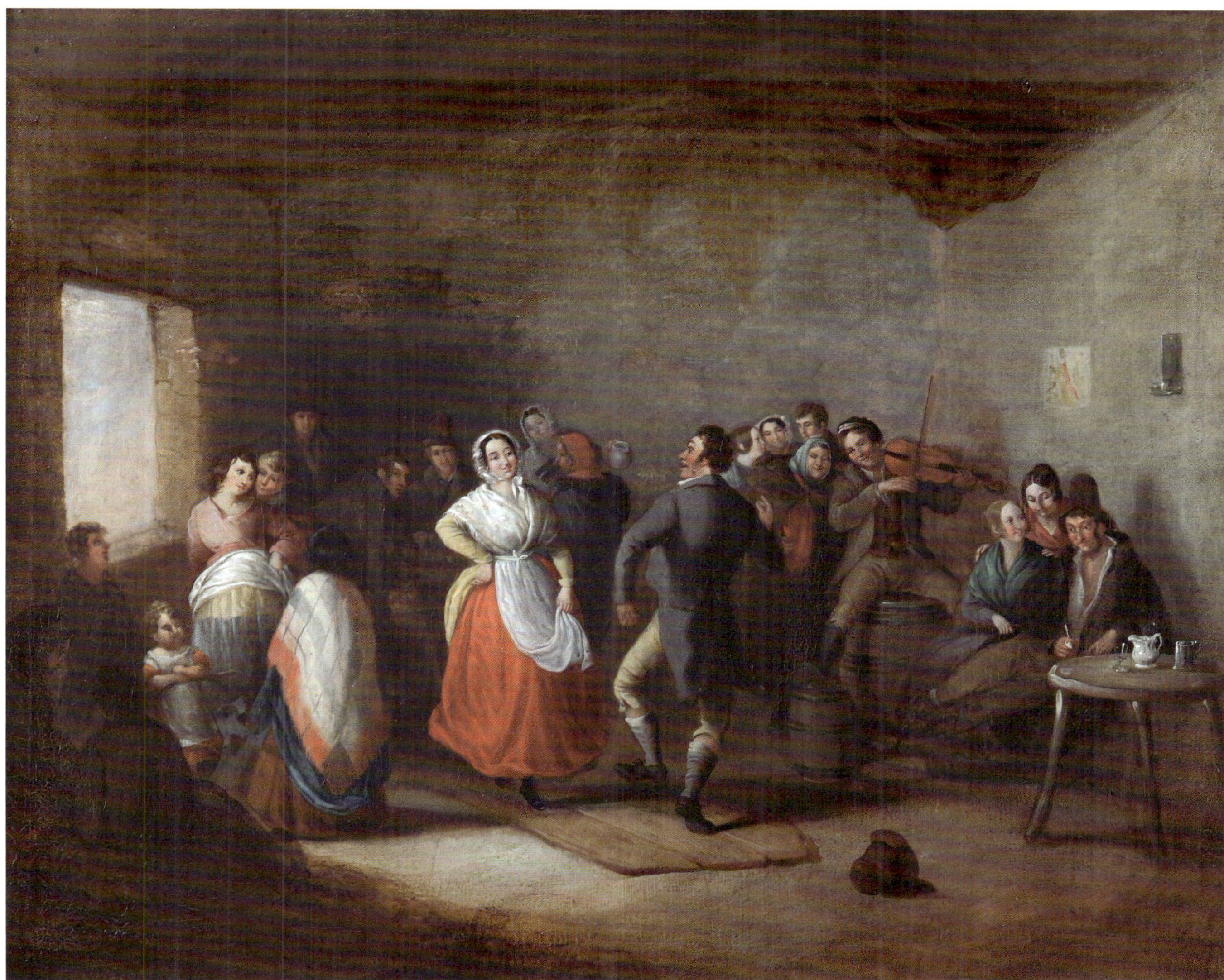

Figure 35

*A Country Dance /
A Wedding Dance*

Daniel Macdonald

1848

always invited and usually attend on such occasions. The second apartment is appropriated
for the neighbours in general; and the third, or an out-house, is devoted to the reception
of buckaughs [sic], shulers, and other beggars. When the marriage is celebrated two
collections are raised amongst the guests, the first for the priest, the other for the piper.
The assembly does not take place until late in the evening, when the marriage ceremony
is performed, and the festivities seldom conclude before day-break the next morning.[172]

If in fact this painting does depict a wedding dance, the bride looks rather old. Prior to the Famine, Irish
people married young (after 1845, postponed marriage and high levels of permanent celibacy were
the norm). Upon marriage, girls donned a matronly cap, and so the dancer here would appear to be
already married. Set codes of feminine conduct were associated with public order and social stability.
For poor, single women, marriage was some assurance against destitution. Marriage patterns were
thus determined by economic forces, arranged by parents, with a view to protecting or enhancing their
interests, however meager their circumstances. Even at the poorest level, marriage was the means by
which inheritance and property were managed. For those more comfortably off, social and economic
compatibility was ensured through the services of a matchmaker. Usually, the eldest son inherited the

Figure 36

The Courtship

Daniel Macdonald

1847

Figure 37

*An Irish Parish Priest
and His Coadjutor*

Daniel Macdonald

1847

family home, and one daughter was provided with a dowry (a dowry coming *into* a house might be used to marry another, otherwise the rest remained at home unmarried, or they emigrated). A girl's dowry, or 'fortune' was the money or property brought by her to her husband. The better-off sent remaining children into the religious life, but even those entering a convent needed a dowry. (Marriage by capture and marriage by purchase were not unheard of either.)

In this painting, the rustic homemade table is the only furniture visible. The fiddler straddles a barrel. And although there is a picture (St. Patrick expelling the snakes from Ireland) and a tin candle-holder on the wall, it would seem as if the painting *is* set in a barn where, in Croker's designation, beggars, boccaughs and shulers were housed during weddings. But, if so, this barn is peopled by respectable, relatively well-off country people, suggesting perhaps that it may simply be a country dance.[173] Weddings were celebrated usually with large amounts of food and drink, following which music and dancing would continue into the early morning, accounting perhaps for the daylight coming through the window. The absence of drink in the painting, usually poured with an unsparing hand at weddings, is another indicator. Croker recounts having seen a piper play without a moment's pause, but given alcoholic sustenance by another holding the jug of porter to his lips, to maintain the flow, so to speak, suggesting that it is not a wedding, although that may simply be accounted for by the growing temperance of the country.[174]

In a life of deprivation, dancing was an expression of vitality, Kevin Whelan sees it as

> a cultural statement, the somatic and kinetic intelligence of which blended into a richly expressive vernacular art. The accomplished traditional dancer rode the rhythm, consummately mastering the movement. But s/he also oscillated along the porous boundary between the respect for tradition and an assertive individuality. For the spectator, the attraction was the expressive tension between tradition and the individual talent; the dancer bound to the strictly prescribed music, could also innovate within and against it. When male and female danced together, there was also sexual theatre — expressed through the heavier 'hit' of the male dancer (culminating in the 'batter', heavy rhythmic drumming with the full foot), counterpoised against the quicker buoyant step of the female performer.[175]

Not surprisingly, the Church took issue with the spontaneity of dancing as providing sexualized contact, in clerically unpolicable places, fuelled by alcohol.

In 1782, a translation of an Irish ballad 'The Pig and the Pot', designed to teach young people the art of love, was published by the *Hibernian Journal* to considerable interest. Given his father's interest in ballads, it was one undoubtedly known by Macdonald. Set in a forest between Cork city and Blarney, it addressed the subject of sexuality, in a less than oblique manner.[176] Courtship was a theme to which Macdonald returned a number of times, as in *The Killarney Milkmaid* (1847) (Crawford Art Gallery) and *The Courtship* (**Fig. 36**). The latter shows a harvest romance — the young man's reaping hook is serving him well. And in *An Irish Parish Priest with his Coadjutor* (**Fig. 37**), we see the blessing, or admonishment for sexual misbehavior, of a couple by a portly priest and his killjoy curate.

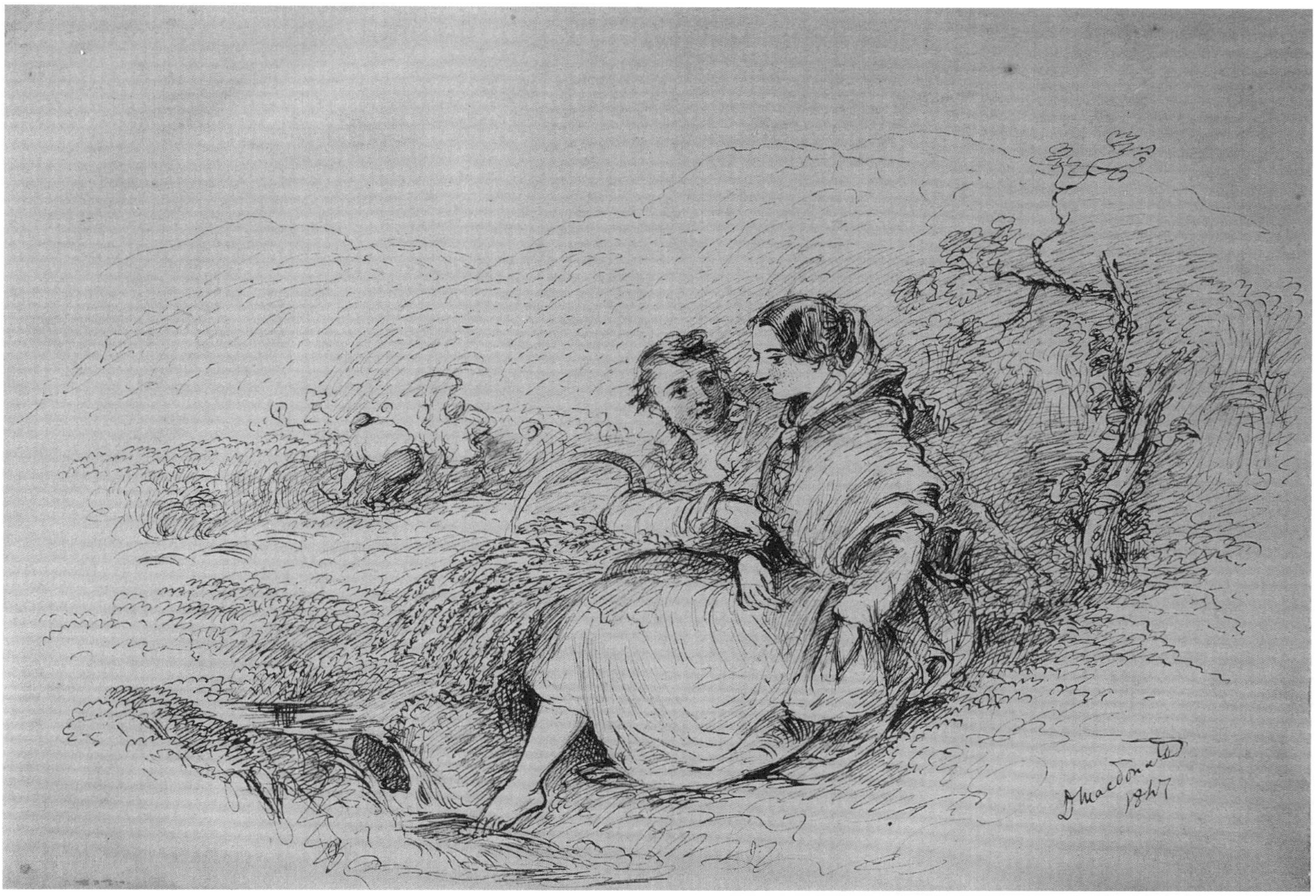

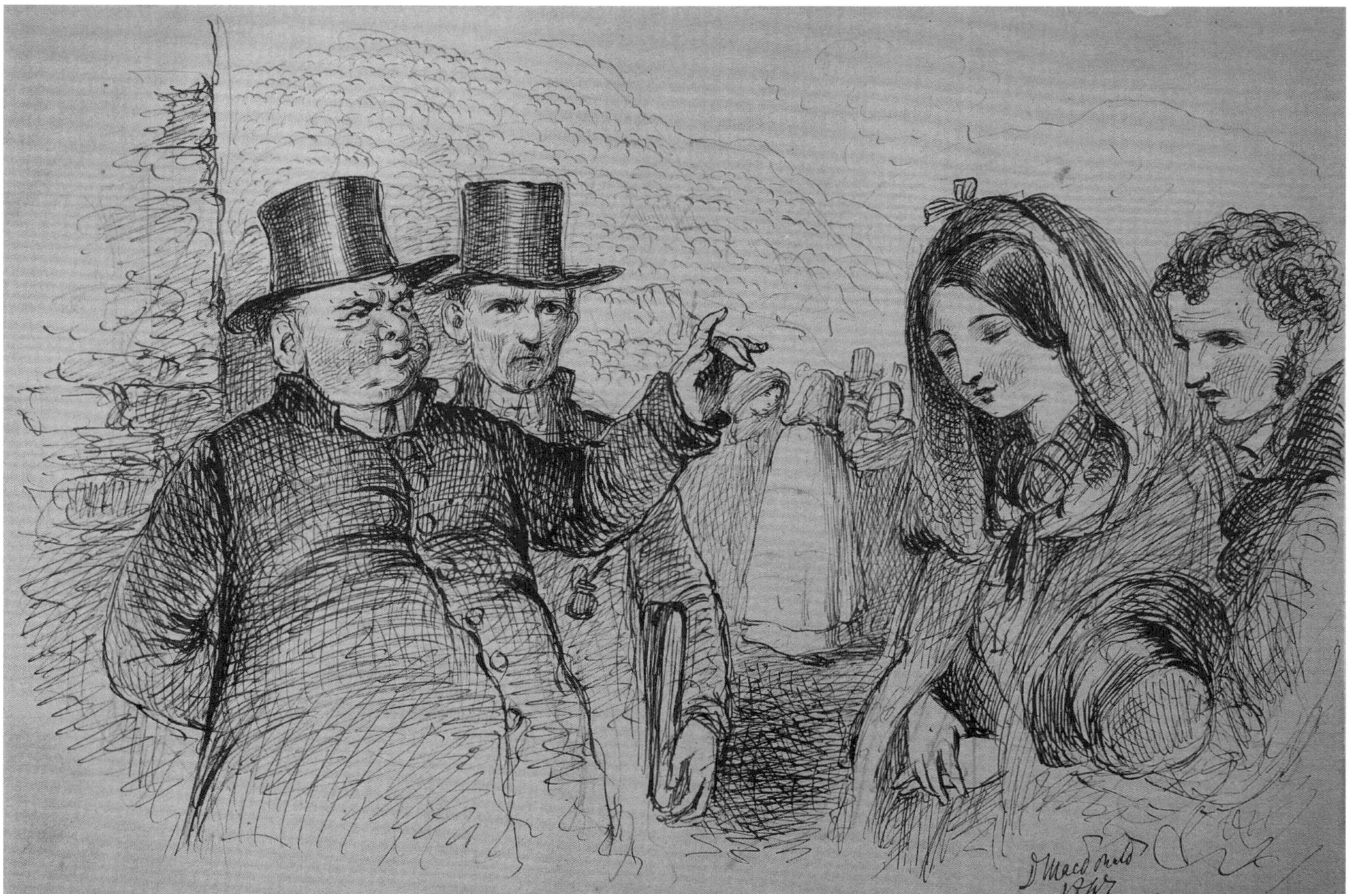

HIGH DAYS AND HOLY DAYS

Figure 38

Preparing for Mass
Daniel Macdonald
1847

From the 1831 census, we know that 80 percent of the population was Catholic, largely concentrated in the west and south, making up the majority of the lower classes in Ireland. Years of persecution under the Penal Laws had weakened the structure and functioning of the Church, but Catholic Emancipation and the right to sit in Parliament brought significant changes.[177] But for the ascendancy class, the election of Daniel O'Connell and the granting of Catholic Emancipation provoked fears for the future of Protestantism. Their anxiety was increased by the British Government's educational policies, which had been designed to put an end to the religious competition in schools. The National System of Education, introduced in 1831, aimed to bring all children together for general literary instruction while separating them for religious doctrine. This only intensified religious rivalry. The necessity of defending Catholicism united all Catholics across the classes and strengthened the notion of Catholicism as a badge of national identity.

Figure 39

*Preparing for Bed:
Scene in an Irish Cabin*
Daniel Macdonald
1847

Macdonald was not immune to the rivalries of class and creed, but there is no malice in his representations. He executed many images featuring aspects of Roman Catholic belief in both oil and sketch form. *Preparing for Mass* **(Fig. 38)** and *Preparing for Bed: Scene in an Irish Cabin* **(Fig. 39)** — watched over by 'Holy Saint Bridget' in the former, and St. Bridget, St. Patrick and Adam and Eve in the latter — show relatively well-off tenant farmers' families, attentive to their religious duties. In one, the family is attending to their spiritual and physical needs before bed; in the other, the young woman is taking off her apron — her cloak and rosary beads are nearby on the chair, and the prayer book on the table, awaiting the family's departure for Mass, although 'the Mammy' with the *duídín* in her mouth looks as if she is going nowhere.

Clay pipes were used by both men and women and were often associated with storytellers, who would keep their audience in suspense by filling the pipe or taking a puff at a crucial moment in a story. And no self-respecting family would wake a loved one without passing out a *duídín*, a pipe filled with a twist of tobacco (the stem often dipped in whiskey or poitín) to each mourner in the room.

These sketches, preliminary to finished oil paintings that remain unlocated, are characteristically Macdonald. They show the artist's attention to the detail and narrative of the material culture of the class. There is an intimacy about these images suggesting that they were observed closely from life, and they are skilfully executed.

Macdonald returned to Ireland in 1847, at the height of the Famine. There are copious sketches dating to that year, including *Soul Beggars* **(Fig. 40)**, his study of what appears to be St. Colman's holy well. Before the Famine, a vernacular Catholicism had established itself in rural Ireland cleaving to traditional beliefs and rituals that included holy wells and calendric customs, becoming decidedly more regulated, controlled and ritualized in the post-Famine period. Geoff Burton says that the text of the day, Philip Dixon Hardy's *The Holy Wells of Ireland* (1836), was written 'from a staunchly and vituperatively Protestant perspective', Macdonald's Holy Well is an altogether different proposition.[178]

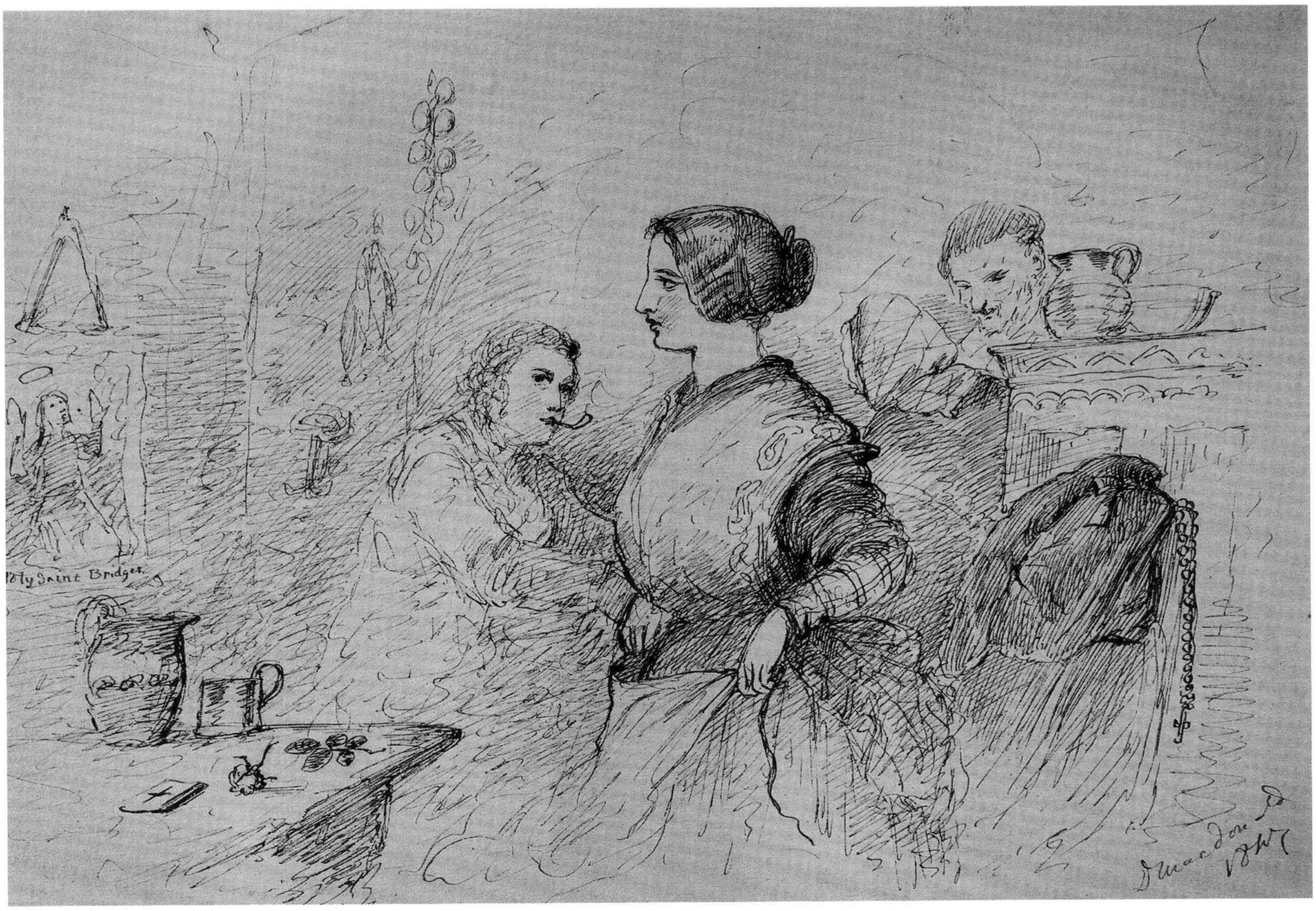
Saint Bridget

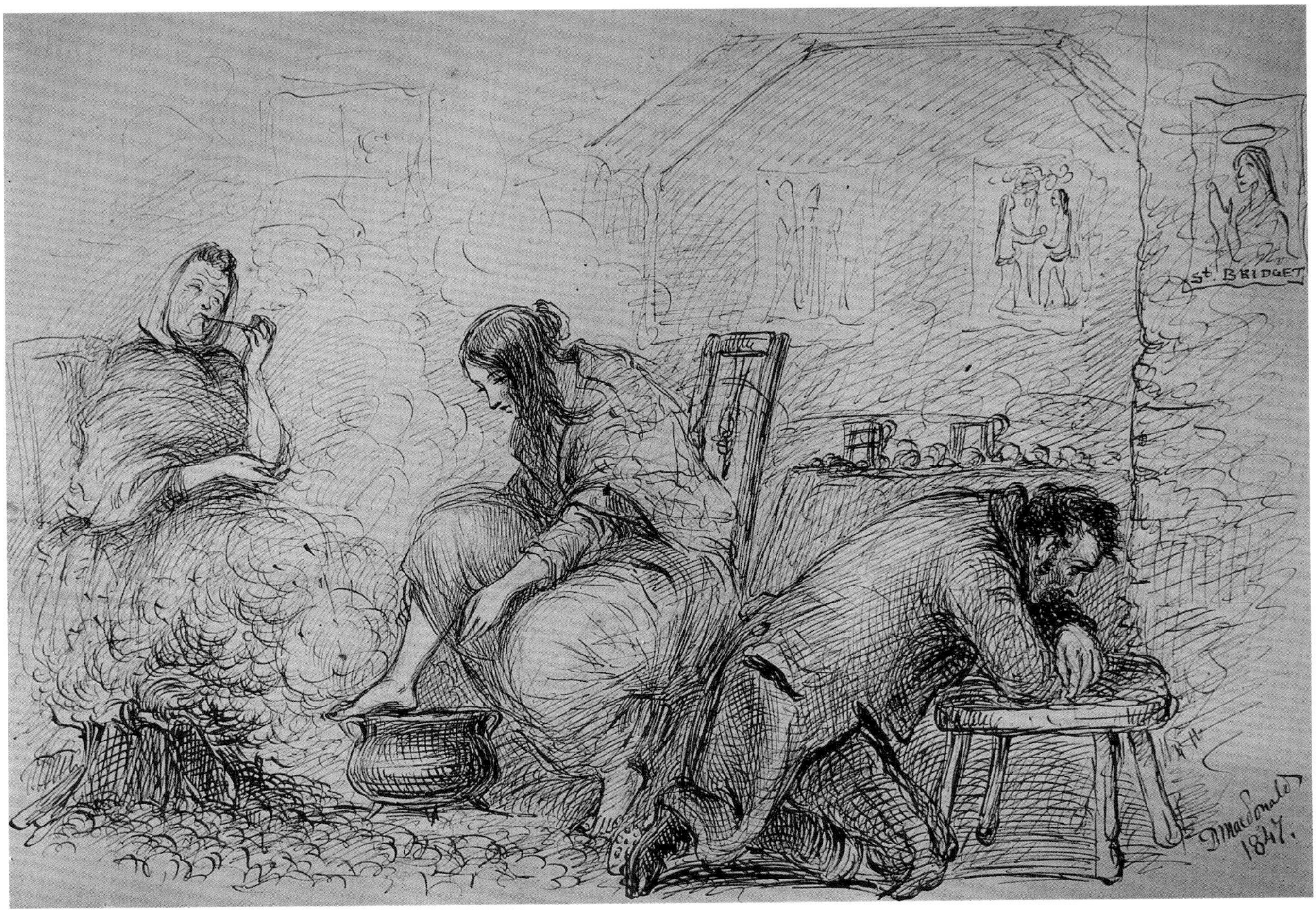
St. BRIDGET
D Macdonald
1847.

There are said to be over 3,000 holy wells in Ireland; at many of these, pagan rituals formerly took place. These were visited at the great festivals of *Imbolc* on February 1, *Beltaine* on May 1, *Lughnasa* on August 1, and *Samhain* on November 1 — especially *Samhain,* when the boundaries between the living and the dead were dissolved, and visions of the Otherworld were said to be seen. Elements of pre-Christian and Christian religious practices melded, thus *Imbolc* became St. Brigid's Day, etc.

In AD 559, Queen Rionach, about to give birth, was cast into the Kiltartin river with as stone around her neck, by her husband who became jealous of a prophecy that their son (St. Colman) would be greater than his father. She survived and gave birth. Divine Providence led two monks — one blind and one lame — to her, and she asked them to baptize her son. The blind monk pulled up some rushes and a well sprung up, splashing his eyes and curing his blindness; the lame monk washed his leg and was cured; and with that water Colman was baptized.

Individual wells became associated with specific ailments, such as fertility or lameness or blindness. Many religious sites comprise a well, a spring, and a sacred tree or standing stone. It was believed that drinking from these waters or bathing in them would bestow wisdom, or cure disease. Holy wells were frequented for various reasons — folk medicine, pilgrimage and popular assembly — fulfilling important medicinal, spiritual and social needs. The term Soul Beggars, as used by Macdonald, is obscure. Beggars often promise to say a prayer for almsgivers, or for the souls of the faithful departed. Given that prayers were the only social capital they had, the idea prevailed that the prayers or curses of someone who had nothing were particularly efficacious.

Figure 40

Soul Beggars

Daniel Macdonald

1847

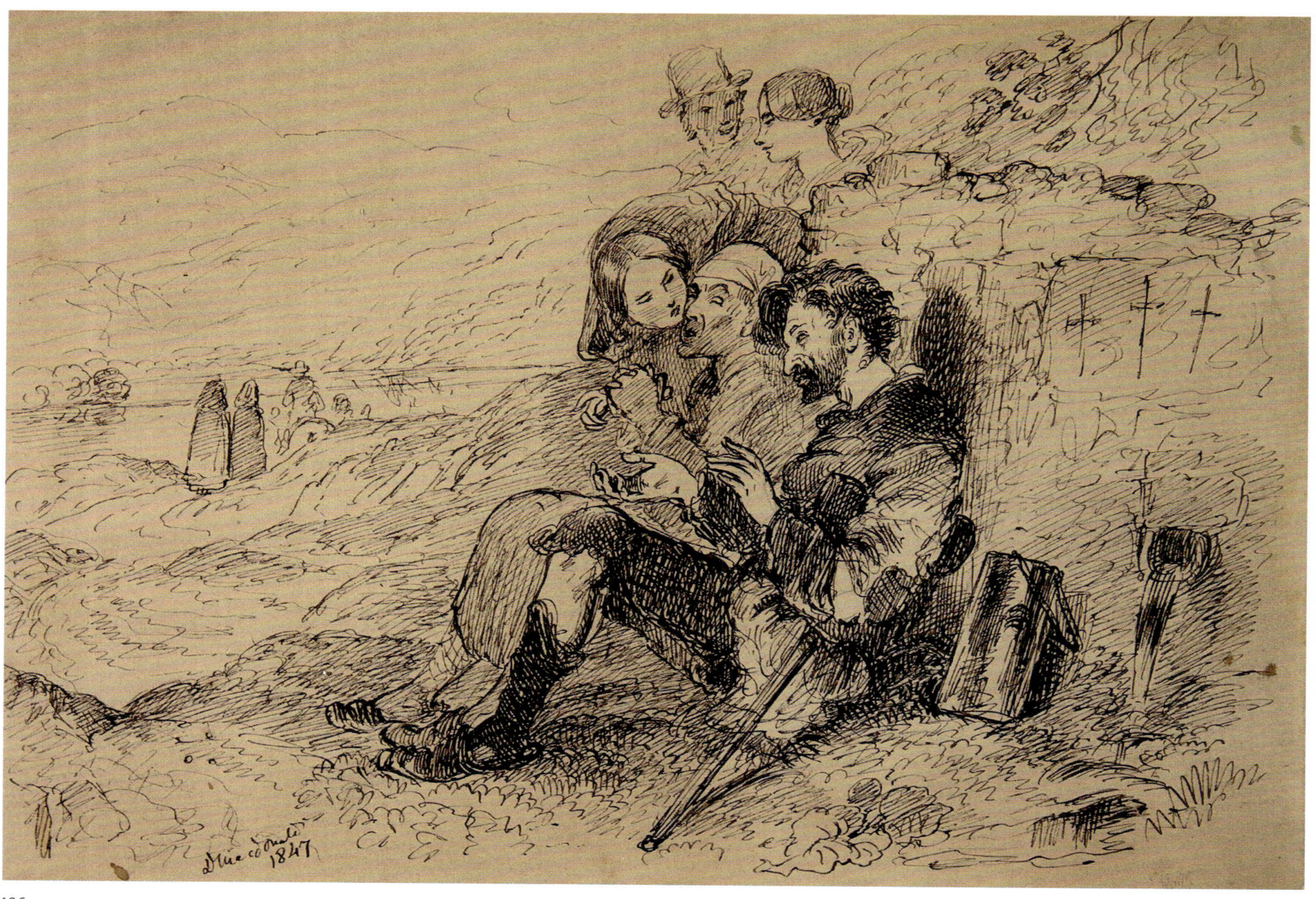

This well is enclosed in an old stone structure. People are both coming and going: pilgrims made 'rounds' at holy wells, circular walks done *deiseal* (in the same direction in which the sun travels). Water is flowing from a rock above, on which three crosses are incised. The bearded man with hand outstretched is lame (*bacach*), and the other blind (*an seandall glic* — the clever old blind man — features in many oral tales as a kind of oracle). A number of Yeats's plays have blind beggars and cripples as vatic figures, often with a holy well in the background, and in *The Cat and the Moon,* set at St. Colman's Well, near Kinvara, Co. Galway, the two main characters are a blind beggar and a lame beggar.[179]

The annual pattern to St. Colman's Holy Well, marking the place of his baptism, took place on October 29th each year. As well as sites of folk medicine, religious devotion and assembly, pattern days were also occasions of much jostling (as we saw in the case of faction fighting) and jollity. Thomas Crofton Croker described the revels of a pattern day in Gougane Barra in 1813:

> After discussing the merits of [the] salmon, and washing it down with some of 'Beamish & Crawford's Porter' we whiled away the time by drinking whiskey-punch, observing the dancing to an excellent piper, and listening to the songs and story-telling which were going on about us. As night closed in, the tent became crowded almost to suffocation, and dancing being out of the question, our piper left us for some other station, and a man, who I learned had served in the Kerry militia, and had been flogged at Tralee about five years before as a White-boy, began to take a prominent part in entertaining the assembly by singing Irish songs in a loud and effective voice. These songs were received with shouts of applause, and … were rebellious in the highest degree. Poor old King George was execrated without mercy; curses were also dealt out wholesale on the Saxon oppressors of Banna the Blessed (an allegorical name for Ireland); Bonaparte's achievements were extolled, and Irishmen were called upon to follow the example of the French people.[180]

As in so many cases, Macdonald captured Ireland on the cusp of cataclysmic change. Just six years later, Sir William Wilde noticed that '[t]he old forms, and customs too, are becoming obliterated. The festivals are unobserved and the rustic festivities neglected or forgotten …'

> The great convulsion which society of all grades here has lately experienced, the failure of the potato crop, pestilence, famine, and a most unparalleled extent of emigration, together with bankrupt landlords, pauperizing poor-laws, grinding officials, and decimating workhouses, have broken up the very foundations of social intercourse, have swept away the established theories of political economists, and uprooted many of our long-cherished opinions. In some places, all the domestic usages of life have been outraged; the tenderest bonds of kindred have been severed, some of the noblest and holiest feelings of human nature have been blotted from the heart, and many of the finest, yet firmest links which united the various classes in the community have been rudely burst asunder. [181]

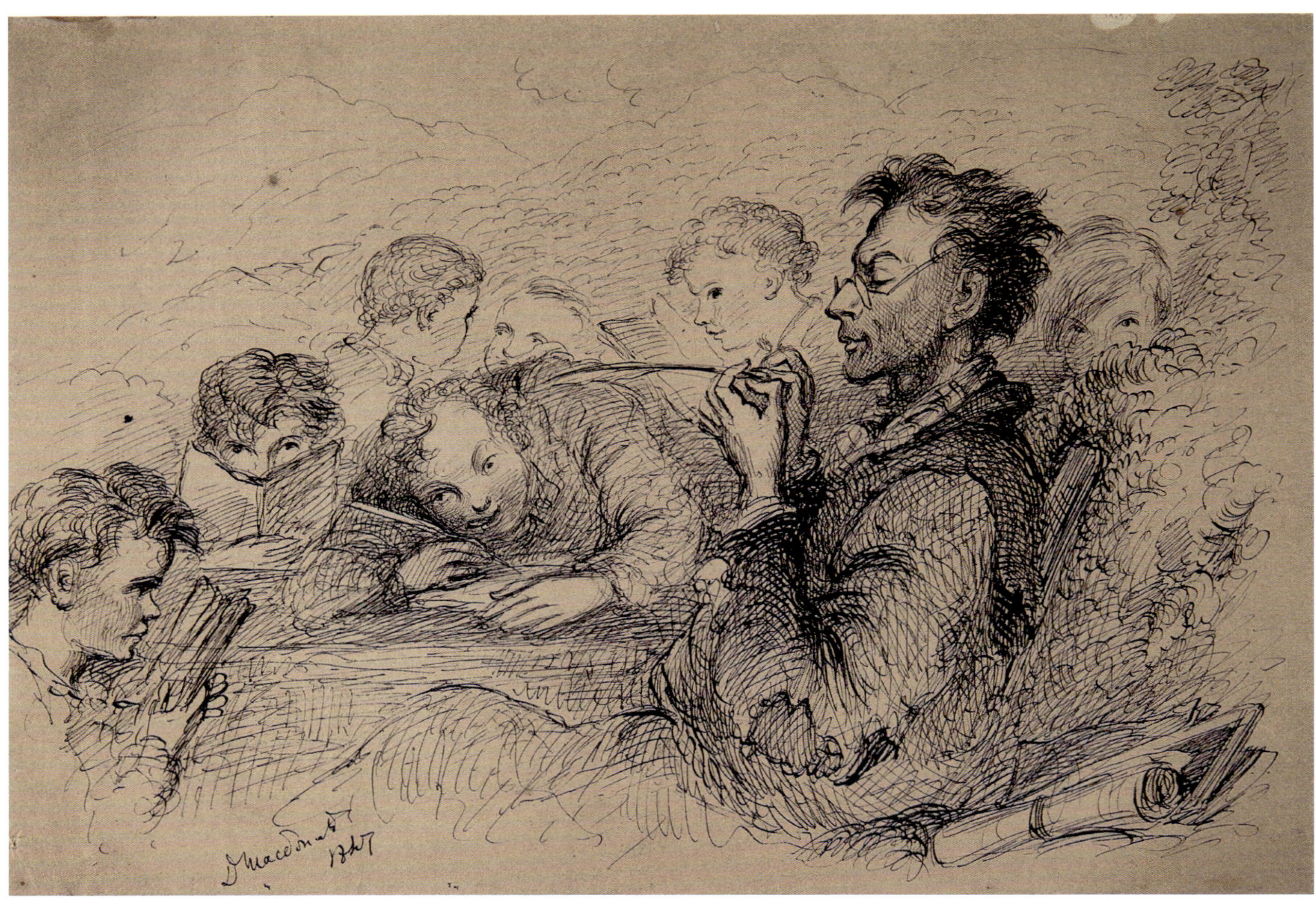

AR SCOIL

Figure 41

The Hedge Schoolmaster

Daniel Macdonald

1847

Macdonald did a number of sketches of hedge schoolmasters and their gossoons. In both *The Hedge Schoolmaster* (**Fig. 41**), and *Mr. Mike Scanlon's School, Ballyshandrahan* (**Fig. 42**) it is the masters on whom Macdonald focuses. In the latter, the master holds forth in his classroom, a *báta*, for correctional purposes in his hand, long enough to extend to the farthest pupil. Glasses pushed up, gums sucked in, he has a slightly bumbling, but highly self-regarding air. The notice pinned to the wall, written it would seem by himself, reads:

> Childre tote to rede, rite & sifer 2d per week. Them as larns manners 2d per week more. By
> Mr Mick Scanlon.

Figure 42

Mr. Mike Scanlon's School, Ballyshandrahan

Daniel Macdonald

1851

In *The Hedge Schoolmaster*, the master is a fine-featured itinerant teacher, intent on sharpening his quill, for purposes educational, and possibly seditious. The class is taking place in the open air, the master leans against a book, propped up against a bank, surrounded by his willing pupils. With one exception, the children are sweet and assiduous. But the master's arched eyebrows and scholarly glasses, his patched clothes and unkempt hair, hint at more on his mind than simple reading, 'riting and 'rithmetic. The density of the cross hatching suggests a ferocity at work. He is shrewd and calculating and used to getting his own way. The standing of schoolmasters in the community was very high. Both William Maginn, and his father before him, for example, ran much-regarded schools in Cork, where the curriculum was both broad and deep. They played many complex roles in Irish peasant life, not least as masters of sedition, feared by the authorities, both Church and state.

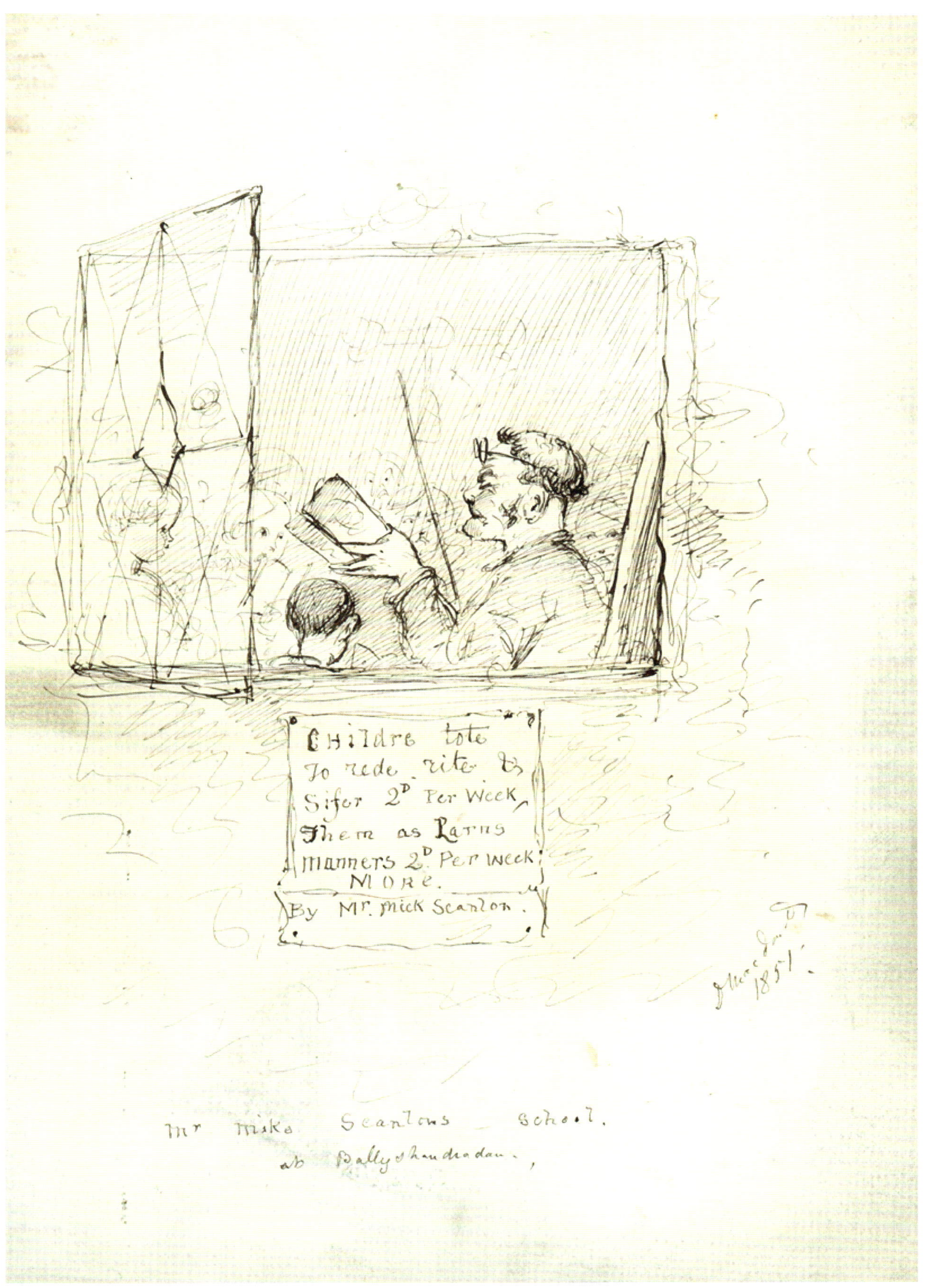

Mr miks Scanlons School.
at Ballyshandradan.

The inference here is that the 'pay' school of Mike Scanlon was somewhat 'less' than the hedge school, where lessons in life and lawlessness were taught, as well as literacy and the classics. In 1824, an official commission established that there were some 11,000 schools with 500,000 pupils and about 12,000 teachers in the 'pay' school system, in addition to 9,000 hedge schools with 400,000 pupils. That is, 40 percent of children received some form of education, however briefly or sporadically, during Macdonald's childhood. Although the matter of education was a deeply political one, nevertheless, hedge schools managed to survive with little interference from the Church or state, the curriculum being defined by individual masters. In addition to the basics, Latin, Greek, and literature in both Irish and English were taught. Even in the late eighteenth century, according to Arthur Young, some level of education was general: 'hedge schools as they are called (they might as well be termed *ditch* ones, for I have seen many a ditch full of scholars) are everywhere to be met with, where reading and writing are taught.'[182] Schooling was largely by the 'individual instruction' method, that is one-on-one. In the early nineteenth century, most schools used the 'monitorial method' whereby the teacher supervised the monitors — slightly older children, who taught the younger ones; in the 1840s, this model gave way to the 'simultaneous method', where the class was taught by the teacher, and the monitors were teachers' aides.[183]

Hedge-school masters were itinerant poets and scholars (and sometimes 'spoilt priests'), and they tended to be erudite and gifted storytellers. Many authored rebellious ballads — 'songs, treasonable, amatory, and laudatory', as Croker called them.[184] *Paddy's Resource* (1795), for example, was a hedge school staple. And they were known to use 'immoral books' in instruction: Cosgrave's *A Genuine History of the Lives and Actions of the Most Notorious Irish Highwaymen, Tories and Raparees* (1795[?]) was a key text in the 'library' of hedge schoolmasters, as were racy chapbooks. In hedge schools, *buachaillí* and *cailíní*, as we see in Macdonald's sketches, were taught together, which the Church also considered immoral.

Protestants, believing Catholicism an inferior, cultish religion, did their utmost to lure Catholics to their schools, and their proselytizing strategies fuelled indignation. Although the hedge schoolmaster came to epitomize Gaelic Ireland, actually, hedge schools insisted on teaching English, believing it to be the language of social mobility, commerce and emigration. As Kevin Whelan put it, '[o]utside the reach of Church and state, they had a foot — and a tongue — in both worlds'.[185] As the chief agent in the transition from Irish to English, masters were thus a strong modernizing and intellectualizing force in nineteenth-century Ireland.

In the post 1798 period, the authorities came down heavily on hedge schools. The hedge schoolmaster played a pivotal role in agrarian society, encouraging militancy in the form of Rockite violence, for example. In many cases, it was he who wrote the threatening notices warning landlords to desist from their avaricious practices, and he was responsible for the diffusion of seditious material and republican ideas as he moved from parish to parish. He was versed in Pastorini's prophecies, carried Whiteboy 'articles' — oaths and regulations for recruiting to secret societies. His polemical writings, ballads, poems and nighttime tales stoked memories of injustices, recent and distant.

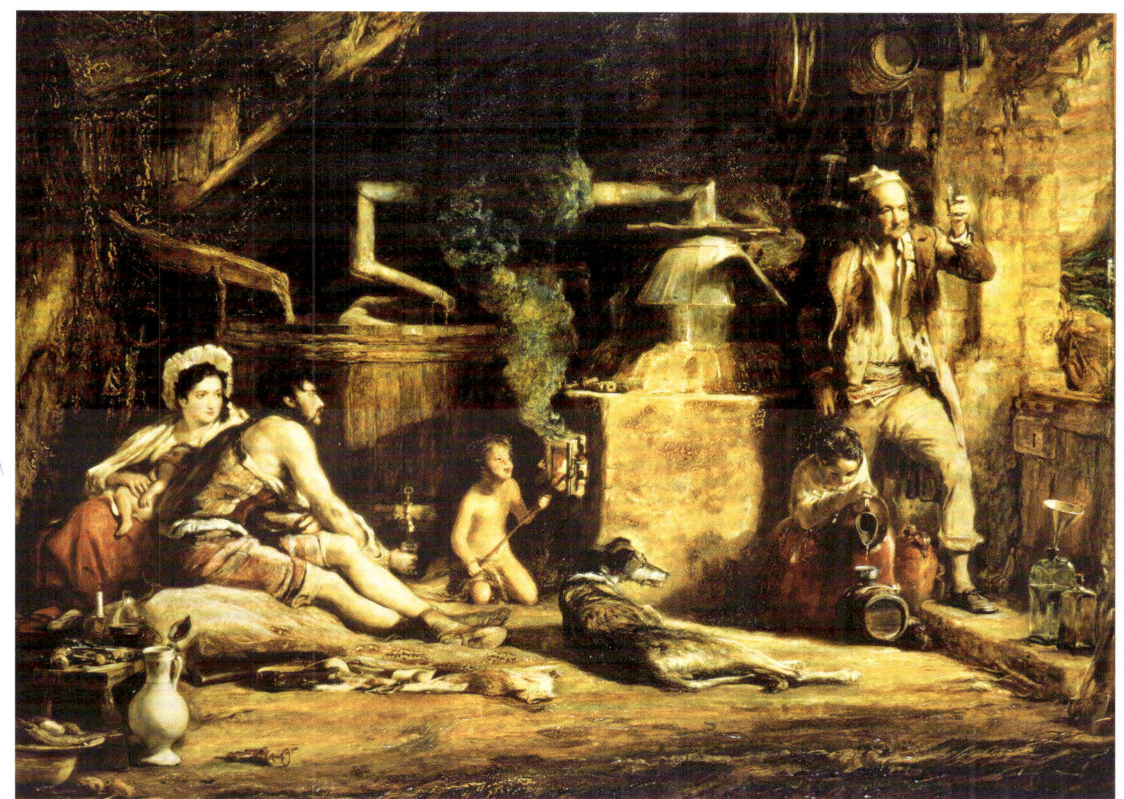

Schoolmasters feature in many works by writers of contemporary ethnography and fiction, such as William Carleton, Lady Morgan, Gerald Griffin and Thomas Crofton Croker, as well as in paintings and drawings.[186] Nathaniel Grogan's *The Country Schoolmaster*, Edmund Fitzpatrick's, *The Irish Schoolmaster* and, of course, Maclise's *Installation of Captain Rock*.

NATIONAL CHARACTER

In 1835, the Scottish artist, David Wilkie, came to Ireland. He was not in search of the poverty and distress evident to all who came, but what Nicholas Tromans describes as 'sensual, even louche, Baroque images of this predominantly Catholic country along the lines of his vision of Spain.' Wilkie thought the Irish a backward, but noble race, 'a people whom no penalties could turn, whom no terror of military violence could overcome.'[187] He produced two remarkable paintings that must have impressed young Macdonald for their subject matter, scale and execution: *The Peep-O'-Day Boys' Cabin in the West of Ireland* (first known as *The Sleeping Whiteboy* (1835–36) (Tate Gallery), and *The Irish Whiskey Still* (1840) **(Fig. 43)**. While these paintings are about Irish criminality and illegality, Wilkie himself saw such activities as representative of 'public events', in other words, Irish social problems, and believed, therefore, that such subjects should be painted 'larger' than mere genre scenes, a perspective also adapted by Macdonald in *The Fighter* and *Tasting the Poitín,* for example[188] **(Fig. 44)**.

The production of and consumption of poitín was a major contributor to social and economic problems, in Ireland, especially violence — of all varieties. The mid 1820s to the late 1830s were periods of record consumption of both poitín and agrarian insurgency in the Munster area, a period that coincided with the boyhood of Daniel Macdonald, to whom this painting is attributed.[189]

Figure 43

The Irish Whiskey Still
Sir David Wilkie
1840

Figure 44 [CROPPED]
FOLLOWING SPREAD

Tasting the Poitín in Ireland
Daniel Macdonald
c. 1844

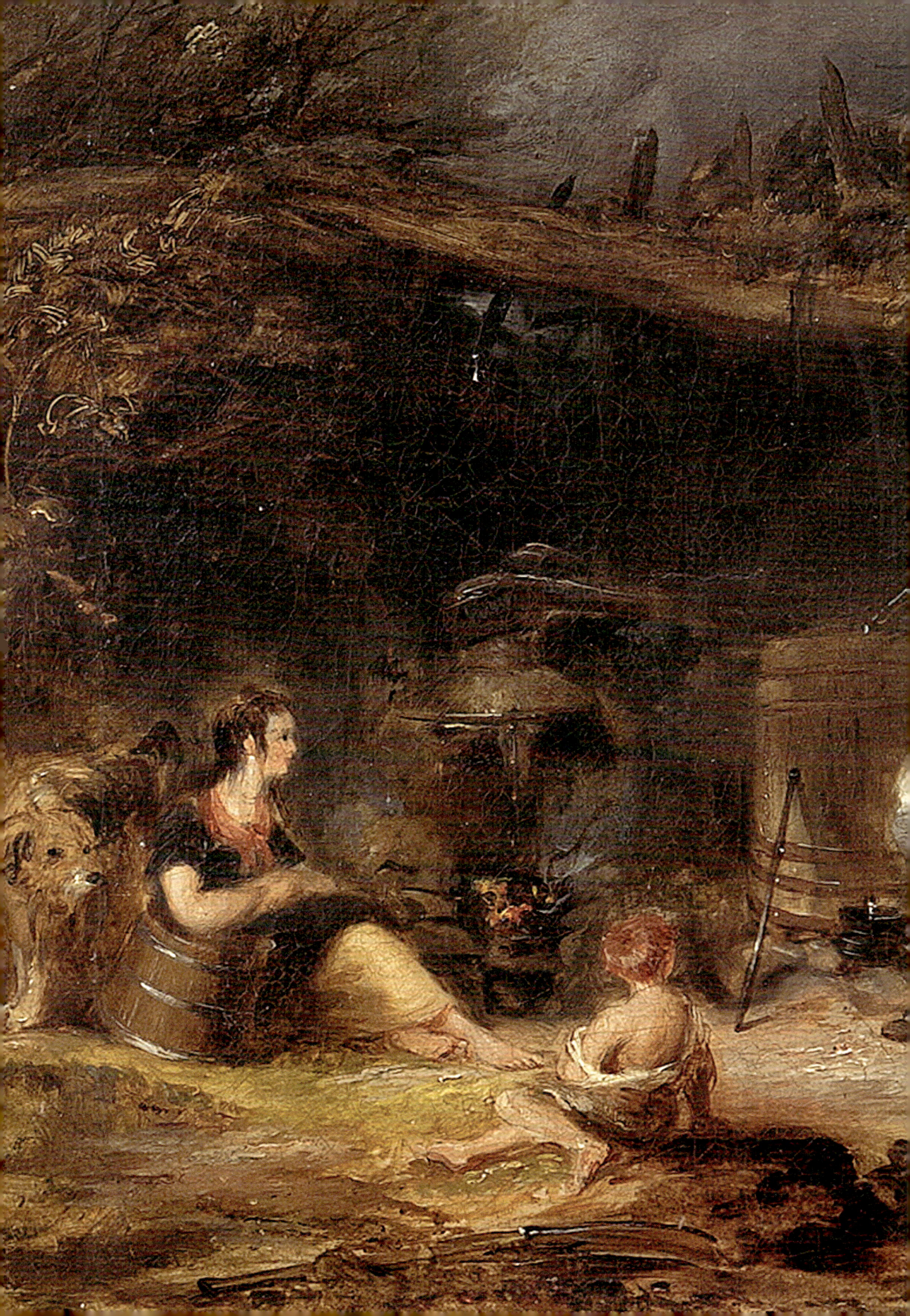

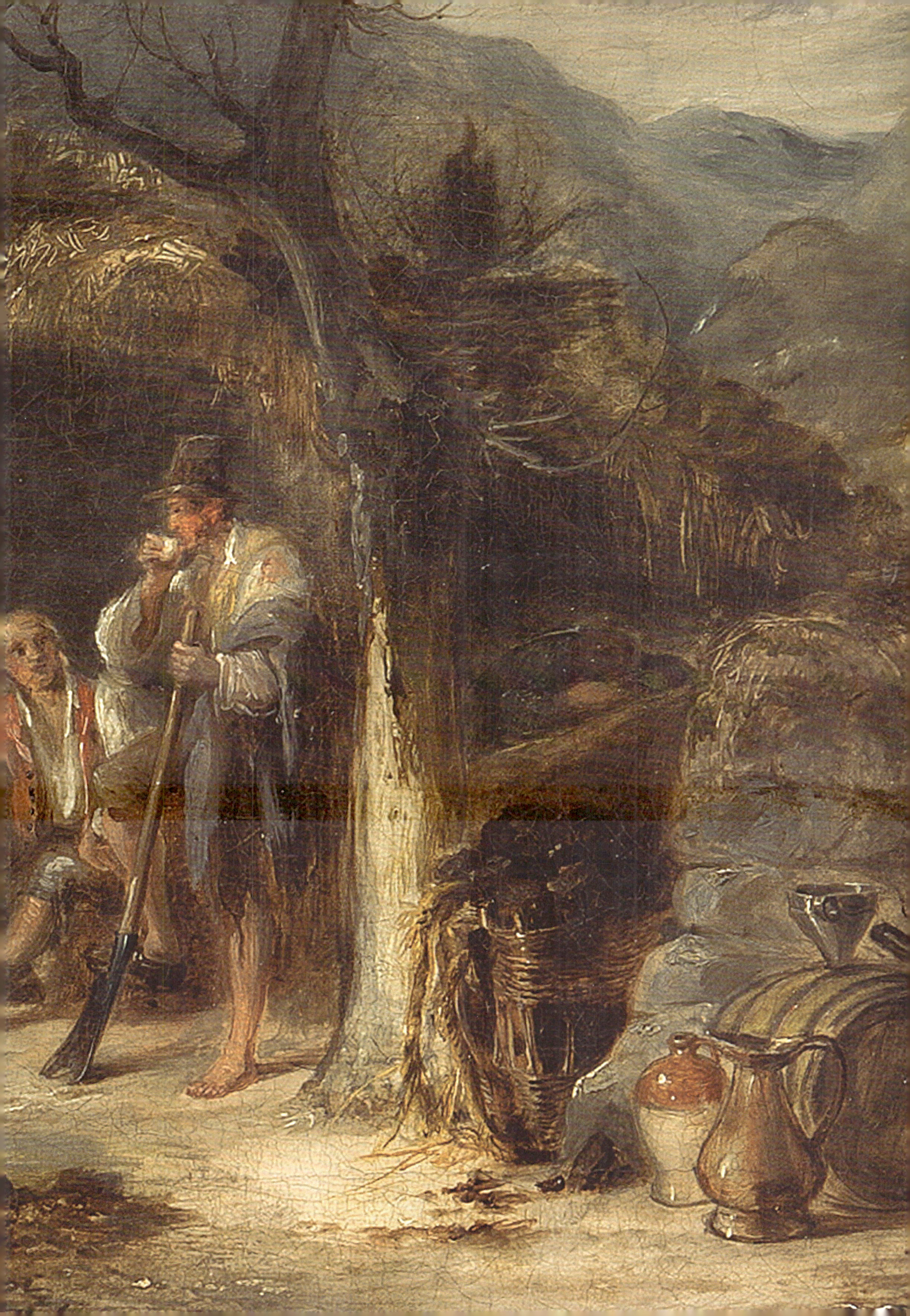

The similarities between *An Irish Peasant Family Discovering the Blight of their Store, Eviction* and *Tasting the Poitín* are discernible. The paintings are emblematically Macdonald, set in the same mountainous area, typical of west Cork. The poitín taster stands on the right with his ragamuffin offspring. It looks as if the same child features in each, and his very own puppy has clearly jumped from one painting to the other. The tombstones, given megalithic stature in *Tasting the Poitín,* resemble the jagged protuberances in Macdonald's *Figures by a Coffin*.

The word poitín derives from the Gaelic word *pota* for pot, referring to the small copper pot used in the process of distillation. Macdonald has closely observed the process and has included other accoutrements: barrel and funnel, 'worm' and earthenware vessel, jug and creel of turf. Other informative vignettes of peasant culture include the father's single brogue. Shoes were precious and essential for digging turf. The artist thus shows him with his one shod foot resting on his *sleán,* the same turf spade as in *An Irish Family Discovering the Blight of their Store.*[190] This is a fascinating record of the social and material culture of illegal distilling in Ireland at this time.

Fintan Cullen notes how the material culture of distilling was often generalized for artistic purposes, but from what is known about Irish stills, Macdonald's version seems realistic enough.[191] As distilling was a long and complicated process, poitín was made in remote areas, out of sight of the law, often on land boundaries so that ownership could be disputed. Distilling needed fire and clean running water, therefore poitín was made in mountainous areas. Here the smoke was less likely to be seen and the distillers could work away from the eyes of 'gaugers', revenue men and constabulary. The open thatch over the hearth suggests just the right amount of cover to keep the fire going and the smoke under wraps from prying eyes (windy or foggy weather, as indicated in the painting, was often chosen to camouflage the activity).

Once the spirit was made, transporting it to sales outlets involved many deceptions, such as hiding it in coffins or under loads of turf. Caesar Otway reported how a 'tinker' made a tin vessel in the shape of his wife, filled it with poitín, and put 'her' to ride pillion behind him to market.[192] Macdonald's painting has an air of intimate clandestinity that is intended to engage and thrill. One has the distinct impression that he visited this distillery — that he has captured the spirit of Ireland, as it were.

Illicit whiskey was hard currency. In poor areas, especially in the west and north west, it constituted an important part of the economy of the peasantry, to the extent that some magistrates and landlords turned a blind eye, so that tenants had sufficient money to pay their rents. However, the national debt led the government to pursue revenue frauds committed through poitín making (as opposed to Parliament Whiskey, for which taxes were paid), but their efforts to suppress illicit stills and circumvent the organized and inventive means by which peasants evaded the authorities, was a game of cat and mouse.

Increases in the price of whiskey contributed to the growth in the production of poitín. Estimates of quantities produced are hard to establish, George Bretherton calculates 8 million gallons of annual production in the 1830s, the equivalent of a gallon for every man, woman and child in the country. Others

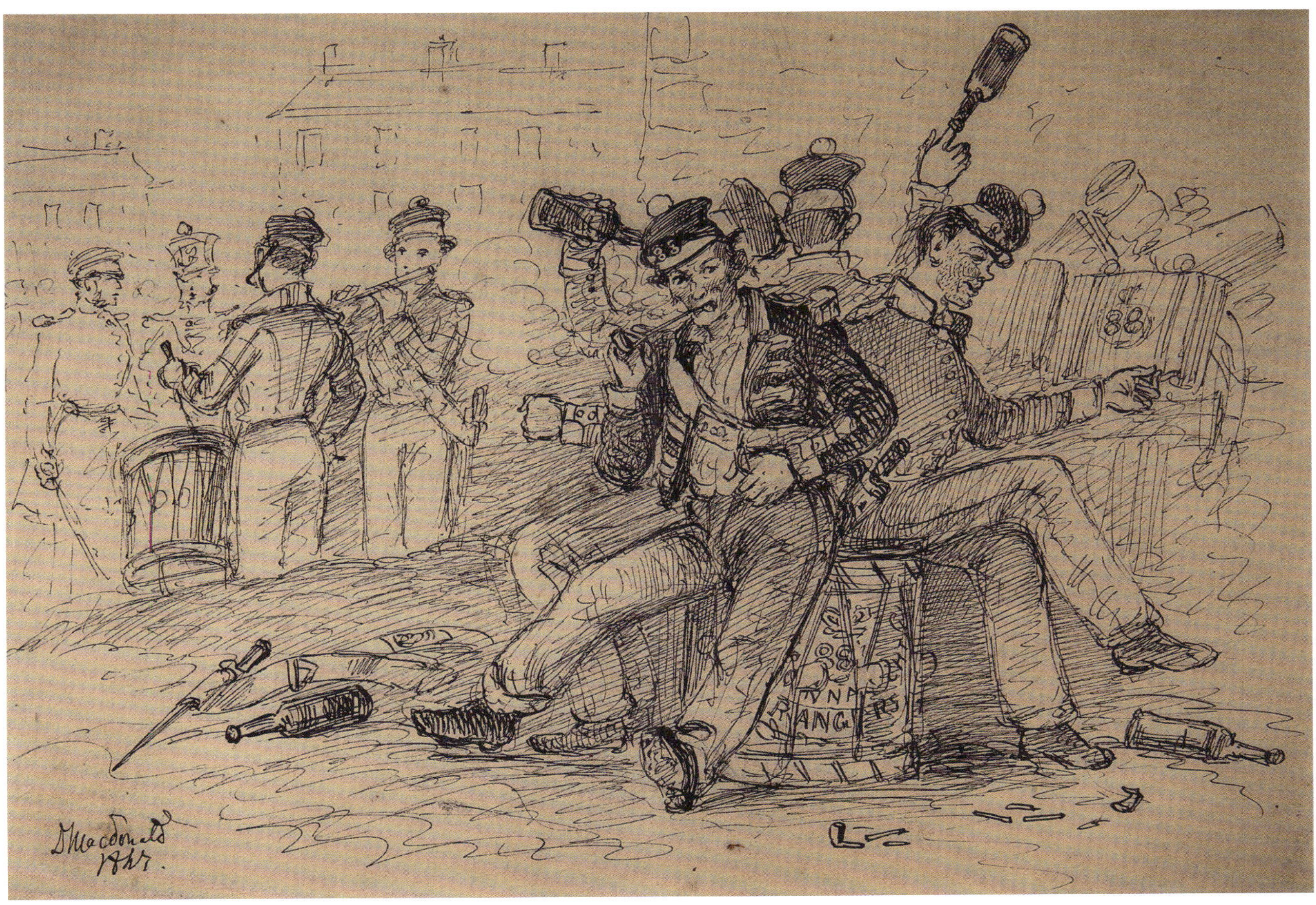

believe this is greatly underestimated.[193] Of course, no-one had the spare potatoes or barley required to make poitín after 1845, from which we can conclude that *Tasting the Poitín* predates the Famine.

Poitín was highly toxic, as evidenced by the figure slumped over the branch of a tree on the right of the painting. As well as being a cause of social ills, it had a reputation as a cause of blindness and other ailments. These effects could be equally attributed to excess consumption and lack of refinement. Croker amusingly described how the self-afflicted would resort to absurd maneuvers to dodge their consciences, no less than the forces of law and order:

> A peasant after suffering the ill consequences of intoxication, will often forswear liquor of any kind for a given period; or will take an oath not to taste spirits within a certain barony, or 'in any house', or 'either in or out of a house,' and though these vows are sometimes religiously observed, yet are they as frequently avoided by various and amusing stratagems: for instance, a man will walk ten miles with the whiskey in his hand until arrived without the prescribed boundary; or in the second case, drink it in the open air; and even when he has pledged himself to drink 'neither in nor out of a house,' his ingenuity has devised a mode of doing so, with one foot within the door and the other without; and when he swears by all he considers holy, to drink, 'not a drop at all at all,' he surmounts his difficulty by eating the bread he has sopped in '*the cratur*'.[194]

Figure 45

Peace was Made for Coward Souls: War, My Boys, For You & Me

Daniel Macdonald

1847

'The Cratur' was ever present. *Peace was Made for Coward Souls: War, My Boys, For You & Me* **(Fig. 45)** depicts a recruiting party in an Irish Town. For Macdonald, the army was an honorable way of life (by this time his brother was a senior officer and well on his way to a career of military and medical brilliance overseas). But the artist was clearly amused by the shenanigans of the recruitment drive. This rambunctious town scene shows members of the army band, sent out to drum up recruits, succumb themselves to the temptations of alcohol and tobacco. Plying potential recruits with alcohol to soften them up, and having a few scoops along the way, was a common occurrence. In 1832, when Ireland's population was 32 percent of the overall UK population, it provided 42 percent of the British army. For many, the army was the only possible source of income, and therefore welcomed, but for others it was a matter, if not of shame, at least of confliction. On the one hand, it was an escape from poverty, and an opportunity to see the world, but at a time of growing national awareness, it had its naysayers. Joining up may not have appealed to the patriotism of the Catholic Irishman, but it was balm to his poverty and discontent.[195]

Recruiting bands were elaborate outfits, moving from town to town, accompanied by brewer's drays with barrels of beer. Here we see the band of the Connaught Rangers in rather disheveled shape. Bayonet down, bottles raised, clay pipes strewn, the drummers have taken to sitting on their drums. The role of the drummer in the army was important. The beat of drums was used to regulate the loading and reloading of weapons during battle; drummers raised morale during fighting; they were used on the battlefield as a means of signalling; and they were also an important feature in stirring up recruitment. Some of those who enlisted under the influence of alcohol would immediately desert upon regaining sobriety, leaving the drummer responsible for failing to secure a committed enlistment.

The role of the Catholic Church in gaining control of the hearts and minds of Irish peasants was thus imbricated with the development of the temperance movement. The first wave of temperance movements was led by Protestant landlords and industrialists who encouraged their workers to join Tontine clubs,

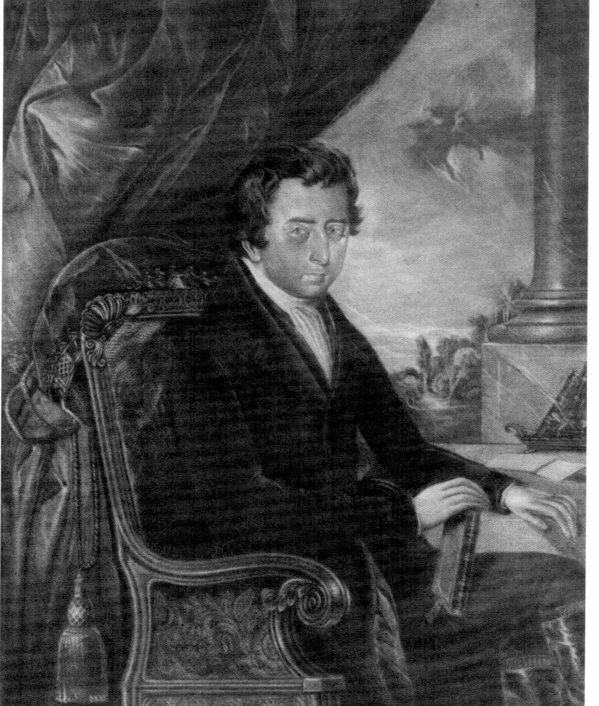

Figure 46

Rev. Theobald Mathew (1790–1856), founder of the Temperance League in Ireland

Daniel Macdonald

in effect savings clubs that required their members to be teetotal. The second wave, led by the Capuchin Father Mathew, advocated freedom from alcohol (and often threw in freedom from England as well). At a very young age, Daniel Macdonald executed a *Portrait of Father Theobald Mathew* **(Fig. 46)**, founder of the Temperance League, in both oil and mezzotint.[196]

The consumption of alcohol is a trope in a number of works by Macdonald. Known as 'unchristened' whiskey, poitín had extensive medicinal and recreational uses, but above all, it typified anti-authoritarianism and contempt for law and order. In the works of Maria Edgeworth and William Carleton, for example, poitín is presented as 'a national toxin'. But whether one identifies with Edgeworth's 'morally structured narratology', or Carleton's wily distillers outwitting corrupt 'gaugers' who collected the taxes, poitín was an integral part of Irish life, proof positive that Ireland could not be subdued.[197] Whiteboys and Rockites did not go home at night to cups of cocoa by the fire. Even the evangelical proselytizer, Caesar Otway recognized that poitín, 'in the estimation of every Irishman—aye, and high-born Englishman too — is so superior in sweetness, salubrity and gusto, to all that machinery, science and capital can produce in a legalized way.'[198] The stereotypes of drunken paddies, reckless rebels and savage aggressors thus conflate in the thrill of the illicitness that is the narrative of poitín.

But there was a remarkable turnaround in the late 1830s, what Paul Townend describes as 'among the more unique and under-examined mass mobilizations of men and women in modern European history: Father Mathew's temperance crusade.' [199] Temperance had begun as a Protestant evangelical movement in America, spreading first to England in the 1820s, reaching Cork in 1835. Initially, Catholics suspected a Protestant proselytizing plot but, in 1838, when Father Mathew assumed command of the Cork Total Abstinence Society, huge numbers flocked to take 'the pledge'; in 1841, he announced that membership had reached a staggering 5.3 million.[200] Even Daniel O'Connell took the pledge in 1840 (though he later wrangled a dispensation, ironically pleading ill health). The paradoxes of temperance were many, not least Father Mathew's own behavior, when he moved himself to the wrong side of the Abolitionism in America. Having signed a petition (along with 60,000 others, including O'Connell) condemning slavery in 1841, in order to avoid alienating his slave-owning friends, he sacrificed his friendship with abolitionists, including Frederick Douglass (who had received the pledge from Mathew in Cork in 1845), who now felt betrayed by him.

Although glimpses of Macdonald's personality are confined to a handful of letters written in his late twenties to Richard Dowden, clearly the friendships of the father extended to the son: Croker, Day, Maginn, Sainthill, Maclise and others. The letters from Macdonald to Dowden, addressed 'My dear friend', reveal a young man of intelligence, wit and charm, at times boyish, romantic and nostalgic.

Dowden was a businessman, botanist and philanthropist, one of the most respected citizens of Cork. A Unitarian Presbyterian, and a liberal, he supported Daniel O'Connell and Repeal. Dowden was a strong advocate of temperance, and worked with Father Mathew. He served on the Cork Poor Relief Committee during the Famine, and on the Cork Anti-Slavery Committee. Like McDaniel, he was an active member of the Royal Cork Institution, where he held the position of Librarian, and of the Cork Literary and Scientific Society, and he was involved in the Mechanics' Institute, the School of Design and other institutions — interests that echoed across the two families. Daniel's correspondence with Dowden was warm and intimate, indicative of the close ties across the generations also. There are several letters from Daniel's mother, Catherine, to Dowden, playfully insisting that Susan, Dowden's only daughter, when visiting London, 'sit' for Daniel. One senses a match was in the air.

In 1847, the older man sent proofs of his forthcoming book, *Walks after Wild Flowers* or *The Botany of the Bohereens* (1852) to the young artist for comment, written while Dowden was stricken with a fever caught from Famine contagion.

Daniel, in turn, wrote to Dowden of his brother John, now a famous naval surgeon on board the *Impregnable*. He described social activities and reminisced about romantic dalliances: 'my first love times and my poetic wanderings through the shady mazes of Dunscombe wood, watching the sun go down in splendor over the far off hills, and in the usual heart burnings on those occasions, and then to see my fair one … walking by moonlight', going on to muse (at all of 30 years-of-age) how 'it makes one young again to think upon old times.'

His description of English parties — plethoric with sugary, 'doughy' food — where he would be required 'to take an old dame with a queer structure of gauze and catgut on her head in to dinner' included two phlegmatic sketches, male and female, of 'Russell Square inmates' (Croker's house).

In London, Daniel retained his boyishness, describing his 'small battery of brass cannon' in their Berners Street Garden, how he and his father 'played at boys again', his father having 'a captaincy in my company and the care of three field pieces'. He described with relish:

> jumping about, charging and ramming home the shots and bringing gunning practice to bear with parabolic curves … the question is who shall jump the highest and who shall fire a volley with the greatest precision. We have pressed two congenials into the service, and I have a belt around my waist, a fur cap with a red nightcap falling from the top in imitation of the horse artillery, and what with the jumping and the firing with the cheers of the belligerents. [201]

It sounds as if life in Berners Street was a lot of fun. Other letters are more businesslike, including one regarding the sending of his pictures on the 'next boat', for the 1852 National Exhibition in Cork, that included small pen sketches of the paintings in question. The organizers of this exhibition were determined to put art and industry to the service of Cork in expiation for the Famine. But tragedy struck. On February 11, 1853, aged 32, Daniel Macdonald died of enteric fever. He was a bachelor and intestate, so his father took over the administration of his affairs, and his sister Jane took over his studio.

From her debut as an artist, Jane exhibited alongside her brother in Cork, London, Manchester, and other venues.* Daniel had lived in London with Jane, her husband William Richard Rogers, and their children. As he died in Jane's house, one supposes that any residual art or papers would have remained there, until the Berners Street household was dispersed in the 1880s when Jane and William divorced. In 1865, their father had died. But as none of Jane's children married, it is likely that Daniel's effects were let go around that time, if not on the death of Jane in 1909. Attempts to trace the descendants of Daniel's siblings have not yielded the discovery of art or papers to date. As so often in such cases, with no descendants to keep the flame alive, he slipped prematurely and undeservedly into obscurity.

Following Daniel's death, Jane took over what would appear to have been his highly successful portrait business. Over the following months, she advertised as 'Sister and Successor to the late Mr. D. Macdonald, Studio, 56 Berners St.' asking that 'The patrons and friends INDEBTED to her late lamented brother will kindly please to pay the sum due of them to Mrs. Rogers, or James Macdonald, administrator' (*Morning Post*, March 7, 1853). And by August 1853, the legal firm, Garrard and James, were appointed to pursue the debtors, suggesting that there must have been a significant amount at stake (*Morning Post*, August 15, 1853).

By 1853, Daniel had attained the reputation of an up-and-coming artist in both Ireland and England. His skill and wit, his audacity and originality were recognized. He had a great future ahead of him, cruelly cut short. Notwithstanding success in London, he never severed his ties to Ireland. The Famine may have subsided, but the aftershocks were such that nothing would be the same again. As Sir William Wilde described:

> … the very rites of sepulture, the most sacred and enduring of all the tributes of affection or respect, have been neglected or forgotten; the dead body has rotted where it fell, or formed a scanty meal for the famished dogs of the vicinity, or has been thrown, without prayer or mourning, into the adjoining ditch. The hum of the spinning-wheel has long since ceased to form an accompaniment to the colleen's song; and that song itself, so sweet and fresh in cabin, field, or byre, has scarcely left an echo in our glens, or among the hamlets of our land. The Shannaghie and the Callegh in the chimney corner, tell no more the tales and legends of other days. Unwaked, *unkeened*, the dead are buried, where Christian burial has at all been observed; and the ear no longer catches the mournful cadence of the wild Irish cry, wailing on the blast, rising up to us from the valleys, or floating along the winding river … [202]

Had Macdonald lived into this post-apocalyptic world, one wonders how he would have represented it.

ENDNOTES

1 Dolores Dooley, *Equality in Community* (Cork, 1996),15; see also Peter Murray, 'Art Institutions in Nineteenth-Century Cork', in Patrick O'Flanagan and Cornelius G. Buttimer, eds., *Cork History and Society*, Dublin, 1993, 813-872.

2 James McDaniel essays include: CLSS/015/009, 1819–1820: Essay No. 22 'Printing from Sand'; Essay No. 109 'Etching on Copper'; Essay No. 124 'On the Harmonic Tones of Musical Strings'; 7 [?Nov] 1825; Essay No. [202] 'Precepts for the direction of amateurs in painting or decorating apartments in distemper'; Essay No. 202 'Precepts for the direction of amateurs in painting or decorating apartments in distemper' (also, copy with sketch of a man); 1826–1827: Essay No. 228 'Creation of coloured pigments for painting'; 6 Dec 1824, 'Address by James McDaniel ... concerning a copybook apparatus using tin plates'; Address by James McDaniel to the President of the CLSS concerning a copybook apparatus using tin plates'.

3 Art Unions were set up following a House of Commons Select Committee on Arts and Manufactures in 1835 to investigate 'the best means of extending a knowledge of the Arts and of the Principles of Design among the people', improving the standard of art and raising artistic awareness (Anthony King, 'George Godwin and the Art-Union of London 1837–1911', *Victorian Studies*, vol. 8, no. 2, December 1964, 101). In Cork, each subscriber paid £1 annually according him the opportunity to win the picture of the year. In the first year alone over £100 was spent on purchasing pictures that were distributed by lot to the subscribers.

4 For the cultural context and life of Corkonians at home and in London, see Terry Eagleton, 'Cork and the Carnivalesque', in *Crazy John and the Bishop: Essays in Irish Culture,* Cork, 1998, 158-211 *passim,* quote 164; and *Recollections of Cork by Thomas Crofton Croker, with corrections by Dr. Maginn,* Trinity College Library, Ms. 1206 (1.6.49–50).

5 Eagleton, 'Cork and the Carnivalesque', 158–211 (158).

6 Quoted in D. J. O'Donoghue, *Geographical Distribution of Irish Ability* (Dublin, 1906) 23; and Mr. and Mrs. S. C. Hall, *Ireland: Its Scenery, Character etc.* (London, 1841–43), vol. 1, 20.

7 S. C. Hall, *Recollections of a Long Life from 1815–1883* (London, 1883), vol. 1,180.

8 Claire Connolly, 'Irish Romanticism, 1800–1839', in *Cambridge History of Irish Literature* (Cambridge, 2006), vol. 1, 407–48 (435).

9 *Fraser's Magazine,* vol. 23, 1841, 737.

10 *Fraser's Magazine,* vol. 23, 1841, 737.

11 John Boyle was the editor of the rather scurrilous and gossipy magazine *The Freeholder.* A notable engagement notice reads: 'It is now finally settled that James Denny, the painter and glazier, is to be Miss Downey's plumber', June 21, 1822.

12 'Letter from Dr. Maginn to William Blackwood' quoted in Margaret Oliphant, *Annals of a Publishing House: William Blackwood and His Sons,* vol. 1 (Edinburgh, 1897), 389.

13 Eagleton, 'Cork and the Carnivalesque', 158–211 (167).

14 *The Art-Union,* February 1845, 83. As editor and proprietor of *The Art-Union/Art Journal,* founded in 1839, Hall, a huge supporter of Maclise, generally gave good coverage to Ireland and specifically to Cork affairs.

15 Bernard Barton, *Metrical Effusions, or Verses on Various Occasions* (London, 1812).

16 Eagleton, 'Cork and the Carnivalesque', 158–211 (199).

17 *Lucas's Cork Directory* (1787) and *Holden's Triennial Directory 1805–1807* list James McDaniel, grocer, at Grand Parade.

18 Maginn glossed the poem with the note: 'McD. Had the ingenuity of inventing an instrument which he called a *bag*-pipe, the bags being omitted'.

19 As evidenced in letters from James McDaniel to Thomas Crofton Croker, Cork City Library, e.g. September 5, 1835.

20 See McDaniel to Croker, Cork City Library, February 27, 1819; he also taught 'Fancy Drawing' in the Misses MacNaughten's Boarding and Day School for young ladies (*Southern Reporter*, December 29, 1827).

21 Although nothing is known of his work as an architect, when witnessing the marriage of his daughter Jane to William Richard Lawrence Rogers in 1846, he recorded his profession as architect.

22 McDaniel translated *The Battle of Gabhra,* a 'wailing dirge' of the Fenian cycle of Irish mythology that tells of the battle against the forces of High King Cairbre Lifechair. (Letter, James McDaniel to Thomas Crofton Croker, Cork City Library, February 27, 1819). His letters are peppered with Latin and French phrases, references to Greek mythology and ancient Irish antiquities, indicating a high level of education.

23 Such as *Interior of Christ Church*, and *Blarney Lane.* Robert Day, 'The Art Catalogue of the First Munster Exhibition', *Journal of the Cork Historical and Archaeological Society,* 1898, vol. 4, no. 40, 307–17 (309).

24 Robert Day, 'Book-Plates Engraved by Cork Artists', *Journal of the Ex Libris Society,* vol. 1, Jan. 1892, 107–11 (108).

25 Day was president of the Cork Cuvierian Society and its successor, the Cork Historical and Archaeological Society, from 1894 to 1914. He had an extensive collection of Irish archaeological artifacts, and was an important antiquary and photographer.

26 Michael Holland, 'Two Typical Cork Sketches', *Journal of the Cork Historical and Archaeological Society,* 1913, vol. 19, no. 98, 76–77.

27 James McDaniel to Thomas Crofton Croker, nd, Cork City Library. The sketch included the ditty:

> *Curious flowr roots shrubs & posies*
> *Greenhouse plants & foreign rosies*
> *Garning in GENL. dun in stile*
> *Inquire within from Patk. Doyl.*
> *N. B. Dry Lodgings*

28 Michael Holland, 'Two Typical Cork Sketches', 77.

29 McDaniel and Croker planned a book on lithography together.

30 James McDaniel to Richard Dowden, nd., Cork City and County Archives, Richard Dowden Papers, IE CCCA / U140: 'For amusement I wrote a squib. It is all about Pusey renegades …': [See Appendix 3].

31 The *Cork Examiner* (March 24, 1865), recorded his death, aged 77, at his residence, Vive Cottage, Peterborough Road, London.

32 *A Modern Visit from the Devil*, by One in Babylon … Second edition with a postscript, and ten illustrations by D. Macdonald (London, 1849), 28.

33 *A Modern Visit from the Devil*, by One in Babylon … Second edition with a postscript, and ten illustrations by D. Macdonald (London, 1849), 5.

34 *A Modern Visit from the Devil*, 8.

35 *A Modern Visit from the Devil*, 9.

36 James McDaniel to Thomas Crofton Croker, August 29, 1819, Croker Correspondence, Cork City Library.

37 Anon, 'Memoir of Samuel Forde — A Cork Artist', *Dublin University Magazine*, vol. 25, no. 147, March 1845, 343.

38 *Considerations on the Utility of the Casts presented by H.R.H. the Prince Regent*, Bolster's (Cork, 1819), 12 and 18.

39 Brian Arkins, *Builders of My Soul: Greek and Roman Themes in Yeats* (Gerrard's Cross, 1990).

40 Thomas Davis, 'National Art,' in *Literary and Historical Essays*, ed. Charles Gavan Duffy (Dublin, 1865), 158. Also, see *Cork Magazine*, vol. 1, no. 1, November 1847, 6–12. Davis alluded to Macdonald's Corkonian forebears, among which were James Barry (1741–1806), Nathaniel Grogan (1739/40–1807) and John Butts (c. 1728–65), and among the next generation, Daniel Maclise (1806–70) John Hogan (1800–58) and Samuel Forde (1805–28). Of the former, for Macdonald, Grogan was the more significant; of the latter, Maclise.

41 *Laocoön and His Sons* was excavated in Rome in 1506; the plaster cast was from the Roman copy in the Vatican Museum, presented to the Cork Society, made under the supervision of Italian sculptor Antonio Canova.

42 Nicola Figgis, 'Nathaniel Grogan' in *Art and Architecture of Ireland, Volume 2: Painting 1600–1900* (Dublin, 2014), 276–77.

43 *Cork Examiner,* March 22, 1847.

44 James McDaniel to Thomas Crofton Croker, September 9, 1835.

45 Daniel Maclise, *Diary,* Royal Academy Archive, 16.

46 Lady Morgan (Sydney Owenson), *The Life and Times of Salvator Rosa,* 2 vols. (London and Paris, 1824).

47 Lady Morgan, *The Life and Times of Salvator Rosa,* 265.

48 For further discussions, see Luke Gibbons, 'Between Captain Rock and a Hard Place: Art and Agrarian Insurgency', in Tadhg Foley and Seán Ryder, eds., *Ideology and Ireland in the Nineteenth Century* (Dublin, 1998), 23–43; and Fintan Cullen, *Sources in Irish Art: A Reader* (Nottingham, 2000).

49 Even Walter Strickland's handwritten note missed the connection, Walter Strickland, Ms. Notes, Ms. 19,685 (A), annotation to vol. II.

50 John Francis Maguire, MP, *The Industrial Movement in Ireland as Illustrated by the National Exhibition of 1852* (Cork, 1853).

51 Daniel Macdonald to Richard Dowden, nd, Cork City and County Archives, references *Jew Dealer and Critics,* discusses transportation to Cork from London for the 1852 exhibition, and features a tiny pen sketch that includes many elements of the Maclise painting that may in time help in the identification of the Macdonald.

52 Joep Leerssen, *Remembrance and Imagination: Patterns in the Historical and Literary Representation of Ireland in the Nineteenth Century* (Cork, 1996), 160.

53 Clare O'Halloran, 'Negotiating Progress and Degeneracy: Irish Antiquaries and the Discovery of the "Folk", 1770–1844', *Folklore and Nationalism in Europe during the Long Nineteenth Century* (Leiden and Boston, 2012), 193.

54 Joep Leerssen, *Remembrance and Imagination* (Cork, 1996), 160.

55 Sir Walter Scott diary, quoted in J. G. Lockhart, *Memoirs of the Life of Sir Walter Scott,* vol. 3 (Edinburgh and London, 1887), 860.

56 In their translation of the latter into German, Jacob and Wilhelm Grimm referenced 'an ancient people' who, because they still spoke Gaelic, 'retain living traces of former times'. *Irische Elfenmärchen* (Leipzig, 1826); cited in Thomas Crofton Croker, *Fairy Legends and Traditions of the South of Ireland,* ed. Thomas Wright, with a memoir by Croker's son ([1825–28] London, nd. [1859?]), xxviii–xxix. The second edition was illustrated by Daniel Maclise (1826).

57 Croker, *Fairy Legends and Traditions*, xxix–xxx.

58 Thomas Crofton Croker, *The Keen of the South of Ireland as Illustrative of Irish Political and Domestic History, Manners, Music, and Superstitions* (London, 1844), xxiv–vi.

59 Joep Leerssen, *National Thought in Europe: A Cultural History* (Amsterdam, 2006), 195.

60 Vaux was a distinguished antiquary and author of important works on the Greek, Roman and Arab worlds.

61 James McDaniel to Thomas Crofton Croker, Cork City Library, August 29, 1819.

62 James McDaniel to Thomas Crofton Croker, Cork City Library, August 29, 1819.

63 Following Croker's death in 1854, most of his library in London was sold, with a published catalogue, *Catalogue of the Greater share of the library of the late Thomas Crofton Croker* whole boxes of material for publication were sold over a three-day period, the McDaniel material probably amongst the rest.

64   Jane MacDonald to Thomas Crofton Croker, Cork City Library, nd.

65   Thomas Crofton Croker, *Researches in the South of Ireland, 1812–22* (Dublin, 1981 [1824]), 223. [Hereafter, *Researches*]

66   Croker, *Researches*, 233, and James McDaniel to Thomas Crofton Croker, January 23, 1820, Cork City and County Archives.

67   James McDaniel to Thomas Crofton Croker, Cork City Library, August 29, 1819.

68   Croker, *Researches*, 170, and James McDaniel to Thomas Crofton Croker, Cork City Library, January 23, 1820.

69   Croker, *Researches*, 85–87, and James McDaniel to Thomas Crofton Croker, Cork City and County Archives, January 23, 1820.

70   Croker, *Researches*, 225.

71   Croker, *Researches*, 168–69, and James McDaniel to Thomas Crofton Croker, Cork City Library, January 23, 1820.

72   *The Freeholder*, December 8, 1827.

73   S. C. Hall, *Retrospect of a Long Life: From 1815 to 1883,* vol. 1 (London, 1883) Notwithstanding his own involvement, Maginn reviewed it in *Blackwood's Magazine*, xviii, July 1825, 55–61.

74   Maginn, *Blackwood's*, xviii, July 1825, 55–61.

75   Croker, *Researches*, 85–87, and James McDaniel to Thomas Crofton Croker, Cork City Library, January 23, 1820.

76   I am indebted to Prof. Angela Bourke for bringing this story to my attention and for sharing her knowledge of Irish folklore so generously with me.

77   Sir William Wilde, 'Irish Popular Superstitions,' in *Ireland: Her Wit, Peculiarities, and Popular Superstitions, with anecdotes, legendary and characteristic, by Distinguished Irish Writers* (Dublin, *c.* 1850), 15.

78   Angela Bourke, 'The Virtual Reality of Irish Fairy Legend', *Éire/Ireland* 31: (1–2) Spring/Summer 1996, 14.

79   Angela Bourke, *Voices Underfoot: Memory, Forgetting, and Oral Verbal Art* (Hamden, CT, forthcoming 2016).

80   Susan Sontag, *Regarding the Pain of Others* (New York, 2003), 18.

81   William Carleton, *The Black Prophet: A Tale of Irish Famine* (Belfast and London, 1847), 14.

82   Angela Bourke, *Voices Underfoot,* forthcoming 2016.

83   Croker, *Researches*, 81.

84   Charles Townshend, 'The Making of Modern Irish Public Culture', *The Journal of Modern History,* vol. 61, no. 3, September 1989, 535–54.

85   Quoted in W. P. Ker, *Epic and Romance* (London, 2013 [1913]), 2–3. For further discussions, see Luke Gibbons, *Gaelic Gothic: Race, Colonization, and Irish Culture* (Galway, 2004); Terry Eagleton, *Heathcliff and The Great Hunger* (London, 1995); Seamus Deane, *Strange Country: Modernity and Nationhood in Irish Writing Since 1790* (Oxford, 1997); and Robert Smart, *Black Roads* (Hamden, CT, 2015).

86   I am grateful to Tom Dunne and Brendan Rooney for discussions on this painting.

87   Claire Connolly, 'Irish Romanticism, 1800–1839', in *Cambridge History of Irish Literature,* vol. 1 (Cambridge, 2006), 407–48 (424).

88   Sinéad Sturgeon, '''Seven Devils": Gerald Griffin's "The Brown Man" and the Making of Irish Gothic', *The Irish Journal of Gothic and Horror Studies*, vol. 11, June 2012.

89   Clare O'Halloran, 'Negotiating Progress and Degeneracy: Irish Antiquaries and the Discovery of the "Folk", 1770–1844', in Timothy Baycroft and David Hopkin, eds., *Folklore and Nationalism in Europe During the Long Nineteenth Century* (Leiden, 2012), 193–206 (201).

90   Croker, *Researches,* 14–16.

91   Croker, *Researches,* 16. The 'private narrative', by Jane Adam, describes the experiences of a loyalist family in Co. Wexford during the Rebellion.

92   Croker, *Researches,* 13–14.

93   Letter (nd) by Croker, in Croker, *Fairy Legends and Traditions of the South of Ireland,* ed. Thomas Wright, with a memoir by Croker's son ([1825–28], London, nd [1859?]).

94   Croker, *Keen of the South of Ireland,* xix–xx.

95   Clare O'Halloran, 'Negotiating Progress and Degeneracy', 206.

96   Arthur Young, *A Tour in Ireland, 1776–1779*, 2 vols. (London, 1892), 166.

97   Paul E. W. Roberts, 'Caravats and the Shanavests: Whiteboyism and Faction Fighting in East Munster, 1802–11', in Samuel Clarke and James S. Donnelly, Jr., eds., *Irish Peasants, Violence and Political Unrest 1780–1914* (Dublin, 1983).

98   Paul E. W. Roberts, 'Caravats and the Shanavests: Whiteboyism and Faction Fighting in East Munster, 1802–11', in Samuel Clarke and James S. Donnelly, Jr., eds., *Irish Peasants, Violence and Political Unrest 1780–1914* (Dublin, 1983), 77.

99   Donnelly shows that there were significant links between Rockism and the more organized and politicized Ribbon movement found in urban centers.

100 Letter from William Maginn to William Blackwood, qtd. in Margaret Oliphant, *Annals of a Publishing House: William Blackwood and his Sons*, vol. 1 (Edinburgh, 1897), 389.

101 Francis Plowden, *The history of Ireland, from its union with Great Britain in January 1801 to October 1810*, 3 vols., vol. 1 (Dublin, 1811), 102.

102 James S. Donnelly, Jr., 'Pastorini and Captain Rock: Millenarianism and Sectarianism in the Rockite Movement of 1821–4', in Samuel Clarke and James S. Donnelly, Jr., *Irish Peasants, Violence and Political Unrest 1780–1914* (Dublin, 1983), 102–37 (103).

103 James S. Donnelly, Jr., 'Pastorini and Captain Rock'. 126.

104 James S. Donnelly, Jr., 'Pastorini and Captain Rock', 102–39.

105 See Anne Hodge and Peter Harbison, 'A Gilded Cage', *Irish Arts Review,* Summer 2014.

106 See Ríonach Uí Ógáin, *Immortal Dan: Daniel O'Connell in Irish Folk Tradition* (Dublin, 1995); and Ruán O'Donnell , 'The Liberator', *Irish Arts Review*, Autumn 2006, 92–97.

107 Gary Owens, 'Constructing the Image of Daniel O'Connell', *History Ireland*, no. 1, Spring 1999, 32–36.

108 Gerald Griffin, *The Rivals; Tracy's Ambition,* vol. 3 ([1829] New York, 1979), 295.

109 *Westminster Review*, April 1, 1824, 492–94.

110 Quoted in Emer Nolan, 'Irish Melodies and Discordant Politics: Thomas Moore's *Memoirs of Captain Rock (1824)*', *Field Day Review*, 2, 2006, 41–54 (52).

111 Emer Nolan, 'Irish Melodies and Discordant Politics', 52.

112 Moore's narrator informed the reader — perhaps speciously — that an explanation of the origin of the name Captain Rock derived from the initials of Roger O'Connor (R-oger O-'C-onnor, K-ing). O'Connor, the eccentric brother of the United Irish leader, Arthur O'Connor, had been sketched on a number of occasions by James McDaniel. Thomas Moore, *The Memoirs of Captain Rock the celebrated Irish chieftain with some account of his ancestors, Written by himself* (London 1824), 6.

113 Morgan Rattler, 'Some Passages in A Visit to the Royal Academy', *Fraser's Magazine*, July 1834, 106–19 (Percival Weldon Banks, graduate of Trinity College Dublin, and barrister, wrote under the pen name of Morgan Rattler for *Fraser's*).

114 Luke Gibbons, 'Between Captain Rock and a Hard Place: Art and Agrarian Insurgency,' in Tadhg Foley and Seán Ryder, eds., *Ideology and Ireland in the Nineteenth Century* (Dublin, 1998), 23–43 (41).

115 Morgan Rattler, 'Some Passages', 106–19.

116 Morgan Rattler, 'Some Passages', 117.

117 Morgan Rattler, 'Some Passages', 118.

118 The titles by which the painting has been known do not correspond to any exhibited work by Macdonald and are understood as descriptive sales titles, henceforth the more accurate descriptive title, *The Fighter,* will be used.

119 Charles Townshend, 'The Making of Modern Irish Public Culture', *The Journal of Modern History*, vol. 61, no. 3, September 1989, 535–54 (549).

120 Máire MacNeill, *The Festival of Lughnasa* (London, 1962).

121 Titles such as *A Genuine History of the Lives and Actions of the Most Notorious Irish Highwaymen, Tories and Rapparees* sold in huge numbers to the literate poor in nineteenth-century Ireland.

122 Croker, *Researches,* 2.

123 Croker, *Researches,* 231.

124 P. D. O'Donnell, *Irish Faction Fighters of the Nineteenth Century* (Dublin, 1975), 19.

125 Gibbons, 'Between Captain Rock and a Hard Place', 40. For the 'feminine' in Ireland of this period, see Margaret Kelleher, *The Feminization of Famine: Expressions of the Inexpressible?* (Cork,1997).

126 Hall, *Ireland: Its Scenery,* 427–28.

127 Hall, *Ireland: Its Scenery,* 170–78.

128 Terry Eagleton, *Heathcliff and the Great Hunger,* 84.

129 *The English Review,* vol. viii, 1847, 261.

130 James Kelly, 'The Duel in Irish History', *History Ireland,* vol. 2, no.1, 1994, 26–30.

131 George Newcomen, 'The tragic tale of Stamer O'Grady and Captain Smyth, Ballinatrae', *The New Ireland Review*, vol. x, September 1898, 30–37.

132 Isaac Weld, *Statistical Survey of the County of Roscommon* (Dublin, 1832), 477.

133 Laurence Geary, 'Epidemic Diseases of the Great Famine', *History Ireland,* 4, 1, Spring, 1996, 27–32 (29).

134 Quoted in Jennifer Hart, 'Sir Charles Trevelyan at the Treasury', *English Historical Review,* ixxv, (1960), 92–110 (94).

135 John Mitchel, *The Last Conquest of Ireland (perhaps),* ed. and introd. Patrick Maume (Dublin, 2005 [1862]), 219.

136 For further discussion, see Niamh O'Sullivan, *The Tombs of a Departed Race: Illustrations of Ireland's Great Hunger* (Hamden, CT, 2014).

137 See Luke Gibbons, *Limits of the Visible: Representing the Great Hunger* (Hamden, CT, 2014); and David Lloyd, 'The Indigent Sublime: Specters of Irish Hunger', *Representations* 92 (Fall 2005), 152–85. One inquest recounted the death of a mother and three children drowned in a dyke, the hand of one child, and part of the foot of another, had been devoured by rats. In Co. Cork, a dead woman was found by the roadside with a dead infant at her breast, the child having bitten off a nipple trying to squeeze a drop of nourishment from her wretched body. Such events were too awful to contemplate, let alone image.

138 For elaborations of the issues involved, see Niamh O'Sullivan, 'Lines of Sorrow': Representing Ireland's Great Hunger', *Ireland's Great Hunger Museum Inaugural Catalogue* (Hamden, CT, 2012); Margaret Crawford, 'The Great Irish Famine 1845–9: image versus reality', *Ireland: Art into History*, Raymond Gillespie and Brian P. Kennedy, eds. (Dublin, 1994), 75–90; Catherine Marshall, *Monuments, Memorials and Visualizations of the Great Famine in Ireland* (Hamden, CT, 2014) and 'Painting Irish History: the Famine', *History Ireland* 4.3, Autumn 1996, 47–49; Emily Mark-FitzGerald, 'Towards a Famine Art History: Invention, Reception, and Repetition from the Nineteenth Century to the Twentieth', in *Ireland's Great Hunger, vol. 2: Relief, Representation, and Remembrance* (Hamden, CT, 2010) and *Commemorating the Irish Famine: Memory and the Monument* (Liverpool, 2013).

139 For further discussions, see James Michael Farrell, '"This Horrible Spectacle": Visual and Verbal Sketches of the Famine in Skibbereen', *Rhetorics of Display,* Lawrence J. Prelli, ed. (Columbia, SC, 2006), 66–89; Margaret Crawford, 'The Great Irish Famine 1845–9', '75–90; Lawrence McBride, 'Historical Imagery in Irish Political Illustration 1880–1910', *New Hibernia Review,* 2.3 (Spring 1998): 9–25; L. Perry Curtis, Jr., *Apes and Angels: The Irishman in Victorian Caricature* (Washington, D.C., 1996).

140 *The Art-Union,* vol. 9, 1847, 82.

141 *The Observer,* February 7, 1847.

142 By 1845, 250,000 acres of Cork alone were under potatoes. Some 3 million people, then approximately one third of the population of Ireland, was almost exclusively dependent on a potato diet. Containing high quantities of starch, some protein, vitamins C, B_1, and riboflavin, and often supplemented with added buttermilk, providing calcium and vitamin A, it was a nutritious diet. Prior to the Great Famine, it was said, there was no hardier race of peasantry. One acre could yield 6.5 to 8.5 tons of potatoes.

143 When available, 12 to 14 lbs of potatoes per day per male adult (women and children ate slightly less) constituted the daily diet. The addition of buttermilk, dripping, salt, and salt herring, if available, turned it into a feast.

144 Croker, *Researches,* 91

145 For a study of Famine illustration, see Niamh O'Sullivan, *The Tombs of a Departed Race: Illustrations of Ireland's Great Hunger* (Hamden, CT, 2014).

146 Daniel Donovan, "Observations on the Peculiar diseases to which the famine of the last year gave origin and on the morbid effects of insufficient nourishment", *The Medical Examiner: A Monthly Record of Medical Science,* vol. 4, June 1848.

147 Descriptions, such as John Kelly's in *The Graves Are Walking The Great Famine and the Saga of the Irish People* (London, 2003), 225, are expanded by contemporary medical understanding of starvation on the human body: 'In the later stages of starvation, the eyelids inflame, the angular lines around the mouth deepen into cavities; the swollen thyroid gland becomes tumor-sized; fields of white fungus cover the tongue, blistering mouth sores develop, the skin acquires the texture of parchment; teeth decay and fall out, gums ooze pus, and a long silky growth of hair covers the face … Hunger edema — a grotesque swelling — is also common.'

148 I am very grateful to Ed O'Riordan for bringing his discovery to my attention, and I thank Terri Kearney for supplementary information on Welply.

149 The once sparse historiography of the Famine is now substantial and includes important work by Christine Kinealy, Cormac Ó Gráda, Peter Gray, James Donnelly, Breandán Mac Suibhne, David Nally, Enda Delaney, Ciarán Ó Murchadha, John Kelly, Laurence M. Geary, and the recent magisterial work edited by John Crowley, William J. Smyth and Mike Murphy, *Atlas of the Great Irish Famine* (Cork, 2012); this is enriched by cross-disciplinary work by Luke Gibbons, David Lloyd, L. P. Curtis, Jr., Kerby Miller, Terry Eagleton, Catherine Marshall, Emily Mark-Fitzgerald and James Michael Farrell.

150 For in-depth study of evictions, see L. Perry Curtis, Jr., *Notice to Quit: The Great Irish Famine Evictions* (Hamden, CT, 2015), and *Depiction of Eviction in Ireland: 1845–1910* (Dublin, 2011).

151 Tom Dunne, 'The Eviction', in *Whipping the Herring: Survival and Celebration in Nineteenth-Century Irish Art,* ed. Peter Murray (Cork, 2006), 134; and *Three Centuries of Irish Art,* ed. Peter Murray (Cork, 2014), 82.

152 Gotthold Ephraim Lessing, on the *Laocoön,* quoted in Hugh Barr Nisbet, *German Aesthetic and Literary Criticism: Winckelmann, Lessing, Hamann, Herder, Schiller, Goethe,* vol. 3 (Cambridge, 1985), 99.

153 The following year, he was described as 'unrivalled' attracting high praise for another *Still-life* representing with 'faultless, startling fidelity', a plaice, a crab, two red herrings, a bunch of radishes, a head of cabbage and a large earthenware crock (*Cork Examiner,* September 6, 1843).

154 Joep Leerssen, *Remembrance and Imagination* (Cork, 1996), 162.

155 For a comprehensive examination of the tourism of Killarney, see William H. A. Williams, *Creating Irish Tourism: The First Century, 1750–1850* (London, 2010), 129–50.

156 William Ockenden, *Letters Describing the Lakes of Killarney and Muckross Gardens* (c. 1760), 134–35.

157 John Bush, *Hibernia Curiosa: A Letter from a Gentleman in Dublin to his Friend at Dover in Kent* (London, 1767) 98.

158 Arthur Young, *A Tour in Ireland, 1776–1779* (London, 1892), 101.

159 John Wilkes, *Encyclopaedia Londinensis, or, Universal dictionary of arts, sciences and Literature,* vol. xi (London, 1812), 718.

160 Quoted in William Williams, *Creating Irish Tourism: The First Century, 1750–1850,* 139–40.

161 William Williams, *Creating Irish Tourism,* 138.

162 Mr. and Mrs. S. C. Hall, *Ireland: its Scenery, Character, etc.,* 3 vols, vol. 1 (London, 1842), 210–11.

163 *Album of original drawings, published in Mr. & Mrs. S. C. Hall's 'Ireland: its scenery, character, &c'',* illustration no. 115, National Library of Ireland.

164 Anne Crookshank and the Knight of Glin, *Ireland's Painters, 1600–1940* (New Haven, 2003), 208.

165 Mairéad Dunlevy and Cormac Ó Gráda, 'A Bowling Match at Castlemary, Co. Cork', in David Dickson and Cormac Ó Gráda, eds., *Refiguring Ireland, Essays in Honour of L. M. Cullen* (Dublin, 2003).

166 For discussions on this painting, see also Brendan Rooney, catalogue entry, *A Time and a Place: Two Centuries of Irish Social Life* (Dublin, 2006), 55–56; and Peter Murray, ed., *Whipping the Herring: Survival and Celebration in Nineteenth-Century Irish Art* (Cork, 2006).

167 Sir William Wilde, 'Irish Popular Superstitions' in *Ireland: Her Wit, Peculiarities, and Popular Superstitions, with anecdotes, legendary and characteristic, by Distinguished Irish Writers* (Dublin, c. 1850), 15.

168 See E. Estyn Evans, *Irish Heritage: The Landscape, The People and their Work* (Dundalk, 1949).

169 Croker, *Researches*, 280.

170 Acquired by R. Robinson (£10) at the distribution of prizes.

171 Arthur Young, *Tour in Ireland, 1776–1779* (London, 1892), vol. 2, 147.

172 Croker, *Researches,* 235; and James McDaniel to Thomas Crofton Croker, Cork City Library, January 23, 1820.

173 Croker, *Researches,* 280.

174 Croker, *Researches,* 281.

175 Kevin Whelan, 'The Cultural Effects of the Famine' in *The Cambridge Companion to Modern Irish Culture,* Joe Cleary and Clare Connolly, eds. (Cambridge, 2005), 143.

176 Brian Henry, *The Pig and the Pot* (Tokyo, 1994).

177 See Thomas Bartlett, *The Fall and Rise of the Irish Nation: The Catholic Question, 1690–1830* (Savage, MD, 1992); K. T. Hoppen's *Ireland since 1800: Conflict and Conformity* (London, 1989); Sean Connolly, *Religion, Law, and Power: The Making of Protestant Ireland, 1660–1760* (Oxford, 1992); Kenneth Hugh Connell, *Irish Peasant Society: Four Historical Essays* (Oxford, 1968).

178 Geoff Burton, digital version of Philip Dixon Hardy's *The Holy Wells of Ireland* (1836), http://www.geoffb.me.uk/wells/wells.html, accessed October 20, 2015.

179 See Anna Rackard and Liam O'Callaghan, *Fish Stone Water: Holy Wells of Ireland* (Cork, 2001), with an introduction by Angela Bourke, to whom I am grateful for insights into this sketch.

180 Thomas Crofton Croker, *Early English Poetry, Ballads, and Popular Literature of the Middle Ages,* vol. 13 (London, 1844), ix–xx.

181 Sir William Wilde, 'Irish Popular Superstitions', 15.

182 Arthur Young, *Tour in Ireland,* 147.

183 John Coolahan, *Irish Education: Its History and Structure* (Dublin, 1981).

184 Croker, *Researches,* 329.

185 Kevin Whelan, *Field Day Review,* 6, 2010, 14.

186 Thomas Francis Dillon Croker, only son of Thomas Crofton Croker, owned the oil version of *Irish Hedge Schoolmaster,* presumably inherited from his father.

187 Nicholas Tromans, *David Wilkie: The People's Painter* (Oxford, 2007), 190.

188 David Wilkie to Robert Vernon, October 15, 1835; quoted in, and for further discussion, see Fintan Cullen, *Visual Politics, The Representation of Ireland 1750–1930* (Cork, 1997), 116–25.

189 Claudia Kinmonth, catalog note, lot 68, Whyte's auctions, November 26, 2012.

190 For further details, see Claudia Kinmonth, *Irish Rural Interiors in Art* (New Haven, 2006).

191 Fintan Cullen, *Visual Politics,* 121.

192 Caesar Otway, *A Tour in Connaught* (Dublin, 1839), 253–55.

193 See John F. Quinn, *Father Mathew's Crusade: Temperance in Nineteenth-century Ireland and Irish America* (Amherst, 2002).

194 Croker, *Researches,* 229.

195 For further discussions, see Keith Jeffery, *An Irish Empire?: Aspects of Ireland and the British Empire* (Manchester, 1996); and John Norris, *Marching to the Drums: A History of Military Drums and Drummers* (Gloucestershire, 2013).

196 Published by himself in Cork, and Colnaghi in London, the latter presented by Walter Strickland to the National Gallery in 1906.

197 See Sinéad Sturgeon, 'The Politics of Poitín: Maria Edgeworth, William Carleton, and the Battle for the Spirit of Ireland', *Irish Studies Review,* 14, no. 4, 2006, 431–45 (431).

198 Qtd. in Sturgeon, 'The Politics of Poitín', 432.

199 Paul A. Townend, *Father Mathew and Irish Identity* (Dublin, 2002),1.

200 Sturgeon, 'The Politics of Poitín', 440.

201 Daniel Macdonald to Richard Dowden, January 1850, Cork City and County Archives, Richard Dowden Papers, IE CCCA/U140.

202 Sir William Wilde, 'Irish Popular Superstitions', 15.

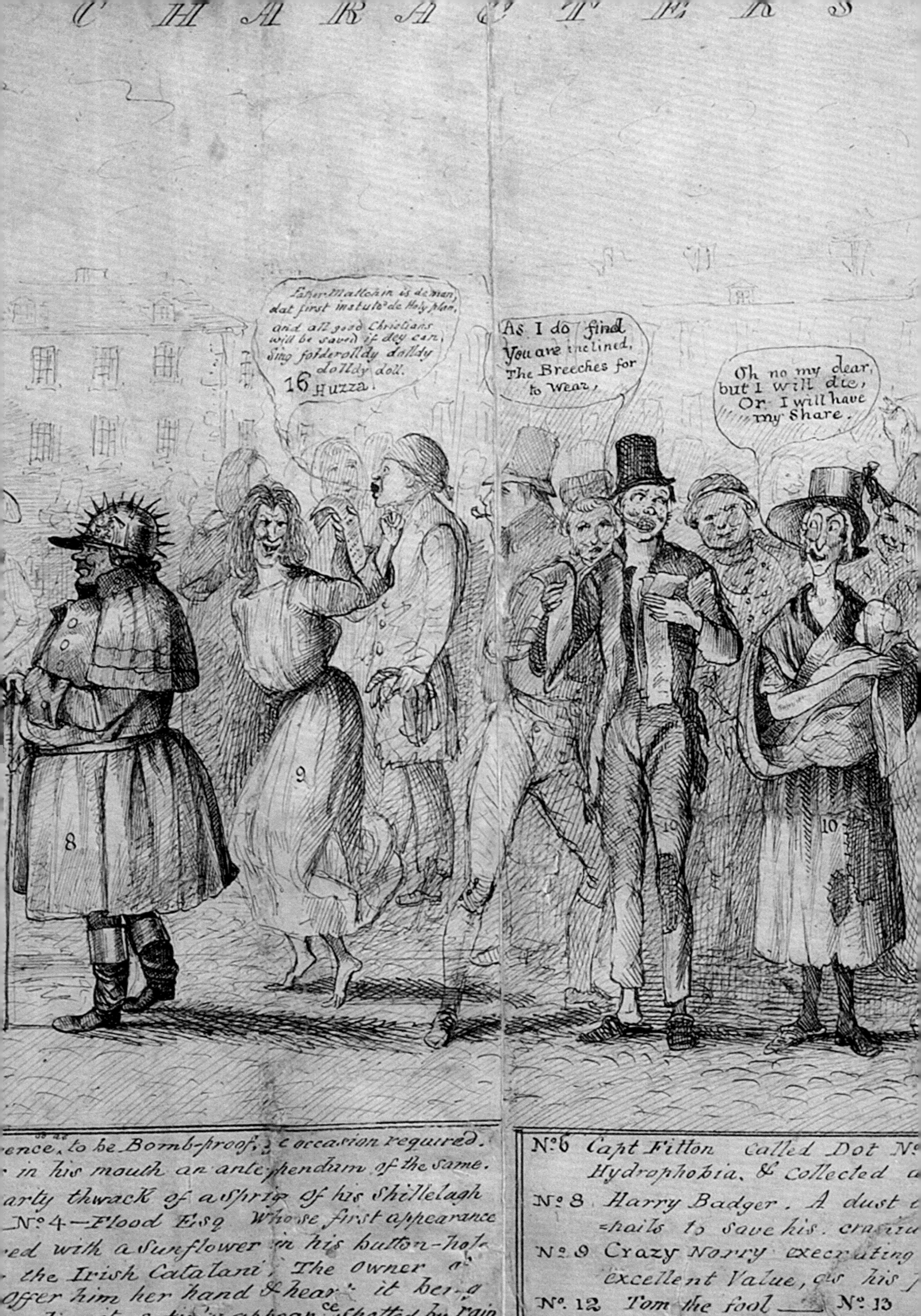

ence, to be Bomb-proof, & occasion required.
in his mouth an ante-pendium of the same.
arty thwack of a sprig of his Shillelagh
N.º 4 — Flood Esq Whose first appearance
ed with a Sunflower in his button-hole
the Irish Catalani. The Owner of
offer him her hand & heart it being
ustin. its satin'y appear.ce Spotted by rain

N.º 6 Capt Fitton Called Dot N.º
Hydrophobia. & collected a
N.º 8 Harry Badger. A dust
=hails to save his. craniu
N.º 9 Crazy Norry execrating
excellent Value, as his
N.º 12 Tom the fool ___ N.º 13

DANIEL MACDONALD EXHIBITION RECORD

1841	**Cork Art Union**	
46	*Dead Game*	
50	*The Dinner at Justice Shallow's (Henry IV)*	
53	*Terriers*	

1842   **Cork Art Union**

10   *Widgeon* etc

34   *Stag Hound*

41   *Bowl Playing*

44   *Hare Starting at the First Yell of the Pack*

50   *Portrait of the late Arthur Crawford Esq.*

81   *A Sídhe Gaoithe/ Fairy Blast* (with poem (fragment))

85   *Portrait of Mr. Caughy of America*

118   *Pen Sketch Portrait of Arthur Crawford Esq. from recollection*

1842   **Royal Hibernian Academy**

115   *'Royalty' — A Stag Hound from Nature*

134   *Dead Widgeon and Cork Harbour Oysters*

190   *Preparing for Bed in an Irish Cabin*

413   *Falstaff, Bardolph and the Page Entertained by Justice Shallow (Henry IV)*

1843   **Cork Art Union**

58   *Still life*

36   *Dogs (King Charles Spaniels)*

9   *Mare*

    Comus

1843   **Royal Hibernian Academy**

2   *Irish Cottagers*

1844   **Cork Art Union**

78   *The Soldier's Billet*

92   *Blind Fiddler*

1847   **British Institution, London**

469   *An Irish Peasant Family Discovering the Blight of their Store*

1849   **British Institution, London**

403   *Landscape Composition*

1850   **British Institution, London**

395   *The Guns of Distress*

1851   **British Institution, London**

324   *The Plougastel Ferry Boat Crossing near Brest*

1852   **Manchester Royal Institution**

168   *Ferry Boat Crossing at Brest*

347   *Anne Page, Shallow* etc

1852   **National Exhibition of the Arts, Manufactures and Products, Cork**

28   *Dead Game*

125   *Going to Bed in an Irish Cabin*

223   *The Gun of Distress*

224   *The Connoisseur*

225   *Old Carrighohan from Dunscombe's Wood*

226   *A Vision of the Sea*

1854   **Manchester Royal Institution**

23   *The Connoisseur in a Jew's Shop*

370   *Peasants of Brittany*

1873   **Loan Museum of Art Treasures, Dublin**

405   *Irish Hedge Schoolmaster Mending a Pen*

1882   **Irish Exhibition of Arts and Manufactures, Dublin**

422   *Irish Wolf Dogs and Pups*

DANIEL MACDONALD INTERIM CATALOGUE

Every effort has been made to document Macdonald's work from known exhibition records, artists' indices, auction records, and public and private collections, nevertheless a number remain unlocated. Erroneous information in artists' dictionaries and indices has been amended where possible. More works, and further details of as yet unknown works will undoubtedly emerge. Please note, measurements may require revision, as it is not always clear when an artwork was measured framed or unframed, and in some cases no dimensions or support details are known. Although incomplete, this catalogue is intended to facilitate future research.

The Tribute, Joseph O'Leary (1833)
Etchings
When I was a Boy (in 'Passages in the Life of an Actor')
The Justice Hall

Figures by a Coffin — a Scene from 'The Collegians' (1840)
Oil on canvas
Signed: D. Macdonald, Cork, July 1840
27.9 × 35.2 in / 71 × 89.5 cm
National Gallery of Ireland
LIT: Nesta Butler in Nicola Figgis, ed., *Art and Architecture of Ireland, Volume 2: Painting 1600–1900* (Dublin and New Haven, 2014)

A Cork Watchman (1840)
Pen and ink
Signed, dated and inscribed: D. Macdonald, Cork, December 31, 1840, 'A Cork Watchman'
10.7 × 8.4 in / 27.2 × 21.2 cm
British Museum
PROV: E. W. G. Macdonald 1903 (with letter to editor of *The Standard*, nd.)

Irish Peasant Travelling in Summer Trim (1841)
Pen and ink
Signed and titled
Album of original drawings, published in
Mr. & Mrs. S. C. Hall's *Ireland: its scenery, character, &c'*, no. 115, National Library of Ireland

Dead Game (1841)
EXH: Cork Art Union, 1841, no. 46; National Exhibition of the Arts, Manufactures and Products, Cork, 1852, no. 28
LIT: *Cork Examiner*, October 3, 1841;
Cork Examiner, November, 26, 1841

Terriers (1841)
EXH: Cork Art Union, 1841, no. 53
LIT: *Cork Examiner*, November 26, 1841
(incorrectly attributed to J. McDonald)

The Dinner at Justice Shallow's, Henry IV (1841)
EXH: Cork Art Union, 1841, no. 50
LIT: *Cork Examiner*, 26 November 1841
(incorrectly attributed to J. McDonald)

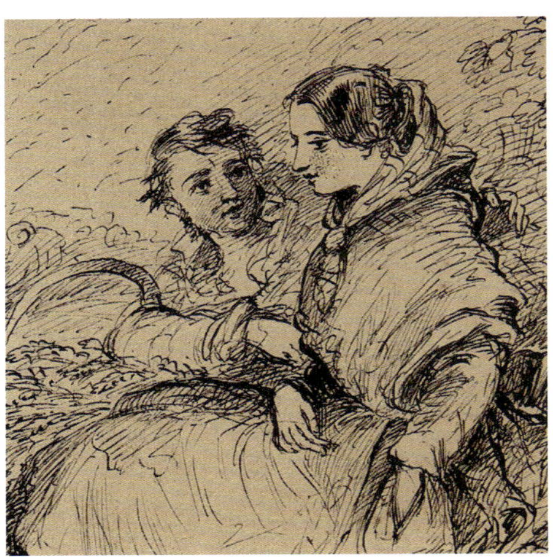

The Eagle's Nest, Killarney (1841)
Oil on canvas
Signed, dated and inscribed: 'Cork 1841'
26.4 × 24.6 in / 67.1 × 62.5 cm
PROV: James Adams, October 13, 2014, lot 768
LIT: *Cork Examiner*, October 3, 1842; Anne Crookshank and the Knight of Glin, *Ireland's Painters, 1600–1940* (New Haven, 2003)

Widgeon etc
EXH: Cork Art Union, 1841, no. 10

Stag Hound
EXH: Cork Art Union, 1841, no. 34

Hare Starting at the First Yell of the Pack (1842)
EXH: Cork Art Union, 1842, no. 44
LIT: *Cork Examiner*, October 13, 1842

Portrait of the late Arthur Crawford Esq. (1842)
EXH: Cork Art Union, 1842, no. 50
LIT: *Cork Examiner*, October 3, 1842

Portrait of Arthur Crawford Esq. from recollection (1842)
Pen Sketch
EXH: Cork Art Union, 1842, no. 118
LIT: *Cork Examiner*, October 3, 1842

Portrait of Mr. Caughy of America (1842)
EXH: Cork Art Union, 1842, no. 85
LIT: *Cork Examiner*, October 3, 1842

Sídhe Gaoithe / The Fairy Blast (1842)
Oil on canvas
35 × 45.2 in / 89 × 115 cm
National Folklore Collection
PROV: Senator E. A. Maguire, presented to National Folklore Commission, 1952

EXH: Cork Art Union, 1842, no. 81; *Amharc Oidhreacht Éireann/ Folk Tradition in Irish Art, an Exhibition of Paintings from the Collection of the Department of Irish Folklore, University College Dublin*, Dublin 1993, no. 11
LIT: *Southern Reporter and Cork Commercial Courier, September 15, 1842; Amharc Oidhreacht Éireann/Folk Tradition in Irish Art, an Exhibition of Paintings from the Collection of the Department of Irish Folklore, University College Dublin*, Dublin 1993; Tom Dunne in Peter Murray ed., *Whipping the Herring: Survival and Celebration in 19th Century Irish Art* (Cork, 2006); Christine Casey, 'Painting Irish folk life: the picture collection' in Críostóir Mac Cárthaigh at "ed., *Treasures of the National Folklore Collection/ Seoda as Cnuasach Bhéaloideas Éireann*, Dublin 2010; Nesta Butler in Nicola Figgis, ed., *Art and Architecture of Ireland, Volume 2: Painting 1600–1900* (Dublin and New Haven, 2014)

Bowl Playing (1842)
Oil on canvas
Unsigned
40 × 51 in / 101.6 × 129.54 cm
Crawford Art Gallery, Cork
PROV: Cork and County Club; Christie's, Glasgow,
May 24, 1988, lot 548
EXH: Cork Art Union, 1842, no. 41
LIT: *Cork Examiner*, October 3, 1842; Brendan Rooney in *A
Time and a Place: Two Centuries of Irish Social Life* (Dublin,
2006); Tom Dunne in Peter Murray, ed., *Whipping the Herring:
Survival and Celebration in 19th Century Irish Art* (Cork, 2006);
Peter Murray, ed., *Three Centuries of Irish Art* (Cork, 2014)

Returning from an Irish Funeral (1842)
Pen and ink on paper
Signed, inscribed and dated: D. Macdonald *inven'* Cork,
Dec' 14th, 1842
13 × 16.5 in / 33 × 42 cm
Ireland's Great Hunger Museum
PROV: Gorry Gallery, November 2014
LIT: Tom Dunne in Peter Murray, ed., *Whipping the Herring:
Survival and Celebration in 19th Century Irish Art* (Cork, 2006);
Peter Murray, Gorry Gallery catalogue, 2014; Nesta Butler in
Nicola Figgis, ed., *Art and Architecture of Ireland, Volume
2: Painting 1600–1900* (Dublin and New Haven, 2014)

'Royalty' — A Stag Hound from Nature (1842)
EXH: Royal Hibernian Academy, 1842, no. 115

Dead Widgeon and Cork Harbour Oysters (1842)
EXH: Royal Hibernian Academy, 1842, no. 134

Preparing for Bed in an Irish Cabin (1842)
EXH: Royal Hibernian Academy, 1842, no. 190; National Exhibition
of the Arts, Manufactures and Products, Cork, 1852, no.125

*Falstaff, Bardolph and the Page Entertained by Justice Shallow
(Henry IV)* (1842)
EXH: Royal Hibernian Academy, 1842, no. 413

Going Home after a Funeral (1842)
Pen and ink on paper
Signed & dated
7.5 × 10.7 in/19.1 × 27.1 cm
Royal Collections Trust
PROV: Queen Victoria, by descent to HRH The Duke of Kent Album
1833–56
LIT: Delia Millar, Delia, *The Victorian Watercolours in the
Collection of Her Majesty The Queen* (London 1995), entry 3730

The Govenor Calling the Hounds (1842)
Pen and ink
Signed and dated
PROV: Cork and County Club

The Castlemary Hunt (1842)
PROV: Cork and County Club

Public Characters (Cork) 1843
Pen and ink
Signed and inscribed: D Macdonald *delt.* Cork, 1843
13.4 × 39.7 in /34 × 101 cm
Clayton Love, on loan to Crawford Art Gallery
LIT: Peter Murray ed., *Whipping the Herring: Survival and
Celebration in 19th Century Irish Art* (Cork, 2006)

Dogs (King Charles Spaniels) (1843)
Oil on canvas
Signed, dated and inscribed: D. Macdonald, Cork, 1843 (and
signed verso)
34 × 38.5 in / 86.4 × 97.8 cm
PROV: Sotheby's, May 21, 1997
EXH: Cork Art Union, 1843, no. 36

Portrait of a Boy Holding a Book with a Flute by his Side
Oil on canvas
Signed and dated: D. Macdonald, Cork, 1843
30 × 24 in /76.2 × 61cm
PROV: Semley Auctioneers, January 23, 2010

Still-life of Crab, Fish and Vegetables (1843)
Oil on canvas
Signed with initials verso
27 × 35 in / 68.6 × 88.9 cm
PROV: Sotheby's, London, November 16, 1988, lot 114
EXH: Cork Art Union, 1843, no. 58
LIT: *Cork Examiner*, September 6, 1843

Dogs (King Charles Spaniels) (1843)
EXH: Cork Art Union, 1843, no. 36
LIT: *Cork Examiner*, September 6, 1843

Comus (1843)
EXH: Cork Art Union 1843 (selected for distribution)
PROV: T. S. Reeves (High Sherriff of Cork) (£9)
LIT: *Southern Reporter and Cork Commercial Courier*,
August 26, 1843; *Cork Examiner*, August, 26, 1843; Nesta
Butler in Nicola Figgis, ed., *Art and Architecture of Ireland,
Volume 2: Painting 1600–1900* (Dublin and New Haven, 2014)

Mare (1843)
EXH: Cork Art Union, 1843, no. 9
PROV: Captain (T.?) Knatchbull, Admiralty
LIT: *Southern Reporter and Cork Commercial Courier*,
August 26, 1843; *Cork Examiner*, August 26, 1843

Irish Cottagers
EXH: Royal Hibernian Academy, 1842, no. 2

Huntsman in Full Gallop (1843)
Pen and ink
Signed and dated 1843
PROV: Cork and County Club

Riding to Cover (1843)
Pen and ink
Signed and dated 1843
PROV: Cork and County Club

Portrait of a Gentleman (1843)
Oil on canvas
Signed and dated: 'D. Macdonald / Cork, 1843'
30 × 24 in / 76.2 × 61 cm
Semley Auctioneers, January 23, 2010

The Fighter (1844)
Oil on canvas
Signed and dated
50.5 × 40.2 in / 128.3 × 102.1 cm
K Club, Sir Michael Smurfit collection
PROV: Christie's Belfast, October 26, 1990,
lot 164; private collection, USA

Blind Fiddler (1844)
PROV: R. Robinson
EXH: Cork Art Union, 1844, no. 92
LIT: *Cork Examiner,* December 11, 1844

The Shower (1844)
Pen and ink on paper
Signed, titled and dated: 'D Macdonald, *The Shower,* 1844.'
10.2 × 14.4 in / 25.9 × 36.6 cm
British Museum
PROV: E. W. G. Macdonald 1903

Portrait of Edward Jesse (1780–1868) (1844)
Chalk and pencil on paper
Inscribed: Mr. Edward Jesse, Writer Natural History
15 × 11 in / 38.1 × 27.9 cm
National Portrait Gallery, London
LIT: Richard Ormond, *Early Victorian Portraits,* 1973; David
Saywell and Jacob Simon, *Complete Illustrated Catalogue,* 2004

The Soldier's Billet (1844)
EXH: Cork Art Union, 1844, no. 78
LIT: *Cork Examiner,* December 20, 1844

Kerry Peasantry (1844)
Pen and ink
Signed and inscribed: D. McDonald *del & fect.*
Inscribed 'Kerry peasantry list'ning to the account of the conviction
of Dan'l O'Connell and the Traversers, at the State Trials in Dublin,
Feb'y 1844'
14 × 9.5 in / 35.6 × 24.1 cm
Kevin Coughlan collection

Portrait of Lieutenant-General Sir John Rowland KBC
(1806–73) (c. 1845)
Attributed to Macdonald
Oil on canvas
30 × 24 in / 76.2 × 61 cm
Crawford Art Gallery
PROV: By descent from General Smyth, Co.
Waterford; Whyte's, February 18, 2003

Portrait of Thomas Dimsdale (1845)
Chalks
Signed and dated: Daniel Macdonald, 1845
21 × 14.5 in / 53 × 37

Turk Mountain, from Ross Road (c. 1845)
Pen and blue-black and brown ink, on blue-grey paper
Titled
9.9 × 14.1 in / 25.1 × 35.7 cm
British Museum
PROV: Presented by Edward Croft Murray

Torc Waterfall, Killarney (1845)
Pen and black ink, touched with colored chalks; on grey paper
Signed, titled, dated and numbered: D. Macdonald, Killarney,
1845, IV
14 × 10 in / 35.5 × 25.1 mm
British Museum
PROV: Presented by Edward Croft Murray

Gap at Dunloe, Killarney (1845)
Pen and brown ink, on blue-grey paper
Signed and dated: D. Macdonald, 1845
10 × 14 in / 25.1 × 35.6 cm
British Museum
PROV: Presented by Edward Croft Murray

*Portrait of Lord Godfrey William Wentworth Boswell Macdonald,
4th Lord Macdonald* (1809–63) (1845)
Initialed and dated: D. MacD, 1845
20.5 × 15 in / 52.1 × 38.1 cm
PROV: Lord Godfrey Macdonald, Kinloch House, Sleat, Isle of Skye

Portrait of Miss Susan Dowden

Irish Peasant Children (1846)
Signed and dated
Oil on canvas
33 × 29 in / 84 × 74 cm
Ireland's Great Hunger Museum, Quinnipiac University
PROV: Gore-Booth family, Lissadell House.
LIT: 'Lines of Sorrow: Representing Ireland's
Great Hunger', *Ireland's Great Hunger Museum
Inaugural Catalogue* (Hamden, CT, 2012)

An Irish Peasant Family Discovering the Blight of their Store (1847)
(also known as *The Discovery of the Potato Blight in Ireland*)
Oil on canvas
Signed
3.5 × 4.1 ft / 84 × 104 cm
National Folklore Collection, University College Dublin
PROV: Christie's London, January 1966, lot 174; Irish Folklore
Commission, UCD (donated by Cecil Woodham-Smith) 1966;
EXH: British Institution, London 1847, no. 469; *Amharc Oidhreacht
Éireann/Folk Tradition in Irish Art, an Exhibition of Paintings from
the Collection of the Department of Irish Folklore, University
College Dublin,* Dublin 1993, no. 15; Cork Rosc, 1971
LIT: Art-Union, March 1, 1847; 'Nothing Vulgar in Rosc Chorcaí',
Sunday Independent, 28 November 1971; Christine Casey,
'Painting Irish folk life: the picture collection' in Críostóir Mac
Cárthaigh, ed., *Treasures of the National Folklore Collection/
Seoda as Cnuasach Bhéaloideas Éireann* (Dublin, 2010); Tom
Dunne in Peter Murray, ed., *Whipping the Herring: Survival
and Celebration in 19th Century Irish Art* (Cork, 2006); Nesta
Butler in Nicola Figgis, ed., *Art and Architecture of Ireland,
Volume 2: Painting 1600–1900* (Dublin and New Haven, 2014)

Captain Mackett RN (1847)
Pen and black ink
Signed, dated and inscribed: D. Macdonald, 1847, 'Johnny'
9.9 × 7.7 in / 25.1 × 19.6 cm
British Museum
PROV: E. W. G. Macdonald, 1903

Tracy Peerage Case (1847)

The six sketches below are mounted together (note: the British
Museum cataloguing of these sketches is inaccurate):
British Museum
PROV: E. W. G. Macdonald, 1903

Man holding fragment of tombstone, with cross (
Tracy Peerage Case, 1847)
Pen and black ink
2.3 × 3.4 in / 5.8 × 8.6 cm

Lord Sudeley (*Tracy Peerage Case,* 1847)
Pen and black ink, and graphite
Inscribed with title and dated '4th May'
3.5 × 2.3 in / 8.9 × 5.8 cm

Lord Brougham and Vaux, Lord Chancellor
(*Tracy Peerage Case,* 1847)
Pen and black ink
Dated and inscribed: '4th May 1847,
Lord Brougham at the Tracy Peerage Case'
3.5 × 2.3 in / 8.9 × 5.9 cm

Delany the Witness (probably) (*Tracy Peerage Case,* 1847)
Pen and black ink

Delany the Witness (*Tracy Peerage Case,* 1847)
Pen and black ink
Inscribed, titled and dated: 'Delany the witness,
Tracy peerage Case', 4 May 1847
3.5 × 2.3 in / 8.8 × 5.9 cm

Lord Radnor (*Tracy Peerage Case,* 1847)
Pen and black ink, over graphite
Inscribed: 'Moore' and 'Lord Radnor'
3.5 × 2.2 in / 8.9 × 5.7 cm

Courtship (1847)
Ink on buff colored paper
Signed and dated: D. Macdonald, 1847
7.5 × 10.6 in / 19 × 27 cm
Crawford Art Gallery

The Killarney Milkmaid (1847)
Ink on buff colored paper
Signed and dated: D. Macdonald, 1847
7.5 × 10.6 in /19 × 27 cm
Crawford Art Gallery

The Hedge Schoolmaster (1847)
Ink on paper
Signed and dated: D. Macdonald, 1847
7.5 × 10.6 in / 19 × 27 cm
Crawford Art Gallery

Preparing for Mass (1847)
Ink on paper
Signed and dated: D. Macdonald, 1847
7.5 × 10.6 in / 19 × 27 cm
Crawford Art Gallery

Preparing for Bed, Scene in an Irish Cabin (1847)
Ink on paper
Signed and dated: D. Macdonald, 1847
7.5 × 10.6 in / 19 × 27 cm
Crawford Art Gallery

After the Duel (1847)
Ink on paper
Signed and dated: D. Macdonald, 1847
7.5 × 10.6 in / 19 × 27 cm
Crawford Art Gallery

An Irish Parish Priest and His Coadjutor (1847)
Ink on paper
Signed and dated: D. Macdonald, 1847
7.5 × 10.6 in / 19 × 27 cm
Crawford Art Gallery

'Mick, you Divil...' (1847)
Ink on paper
7.5 × 10.6 in / 19 × 27 cm
Crawford Art Gallery

'Peace was made for coward souls:
War my boys for you and me' (1847)
Ink on paper
Signed and dated: D. Macdonald, 1847
7.5 × 10.6 in / 19 × 27 cm
Crawford Art Gallery

Soul Beggars (1847)
Ink on paper
Signed and dated: D. Macdonald, 1847
7.5 × 10.6 in / 19 × 27 cm
Crawford Art Gallery

Welply Tribute (1847)
LIT: *Cork Examiner,* January 11, 1847

Portrait of Sir William Mordaunt Sturt Milner, 4th Bt (1848)
(by James Henry Lynch, printed by Day & Son,
after Daniel Macdonald)
Lithograph, 1848
21.4 × 14.5 in / 54.4 × 36.8 cm
National Portrait Gallery, London

A Wedding Dance (1848) (or *A Country Dance*)
Oil on canvas
29.7 × 35.4 in / 75.5 × 90 cm
Crawford Art Gallery,
LIT: Nesta Butler in Nicola Figgis, ed., *Art and Architecture of Ireland, Volume 2: Painting 1600–1900* (Dublin and New Haven, 2014); Peter Murray, ed., *Three Centuries of Irish Art* (Cork, 2014)

A Modern Visit from the Devil (1848 and 1849)
Thirteen untitled pen and ink sketches

Landscape Composition (1849)
EXH: British Institution, 1849, no. 403

The Guns of Distress (1850)
EXH: British Institution, 1850, no. 395; National Exhibition of the Arts, Manufactures and Products, Cork, 1852, no. 223

Portrait of Charles James Hale Monro (1850)
Chalks
25.5 × 20 in / 65 × 51

Portrait of Seymour Vassal Hale Monro (1850)
Chalks
25.5 × 20 in / 65 × 51

The Eviction (c. 1850)
Attributed to Daniel MacDonald
Oil on canvas
24.8 × 29.5 in / 63 × 74.9 cm
Crawford Art Gallery
PROV: Adams, May 28, 2003, lot 4; Adams, April 15, 2008, lot 601
EXH: *Whipping the Herring: Survival and Celebration in 19th Century Irish Art* (Cork, 2006)
LIT: Tom Dunne in Peter Murray, ed., *Whipping the Herring: Survival and Celebration in 19th Century Irish Art* (Cork, 2006); Peter Murray, ed., *Three Centuries of Irish Art* (Cork, 2014); Nesta Butler in Nicola Figgis, ed., *Art and Architecture of Ireland, Volume 2: Painting 1600–1900* (Dublin and New Haven, 2014)

Dan at Cork (1850)
Pen and ink
Initialed and dated: D. Macd., 1850
14.5 × 10 in / 36.8 × 25.4 cm
Kevin Coughlan collection

Daniel O'Connell says: 'Now boys be asy — For the sake of John, and Tom, and the Lamb of Ardagh — The Lion of the Fold of Judah — and Ah! boys, the Dove of Galway !! Be asy. Three cheers for The Queen. Ah boys, we love our dear Queen — our sweet Queen — and three cheers for those dear gentlemen of the Millingtary come out today for our protection. Ah boys, we love the Millingtary. Hurrah, hurrah, hurrah. One cheer more. Hurrah, hurrah, hurrah.'

The Plougastel Ferry Boat crossing near Brest (1851)
51 × 61 in / 129.5 × 154.9 cm
EXH: British Institution, 1851, no. 324; Manchester Royal Institution, 1852, no. 168
LIT: *Morning Chronicle*, February 10, 1851

Anne Page, Shallow etc. (1852)
EXH: Manchester Royal Institution, 1852, no. 347

The Connoisseur in a Jew's Shop (1852)
EXH: National Exhibition of the Arts, Manufactures and Products, Cork, 1853, no. 224; Royal Institution Manchester, 1854, no. 23
LIT: Daniel Macdonald to Richard Dowden, nd; National Exhibition of the Arts, Manufactures and Products, Cork, 1853; John Francis Maguire, MP, Mayor of Cork, *The Industrial Movement in Ireland as Illustrated by the National Exhibition of 1852* (Cork, 1853); *Southern Reporter and Cork Commercial Courier,*1 July 1852; *The Coleraine Chronicle,* June 26, 1852 (from Cork Constitution); *Manchester Courier and Lancashire General Advertiser,* October 21, 1854: Walter Strickland, Ms. Notes Ms. 19,685 (A), annotation to vol. II

Old Carrighohan from Dunscombe's Wood (1852)
Oil on canvas
EXH: National Exhibition of the Arts, Manufactures and Products, Cork, 1852, no. 225
LIT: National Exhibition of the Arts, Manufactures and Products, Cork, 1852; *Coleraine Chronicle,* June 26, 1852; *Cork Constitution; Cork Examiner,* September 10, 1852

A Vision of the Sea (1852)
EXH: National Exhibition of the Arts, Manufactures and Products, Cork, 1852, no. 226

Why what do I see yonder? (1853)
Chalks on paper
Signed, dated and inscribed: D. Macdonald, 1853, 'Why what do I see yonder?'
10.1 × 14,4 in / 25.6 × 36.5 mm
Purchased from E. W. G. Macdonald, 1903
British Museum
LIT: Nesta Butler in Nicola Figgis, ed., *Art and Architecture of Ireland, Volume 2: Painting 1600–1900* (Dublin and New Haven, 2014)

Peasants of Brittany
EXH: Manchester Royal Institution, 1854, no. 370

Irish Hedge Schoolmaster Mending a Pen
EXH: Loan Museum of Art Treasures, Dublin, 1873, no. 405

Irish Wolf Dogs and Pups
EXH: Irish Exhibition of Arts and
Manufactures, Dublin, 1882, no 433

Tasting the Poitín in Ireland
Attributed to Daniel Macdonald
Oil on canvas
14 × 18 in / 35.6 × 45.7 cm
Heide Roche collection
PROV: Whytes, November 26, 2012, lot 68
LIT: Claudia Kinmonth, Whyte's catalogue, November 26, 2012;
Peter Murray, ed., *Whipping the Herring: Survival and
Celebration in 19th-Century Irish Art* (Cork, 2006)

Portrait William Sandys Wright Vaux
Graphite, on blue-grey paper
Initialed: Macd
8 × 6.9 in / 20.4 × 17.5 mm
British Museum
PROV: E. W. G. Macdonald, 1903

Old Town in Surrey
Watercolor
6.3 × 10 in / 16 × 25.4 cm
PROV: Waddington's, Canada, February 27, 2008, lot 189

The Awakened Conscience
Watercolor
6 × 9 in / 15.2 × 22.9 cm
PROV: Waddington's, Canada, September 26, 2007, lot 189

Rev. Theobald Mathew (1790–1856)
Mezzotint
Signed: D. Macdonald, pinxt et Sculpt
14.8 × 11.6 in / 37.6 × 29.5 cm
Published: London, Colnaghi; and Cork, himself
Presented: Mr. W. G. Strickland, 1906
National Gallery of Ireland

Portrait of Theobald Mathew
Oil on canvas

Portrait Robert Day FSA, MRIA (as a boy)

The Dancing Master

Mr Mike Scanlon's School, Ballyshandrahan (1851)
Signed and dated: D. Macdonald, 1851
PROV: Kiefer Auctions, January 24, 2009

Portrait of a Girl
PROV: Semley Auctioneers, January 25, 2014, lot 132

A Pair of Portraits (perhaps father and son)
Oil on canvas
30 × 24 in / 76.2 × 61 cm
PROV: Mallams, September 26, 2001, lot 25

Fisherfolk on Beach
Watercolor
Signed
6.8 × 9.8 in / 17.3 × 24.9 cm
PROV: Waddington's Canada. June 27, 2013, lot 5

The Ferry Boat Arriving
Oil on canvas
Signed: D. Macdonald
Inscribed indistinctly in pencil on stretcher 'by D. Macdonald'
16 × 26 in / 40.6 × 66 cm
PROV: Waddington's, Canada, October 4, 2012, lot 27

Spectators of Punch
Pen and ink
PROV: Adams, October 5, 2010, lot 363

Tom Bearing Important Despatches to Ballydrisheen
Pen and ink
PROV: Adam's, October 5, 2010, lot 363

*A Night in Bristol, Mr. Mark Antony Wiggins,
Pitching into the Bugs* (1850)
Pen and ink
PROV: Adam's, October 5, 2010, lot 363

Huntsmen, Horses and Hound
Pen and ink
PROV: Cork and County Club

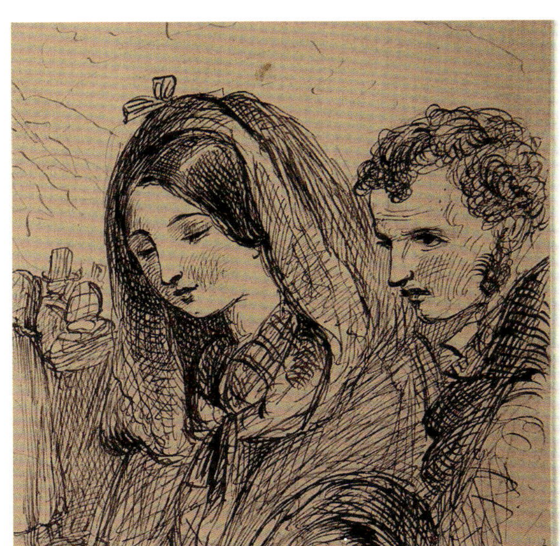

JAMES MCDANIEL WORKS (1788–1865)

Given that James McDaniel changed his name to Macdonald in the mid 1830s, caution should be exercised in the case of works exhibited as J. Macdonald, given that his daughter Jane was also an artist (for which reason, she came to call herself Jane Masters Macdonald / Jane Masters Rogers).

DEFINITE ATTRIBUTIONS:

1815   **First Munster Exhibition, Cork**

7   *Cupids Catching a Hare,* pen sketch

119   *Music, Painting, Poetry,* humorous pen sketch (engraved by R. Dorman, and illustrated in M. Holland, 'Two Typical Cork Sketches', Journal of the Cork Historical and Archaeological Society, 1913, vol. 19, no. 98, 76–77)

129   "*'Poeta Nascitur',* (a poet is born not made) *a literary character in this city, equally a disciple of the Muses and Bacchus.*" Humorous pen sketch. Same fig as above (carries … 'controversy')

1817   **Cork Society for Promoting the Fine Arts**

76   *Ruins Composition* (pen sketch):

*'Lo mouldering, wild unknown
What fanes, what towers o'erthrown
What tumbling chaos marks the waste of time'*

(*Ode to Time*, occasioned by seeing the ruins of an old castle, James Beattie, LLD, 1806)

128   *Music, Painting and Poetry,* humorous pen sketch

1828   **Mechanics' Institute Exhibition, Cork**

40   *Landscape*

1832   **Royal Hibernian Academy, Dublin**

144   *Landscape-Composition*

1833   **Cork Society for Promoting Fine Arts**

81   *Composition*

1833   ***The Tribute,* Cork 1833, a volume of prose and poetry, "The Phrenologist" (etching)**

1835   **The Society of Native and Resident Artists, Cork**

121   *The Ghost Story*

122   *Conversation*

123   *Sunday Morning*

124   *Farmyard*

125   *Poebur (peebur) un Thuig[?]*

1841   **Cork Art Union**

8   *Portrait of a Gentleman*

DATED:

The Bird's Nest (1852)
Oil on canvas
Signed and dated
16.5 × 20.5 in/42 × 52 cm
PROV: Philips, no. 30, 24 September 1979

UNDATED:

Christ Church Pew
Pen and ink sketch
PROV: Robert Day FSA

Blarney Lane
Pen and ink sketch
PROV: John Marks, Master in Chancery; Mr. Blake; Robert Day FSA

Portrait of Harry Badger
Lithographed by Guy & Co., Cork.

Hanging around the old courthouse in South Main Street, Cork, dressed in yellow buckskin trousers, and a red coat of pseudo military cut, Harry Badger wore an extraordinary contraption on his head, a brass helmet with iron spikes, to prevent local children from knocking it off. A popular eccentric, Harry prided himself on his ability to eat anything. When a mouse was slipped into his pint of porter, Harry did not disappoint. (See Michael Lenihan, *Hidden Cork: Charmers, Chancers and Cute Hoors*)

Harry Badger also appears in *Public Characters* by Daniel Macdonald.

James McDaniel to Richard Dowden, nd., Cork City and
County Archives, Richard Dowden Papers, IE CCCA/U140:

> 'For amusement I wrote a squib. It is all about Pusey renegades
> … but as he finds Puseyism will never lead to Canterbury
> (while Lord John R. steers the helm) he dexterously assumes
> the orthodox masks and figures of staunch opponents
> to Pope and Papacy, and recommends an augmentation
> to the Bishops' Bench to give stability to the established
> which is reeling to and fro like a drunken man …

> *They naturally go Rome-ing, some go 'the whole hog' —*
> *others are wavering but all are pining for Maryolotary*
> *as firmly established by the man as sits in his throne*
> *propped up by French bayonets with three hats on his*
> *head as Hogarth represented him in one of the illustrations*
> *to Swift's Tale of a Tub thus [?] a triple crown:*

No. 1. Nursery Rhimes of Mother Church, Volo Episcopare

Master Hook (Vicar of Leeds) having been a naughty boy for
hiring a Jesuit curate and sending Pusey converts to Mass, all
of a sudden turns to the right [?] about face, jumps up into his
mother's lap and she dances him affectionately to the tune of

> *Dance for your Mammy,*
> *My Pusey Baby:*

Master Hook having been so naughty as to present the scarlet
lady to his natural mother and fearing that he would get no
more sugar plums calls Cardinal Wiseman's mother's name
out of the apocalypse. Confesses his own naughtiness and
begs mother Church may indulge him with more of the song
(such is the cunning of children). Dandying the wayward boy
on her knee, she proceeds with a climax of peroraration thus

> *'Episcopare Volo'*
> *Rome's candidates for Mitres play*
> *Parts insincere and Hollow*
> *Cries Wiseman as he runs away*
> *While Sacerdotes follow*
> *Episcopare Nolo*
>
> *I'll call a special chapter*
> *I'll make my child a dean*
> *I'll send him to St George's*
> *To preach before the Queen*
> *Dance for your Mammy etc*

Master Hook having a predeliction for certain venerable
localities in Mother Church's gifts tells the old lady that
he could not contentedly live any where but in York or
Cantebury and then urges her to go on, she thus proceeds

> *I'll buy my children a mitre*
> *I'll buy my children a Crook*
> *A Cassock and lawn sleeves likewise*
> *And he'll be Bishop Hook*
>
> *Dance for your Mammy etc*

Master Hook making much ado about occupying an old
mansion as Lambeth his kingdom [?] Mother preaches patience
under present circumstances and engages to do more for
him after a while, and placing a golden ball on the apex of
his highest steeple to complete her climax thus proceeds

> *My Pusey Pet your patience try*
> *Till dainty things I dish-up*
> *When Ebor or Cantwar [?] shall die*
> *I'll make you an Archbishop*
> *Dance for your Mammy etc*

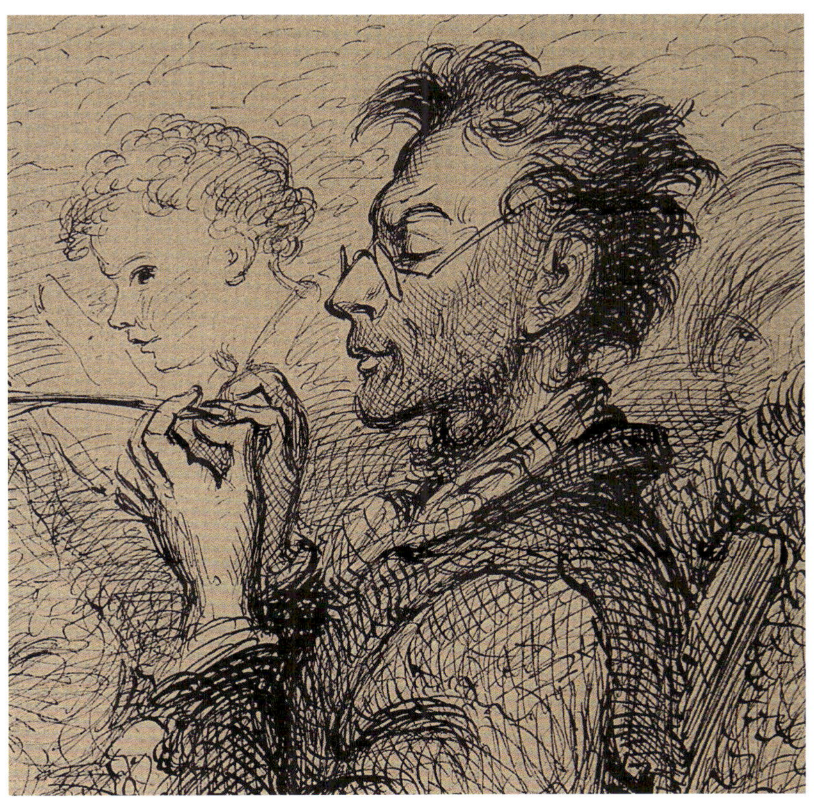

JANE MASTERS MACDONALD ROGERS BIOGRAPHY (1824–1909)

From her debut in 1842 at the age of 18, Jane Masters Macdonald exhibited alongside her brother Daniel (after marriage, she signed herself Jane Masters Rogers). Working across a wide range of genres, her art was generally positively received. Her first contributions to the *Cork Art Union*, *Shylock* and *Learning to Walk* were described as the work of 'a clever young artist':

> *Is this the Jew/That Shakespeare drew?* Now we do concede that this whole picture has more of the melodrama that the tragedy in it. We think Shylock could be better represented without a hat, and with a pale countenance: he looks at us too like a Calabrian brudit (sic). Yet, for all this, it is a good picture. Its execution is praiseworthy; the sealed bond, the hands, in spite of the showy profusion of rings, and the knife; though Kean, we think, instead of using a strop, with a less deliberate air of dainty preparation, and a more natural indication of ferocity, was accustomed to tear the sides of it along the floor. Let us see: *Shylock*. By Miss Jane McDonald. Shame on our criticism, once and again! Why did we not look before us? We have not done the picture justice. The whole effect, allowing for what we have objected, and which it is too late to retract, is really admirable; and when we think it is the production of a lady, we warmly congratulate her on her entrance into the artistic lists, and predict for her, is she will persevere, the certainty of a very pleasing and honorable distinction.

The reviewer went on to describe *Learning to Walk* as 'a very pretty and very amiable picture', conceding that there are marks of juvenility about it, 'but these are only the stronger indication of promise, inasmuch as there is a fidelity of expression, and a graphic power of detail in it which show it to be the work of no mean aspirant, and recommend it, at once to our approbation' (*Cork Examiner*, October 3, 1842). In 1844, when she exhibited *Shrovetide (Match-making)*, she showed herself, like her brother, to be versed in rural lore, the *Cork Examiner* gave it an uncommon amount of attention:

> This is indeed a charming picture, and more than charming — it is full of talent, abounding with promise. It is natural, clever, spirited and pleasing; the design is ably executed, and the detail is accurate and careful. Without an appeal to the catalogue, the picture could be understood at a glance, the subject is so manifest. Seated near and round a table, plentifully covered with 'the eating and drinking' — with whiskey galore, and porter, and bread — are several figures. There is a match-maker with his leering half-closed eye, just squinting at the progress of the good work … . We understand this personage owes not his existence on canvas to the imagination of the fair artist; the original stands high in his profession and rejoices in the mysterious *sobriquet* of 'Johnny The Needles'. He is a walking prototype of a small scale of *Debrett's Peerage* — can tell the ancestry of every farmer for twenty miles round, and knows to a shilling, to a blanket, or to a skillet, the fortune of every 'likely' girl, within the same rather extended circle. His diplomatic triumphs are written in every line of his expressive countenance. Seated near him is a fine clean-skinned boy, who with great earnestness is forcing on a nice, tidy, rosy-cheeked country-girl something in a jug — the fair damsel, who evidently seems a little the softer from the combined effects of the love and the 'something', placing her hand on the top of her glass, with an air of once conscious of her danger, and strongly expressive of refusal. At a little distance sits the father, the man of the house, who looks with a favorable eye on the courtship. In a remote corner of the large kitchen are females, one the *van-a-thee*, the woman of the house, the other a crony or a gossip, both intent on inspecting a blanket which they both concur in admiring, and which, without doubt, forms part of the young damsel's dowry. Near the old man, leans a young boy, with a beautiful face and most spirited expression, one that would remind you much of Maclise's best heads. At the other end of the room is a wandering *Boccogh*, a sturdy travelling beggar — with bold, impudent face, unkempt lock, and laden with a multitude of wallets. This worthy who appears quite 'at home', is raising his hand to the dresser to take down a cup, and join in the more spiritual part of the business … . Then the detail of sparkling glass, and shining pint — the bread cut, and the loaf, the broken crusts, and the knife, with the rosy 'Sweet William' apples placed before the *cushla ma chree* of the solf-hearted bachelor — all these are of inimitable, in fact equal to any terms of praise. But the crowning bit of all is a glorious 'pig's countenance', prophetically reposing as it were, on a few heads of the choicest greens. It is more than nature — it is absolutely irritating to any empty stomach, or to a devout observer of 'ember days'. We must not forget the girl of all work, who stands behind the lovers, and who, with sparkling eye and appreciating smile, seems to have arrived at a settled conviction that match-making was not a bad thing at all, and that she herself had no conscientious objection to be No. 1 in the present, or in similar negotiation. We have just described, more minutely, perhaps than we could conveniently do, this creditable picture, which if not the best, is one of the best in the exhibition. The tone, the drawing, the colouring and the detail, are all worthy of the highest commendation.' (December 20, 1844)

Reviews continued in a positive vein until *'One of earth's fairest womankind'* (1854) was exhibited at the Royal Manchester Institution and denounced for its indelicacy:

> We take exception to the manner in which Mrs. J. M. Rogers has chosen to embody the idea contained in the three lines from Moore's *Lives of the Angels*. We can understand how want may make an artist so far forget himself as to pander to libidinous taste, and produce the disgraceful prints which may be sometimes seen in our streets; but how a lady can so far forget the delicacy which belongs to her sex as to produce a work like this to be exhibited before mixed assemblies, we are at a loss to understand; and we cannot but think that the council of the institution might have marked their sense of the impropriety by assigning it a place more out of sight, where it would of necessity have raised a blush on the check of modesty. (*Manchester Courier and Lancashire General Advertiser*, November 4, 1854)

Jane continued to exhibit regularly until, rather ingloriously, her career came to an end with a showing in the Royal Hibernian Academy in 1876, to which the *Freeman's Journal* took exception:

> No. 124 bears a title redundant and ambitious — *Irish Peasantry Returning from a Repeal Meeting through a Pass in the Kerry Mountains*. Mrs. Rogers, the artist, has been bold enough in her subject and correspondingly inadequate in her treatment. She lacks almost all the requirements which her suggestion demands — a mastery over colours, a high capacity for grouping, a thorough acquaintance with drawing, and a combination of portrait and landscape painting. Very few artists can boast all these powers, and Mrs. Rogers, we regret to say, can boast but few of them. Her picture is hung considerably above the line. (March 8, 1876)

However, from an auspicious start in Cork, Jane did quite well as an artist in London. In 1846, she married William Richard Rogers MD (1817–1901). Rogers was born in Dublin, studied at University College London and Heidelberg University, and 'walked the hospitals of France and Italy'. He was a Fellow of the Royal Medical and Chirurgical Society of London, a licentiate of the Royal College of Physicians, and member of the Obstetrical Society of London. He was a distinguished obstetrician, gynecologist and *accoucheur*. At this time, women of class were attended at home by their physician. With a home visit fee of 3 guineas, private medicine was well remunerated, but Rogers's commitment to public health seems to have been both progressive and altruistic, and he was reputedly much loved by patients and colleagues. He was physician to the Samaritan Free Hospital, and consulting surgeon to the Grosvenor Hospital for Women and Children where he specialized in puerperal cases and uterine cancer, receiving commendations for treating difficult cases with considerable success.[1] He lectured 'the poorest class' on health and hygiene in an attempt to combat the remarkable levels of infant mortality at the time. During a massive outbreak of cholera in 1854, Rogers distinguished himself — the index case being a patient of his.[2]

Jane and William lived their married lives at 56 Berners Street, where also resided her father James, and brother Daniel. They had six children (not all of whom thrived; two spent time in a 'lunatic asylum'). Their eldest son continued the family tradition, becoming a surgeon in the Royal Navy. Kate, their eldest daughter, was also an artist, exhibiting, but rarely, at the Royal Society of British Artists, Suffolk Street, and the New Watercolour Society. She caused quite a stir when her uncle, the Rev. James Alexander, recorded a psychical experience relating to the death of her grandmother, Catherine McDaniel/Macdonald in 1877. Psychical experiences were the subject of much interest at the time, both from religious and 'scientific' perspectives. Kate reported experiencing 'a presence' of her grandmother, living at that time with James Alexander, minutes before she died. The Society for Psychical Research employed a number of investigators to ascertain the 'veracity' of such episodes, one being James Alexander himself.[3]

But well into the marriage, things unraveled. In 1888, after 42 years of marriage, William's 'habitual adultery' was discovered, resulting in divorce, a rare occurrence at the time.[4] Jane died in 1909 in Brighton, her estate was valued at a not inconsequential £1,470, 18 s, 2d. None of the Rogers children married. On Jane's death, Kate inherited, and when she died, she left everything to her cousin, Catherine Macdonald Wilson, daughter of James Alexander Macdonald and Harriet Mackie. The cousin married Sir William Courthope Townshend Wilson, Vice Chancellor of the County Palatine of Lancaster. Attempts to follow the line and find the effects of Daniel have not yielded results.

---

[1] See obituary, *The Lancet*, 6 April 1901.

[2] See Steven Johnson, *The Ghost Map: The Story of London's Most Terrifying Epidemic—and How it Changed Science, Cities, and the Modern World* (New York, 2006).

[3] Her 'visual hallucination' was recorded in Edmund Gurney, Frederick William Myers and Frank Podmore, *Phantasms of the Living* (London 1886), 528. This investigation of the connection between ghost-seeing and telepathy is a key source on Victorian psychical research.

[4] http://discovery.nationalarchives.gov.uk/details/r/C7985755 (accessed December 2, 2015)

JANE MASTERS MACDONALD ROGERS WORKS (1824–1909)

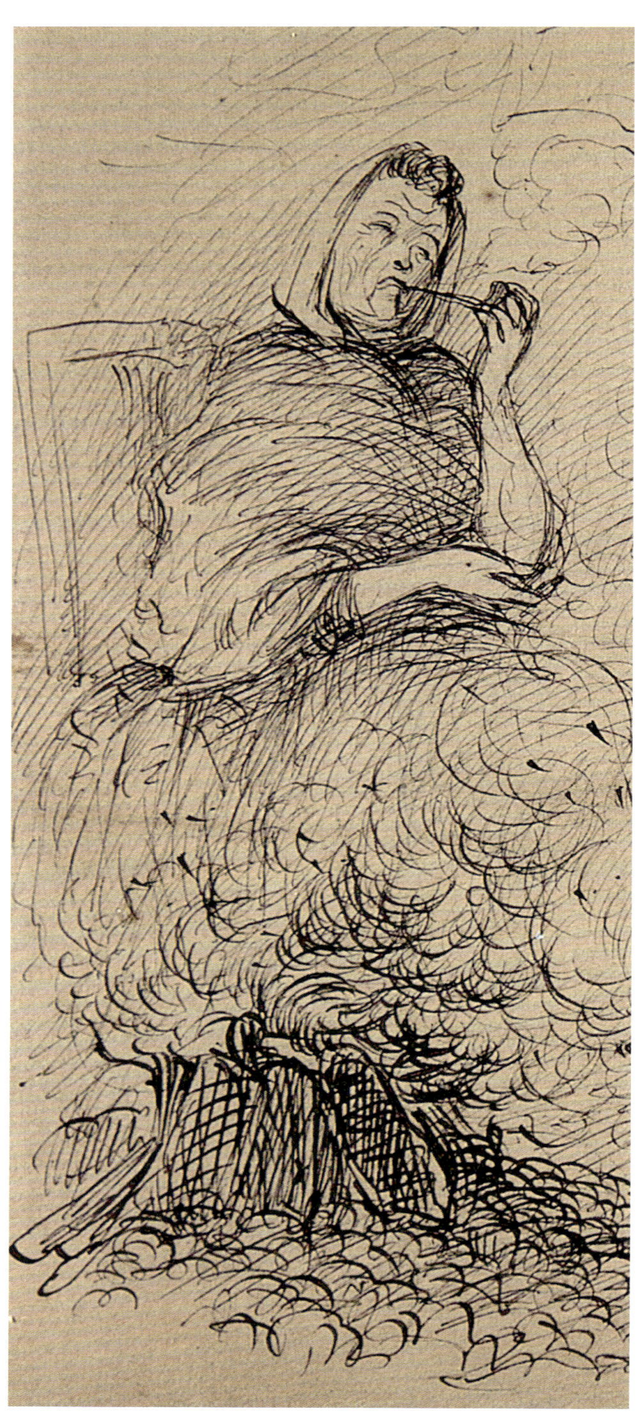

EXHIBITED WORKS

1841 **Cork Art Union**

38 *An Irish Hood*

56 *The Mourner*

96 *Portrait of a Lady*

1842 **Cork Art Union**

42 *Shylock*

*Portia: Have by some Surgeon, Shylock
On your charge, to stop his wounds
Lest he do bleed to death.*

Shylock: Is it so nominated in the Bond?

67 *Learning to Walk*

1842 **Royal Hibernian Academy**

211 *Landscape — Fall of the Leaf and
Children Wood Gathering*

258 *The Holy Family*

259 *Children at a Potato Stall*

1843 **Royal Hibernian Academy**

96 *Bacchante*

1844 **Royal Hibernian Academy**

58 *Shrovetide (match-making)*

1847 **Royal Academy**

478 *An Irish Peasant*

1848 **Royal Academy**

154 *Simeon and the Infant Saviour,
'Lord now lettest thou thy servant depart in peace, etc.'
(Luke, ii. 29)*

1849 **British Institution**

78 *Learning to Walk,
2.3 × 2.10 ft*

1850 **Royal Academy**

5 *William Ross Esq.*

1853 **British Institution**

431 *Nymph of Flora*

1854 **Royal Academy**

984 *An Officer of the 10th Hussars*

1854 **Royal Manchester Institution**

252 *Simeon and the Infant Saviour
'Then took he Him in his arms,
and Blessed God' (Luke ii. 28)*

  Portrait of a woman (1863) [Flora Macdonald]

435 *The Angel at the Sepulchre*

468 *Blackberry Gathering*

141 *One of earth's fairest womankind*
Half veiled from view, or rather shrined,
In the clear crystal of a brook
(Moore, *Lives of the Angels*)

179 *A Roman Flower Girl*

37 *A Miser*

1855 **Royal Academy**

971 *Portrait of a Lady*

996 *Portrait of a Lady*

1103 *An Officer of the Turkish Contingent*

1856 **Royal Academy**

365 *Sir William C. Ross RA*
British Institution

319 *Enamel on Porcelain, after Raphael*

1858 **Royal Academy**

746 *William Richard Laurence, eldest son of Dr. Rogers*

876 *F. Sibson Esq., MD, FRS*

1859 **Royal Academy**

892 *Kate*

1863 **Royal Academy**

735 *Flora Macdonald**

780 *Ida*

1865 **Royal Academy**

674 *Portrait of a Young Lady*

1866 **Royal Academy**

759 *The Tale of 'Blue Beard'*

1871 **Royal Hibernian Academy**

50 *Belgian Peasant*

109 *A Sketch from Life*

1873 **Worcester Fine Arts Exhibition**

1876 **Royal Hibernian Academy**

124 *Irish Peasantry Returning from a Repeal Meeting*
through a Pass in the Kerry Mountains

1880 **Exhibition of painting on China**

497 *Our Sunbeam*

Portrait of the Hon. Elizabeth Allworth, Cork,
Mezzotint (large quarto new plate of the 1811 original,
then out of print)
LIT: Letter to Thomas Crofton Croker, nd.

Portrait of a Spaniel
Oil on canvas
Signed and dated J. M. Rogers '87
18 × 16 in / 29 × 27 cm
PROV: Echoes Antiques, Seaford, NY, USA,
September 27, 2014, lot 125

Portrait of a woman (1863) *[Flora Macdonald]*
Pastel on paper
Signed, dated and inscribed lower left: J. M. Rogers, 1863, London
67.3 × 52.6 cm
Geffrye Museum
Gift 1972, Raymond Mander, London
Also known as 'Miss Floe'.

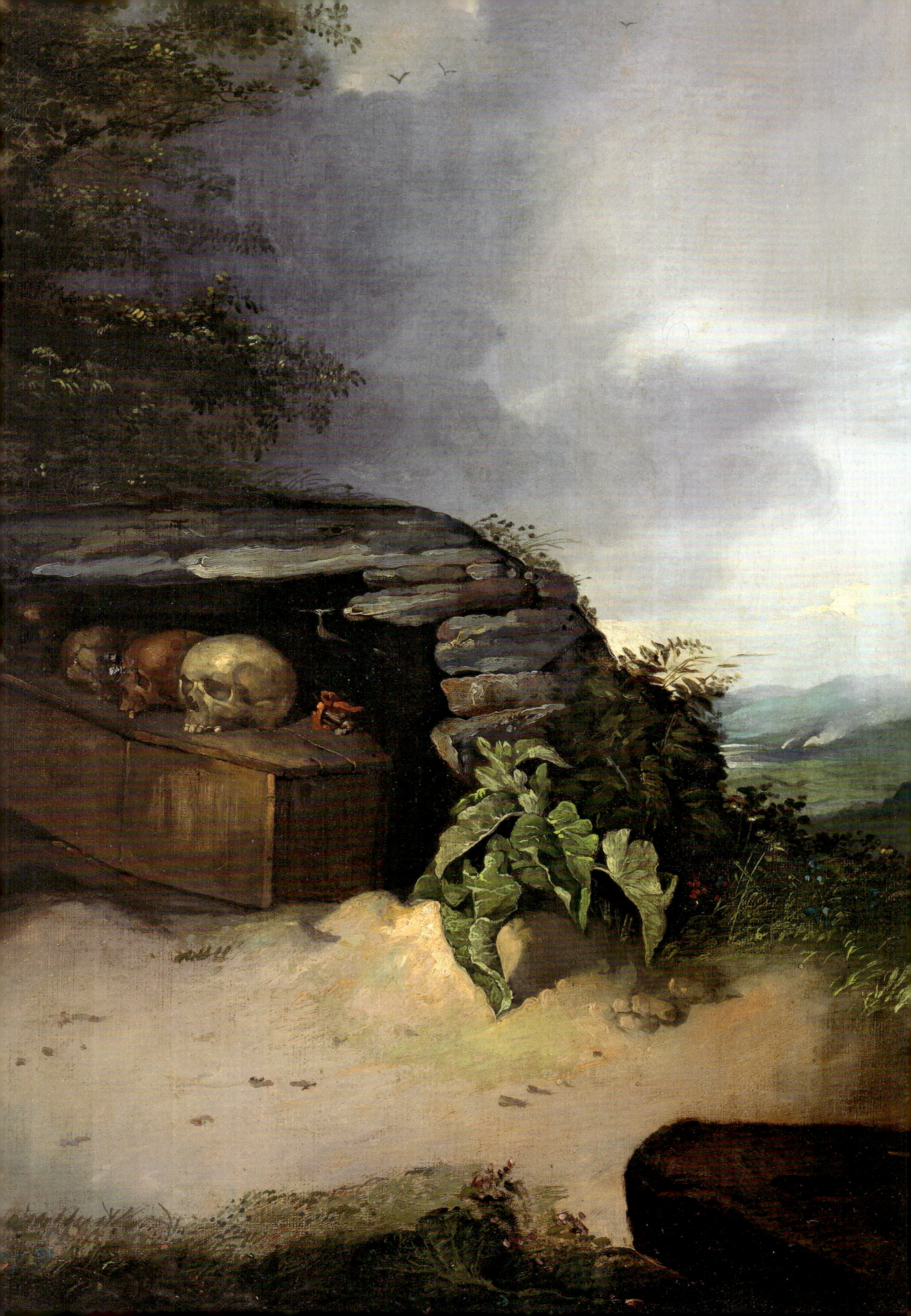

BIBLIOGRAPHY

Anonymous. 'Memoir of Samuel Forde — A Cork Artist', *Dublin University Magazine*, 25, 147 (1845) 338–57

Arkins, Brian. *Builders of My Soul: Greek and Roman Themes in Yeats* (Gerrard's Cross, 1990)

The Art-Union (London, February 1845)

Bartlett, Thomas. *The Fall and Rise of the Irish Nation: The Catholic Question, 1690–1830* (Savage, MD, 1992)

Barton, Bernard. *Metrical Effusions, or Verses on Various Occasions* (London, 1812)

Bates, William. *The Maclise Portrait-Gallery of Illustrious Literary Characters with Memoirs* (London, 1883)

Bourke, Angela. 'The Virtual Reality of Irish Fairy Legend', *Éire/Ireland*, 31: (1–2) Spring/Summer, 7–25

———. *Voices Underfoot: Memory, Forgetting, and Oral Verbal Art* (Hamden, CT, forthcoming 2016)

Bush, John. *Hibernia Curiosa: A Letter from a Gentleman in Dublin to his Friend at Dover in Kent* (London, 1767)

Butler, Nesta. *Art and Architecture of Ireland, Volume 2: Painting 1600–1900,* ed. Nicola Figgis (Dublin and New Haven, 2014)

Carleton, William. *The Black Prophet: A Tale of Irish Famine* (Belfast and London, 1847)

Casey, Christine and Bo Almqvist. *Amharc Oidhreacht Éireann/Folk Tradition in Irish Art, an Exhibition of Paintings from the Collection of the Department of Irish Folklore, University College Dublin* (Dublin, 1993)

Casey, Christine. 'Painting Irish Folk Life: The Picture Collection' in Críostóir Mac Cárthaigh, ed. *Treasures of the National Folklore Collection/Seoda as Cnuasach Bhéaloideas Éireann* (Dublin, 2010)

Connell, Kenneth Hugh. *Irish Peasant Society: Four Historical Essays* (Oxford University Press, 1968)

Connolly, Claire. 'Irish Romanticism, 1800–1839', *Cambridge History of Irish Literature* (Cambridge, 2006) 407–48

Connolly, Sean. *Religion, Law, and Power: The Making of Protestant Ireland, 1660–1760* (Oxford, 1992)

Considerations on the Utility of the Casts presented by H.R.H. the Prince Regent (Cork, 1819)

Coolahan, John. *Irish Education: Its History and Structure* (Dublin, 1981)

Cork Examiner March 24, 1865

Crawford, Margaret. 'The Great Irish Famine 1845–9: Image Versus Reality'. in Raymond Gillespie and Brian P. Kennedy, eds. *Ireland: Art into History* (Dublin, 1994) 75–90

Crofton Croker, Thomas. *Early English Poetry, Ballads, and Popular Literature of the Middle Ages,* vol. 13 (London, 1844)

———. *Fairy Legends and Traditions of the South of Ireland* (London, 1825)

———. *Recollections of Cork* [Ms. 1206 (1.6.49–50)], Trinity College Library

———. *Researches in the South of Ireland* (Dublin, 1981 [1824])

———. *The Keen of the South of Ireland: As Illustrative of Irish Political and Domestic History, Manners, Music, and Superstitions* (London, 1844)

Crookshank, Anne and The Knight of Glin. *Ireland's Painters, 1600–1940* (New Haven, 2002)

Crowley, John, William J. Smyth and Mike Murphy, eds. *Atlas of the Great Irish Famine* (Cork, 2012)

Cullen, Fintan. *Visual Politics: The Representation of Ireland, 1750–1930* (Cork, 1997)

———. *Sources in Irish Art: A Reader* (Nottingham, 2000)

Curtis, L. Perry, Jr. *Notice to Quit: The Great Famine Evictions* (Hamden, CT, 2015)

———. *Apes and Angels: The Irishman in Victorian Caricature* (Washington, DC, 1971)

———. *Depiction of Eviction in Ireland: 1845–1910* (Dublin, 2011)

D'Alton, Ian. *Protestant Society and Politics in Cork, 1812–1844* (Cork, 1980)

Davis, Thomas. 'National Art', in Charles Gavan Duffy, ed. *Literary and Historical Essays* (Dublin, 1865)

Day, Robert. 'Book-Plates Engraved by Cork Artists', *Journal of the Ex Libris Society,* 1 (1892) 107–11

Deane, Seamus. *Strange Country: Modernity and Nationhood in Irish Writing Since 1790* (Oxford, 1997)

Donnelly, James S., Jr. 'Pastorini and Captain Rock: Millenarianism and Sectarianism in the Rockite Movement of 1821–4', in Samuel Clarke and James S. Donnelly, Jr., eds. *Irish Peasants, Violence and Political Unrest 1780–1914*, eds. (Dublin, 1983) 102–37

Donovan, Daniel. 'Observations on the Peculiar Diseases to Which the Famine of the Last Year Gave Origin and on the Morbid Effects of Insufficient Nourishment', *The Medical Examiner: A Monthly Record of Medical Science*, 4 (1848)

Dooley, Dolores. *Equality in Community: Sexual Equality in the Writings of William Thompson and Anna Doyle Wheeler* (Cork, 1996)

Dunlevy, Mairéad and Cormac Ó Gráda. 'A Bowling Match at Castlemary, Co. Cork', in David Dickson and Cormac Ó Gráda, eds. *Refiguring Ireland, Essays in Honour of L. M. Cullen* (Dublin, 2003)

Dunne, Tom. 'The Eviction' in Peter Murray, ed., *Whipping the Herring: Survival and Celebration in Nineteenth-Century Irish Art* (Cork, 2006)

———. 'The Eviction' in Peter Murray, ed. *Three Centuries of Irish Art* (Cork, 2014)

Eagleton, Terry. 'Cork and Carnivalesque' in *Crazy John and the Bishop* (Cork, 1998) 158–211

———. *Heathcliff and the Great Hunger: Studies in Irish Culture* (London, 1995)

The English Review, viii (1847)

Evans, E. Estyn. *Irish Heritage: The Landscape, The People and their Work (Dundalk, 1949)*

Farrell, James Michael. '"This Horrible Spectacle": Visual and Verbal Sketches of the Famine in Skibbereen', in *Rhetorics of Display*, Lawrence J. Prelli, ed. (Columbia, SC, 2006), 66–89

Figgis, Nicola. 'Nathaniel Grogan' in *Art and Architecture of Ireland, Volume 2: Painting 1600–1900* (Dublin, 2014) 276–77

Mark-FitzGerald, Emily. 'Towards a Famine Art History: Invention, Reception, and Repetition from the Nineteenth Century to the Twentieth', in *Ireland's Great Hunger, vol. 2: Relief, Representation, and Remembrance* (Hamden, CT, 2010)

———. *Commemorating the Irish Famine: Memory and the Monument* (Liverpool, 2013)

Foley, Michael. *'Read all about It': Newspapers and the Great Hunger* (Hamden CT, 2015)

Fraser's Magazine, 23 (1841)

The Freeholder, 8 December 1827

Geary, Laurence. 'Epidemic Diseases of the Great Famine', *History Ireland*, 4, 1 (1996) 27–32

Gibbons, Luke. 'Between Captain Rock and a Hard Place: Art and Agrarian Insurgency', in Tadhg Foley and Seán Ryder, eds. *Ideology and Ireland in the Nineteenth Century* (Dublin, 1998) 23–43

———. 'Topographies of Terror: Killarney and the Politics of the Sublime', *South Atlantic Quarterly*, 95 (1996) 23–44

———. *Limits of the Visible: Representing the Great Hunger* (Hamden, CT, 2014)

———. 'Race against Time: Racial Discord and Irish History'. *Transformations in Irish Culture* (Cork, 1996) 149–63

Griffin, Gerald. *The Rivals, and Tracy's Ambition* (Dublin, 1829)

Hall, Mr. and Mrs. Samuel Carter. *Ireland: Its Scenery, Character, etc.* 3 vols. (London, 1840–43)

Hall, S. C. *Retrospect of a Long Life: From 1815 to 1883,* 2 vols., vol. 1 (London, 1883)

Hart, Jennifer. 'Sir Charles Trevelyan and the Treasury', *English Historical Review* LXXV (1960) 92–110

Henry, Brian. *The Pig and the Pot* (Tokyo, 1994)

Holden's Triennial Directory (1805–07)

Hodge, Anne and Peter Harbison. 'A Gilded Cage', *Irish Arts Review,* Summer 2014.

Holland, Michael. 'Two Typical Cork Sketches', *Journal of the Cork Historical and Archaeological Society*, 19, 98 (1913) 76–77

Johnson, Steven. *The Ghost Map: The Story of London's Most Terrifying Epidemic—and How it Changed Science, Cities, and the Modern World* (New York, 2006)

Kelleher, Margaret. *The Feminization of Famine: Expressions of the Inexpressible?* (Cork, 1997)

Kelly, James. 'The Duel in Irish History', *History Ireland*, 2, 1 (1994) 26–30

Kelly, John. *The Graves Are Walking* The Great Famine and the Saga of the Irish People (London, 2003)

Ker, W. P. *Epic and Romance* (London, 2013 [1913])

Kinealy, Christine. *Apparitions of Death and Disease: The Great Hunger in Ireland* (Hamden, CT, 2014)

Kinmonth, Claudia. Catalogue note, Whyte's Auctions (November 26, 2012)

———. *Irish Rural Interiors in Art* (New Haven, 1993)

The Lancet, April 6,1901

Leerssen, Joep. *National Thought in Europe: A Cultural History* (Amsterdam, 2006)

———. *Remembrance and Imagination: Patterns in the Historical and Literary Representation of Ireland in the Nineteenth Century* (Cork, 1996)

Lessing, Gotthold Ephraim. 'On the Laocoön' in Hugh Barr Nisbet, ed. *German Aesthetic and Literary Criticism: Winckelmann, Lessing, Hamann, Herder, Schiller, Goethe* (Cambridge, 1985)

Lockhart, JG. *Memoirs of the Life of Sir Walter Scott, vol. 3 (Edinburgh and London, 1887)*

Lucas's Cork Directory (1787)

Macdonald, Daniel. Appointments for the week of June 23, 1845. Richard Dowden Papers [IE CCCA/U140], Cork City and County Archives

———. Letter to James McDaniel, nd. Richard Dowden Papers [IE CCCA/U140], Cork City and County Archives

———. Letter to Richard Dowden, January 1850. Richard Dowden Papers [IE CCCA/U140], Cork City and County Archives

———. Letter to Richard Dowden, nd. Richard Dowden Papers [IE CCCA/U140], Cork City and County Archives

Mackenzie, Alexander. *History of the Macdonalds and Lords of the Isles: With Genealogies of the Principal Families* (London, 2013 [1881])

MacNeill, Máire. *The Festival of Lughnasa* (London, 1962)

Maginn, William. *Blackwood's Magazine,* xviii (July 1825) 55–61

Maguire, John Francis. *The Industrial Movement in Ireland, As Illustrated by the National Exhibition of 1852* (Cork, 1853)

Manchester Courier and Lancashire General Advertiser, October 21,1854

Marshall, Catherine. *Monuments, Memorials and Visualizations of the Great Famine in Ireland* (Hamden, CT, 2014)

McDaniel, James. Letter to Thomas Crofton Croker, July 1, 1819. Cork City Library

———. Letter to Thomas Crofton Croker, August 29, 1819. Cork City Library

———. Letter to Thomas Crofton Croker, April 19, 1830. Cork City Library

———. Letter to Thomas Crofton Croker, September 9, 1835. Cork City Library

———. Letter to Thomas Crofton Crocker. 5 September 1836. Cork City Library

Lady Morgan (Sydney Owenson), *The Life and Times of Salvator Rosa*, 2 vols. (London and Paris, 1824)

Morning Post, May 5, 1847

Murray, Peter, ed. *Whipping the Herring: Survival and Celebration in Nineteenth-Century Irish Art* (Cork, 2006)

———. *Three Centuries of Irish Art* (Cork, 2014)

———. 'Art Institutions in Nineteenth-Century Cork', in Patrick O'Flanagan and Cornelius G. Buttimer, eds. *Cork History and Society* (Dublin, 1993) 813–72

Nally, David P. *Human Encumbrances: Political Violence and the Great Irish Famine* (Notre Dame, IN, 2011)

Newcomen, George. 'The Tragic Tale of Stamer O'Grady and Captain Smyth, Ballinatrae', *The New Ireland Review*, x (1898) 30–37

Nolan, Emer. 'Irish Melodies and Discordant Politics: Thomas Moore's *Memoirs of Captain Rock* (1824)', *Field Day Review*, 2 (2006) 41–53

O'Donnell, P. D. *Irish Faction Fighters of the Nineteenth Century* (Dublin, 1975)

O'Donnell , Ruán. 'The Liberator', *Irish Arts Review*, Autumn 2006, 92–97

O'Donoghue, D. J. *The Geographical Distribution of Irish Ability* (Dublin, 1906)

O'Halloran, Clare. 'Negotiating Progress and Degeneracy: Irish Antiquaries and the Discovery of the "Folk", 1770–1844', in Timothy Baycroft and David Hopkin, eds. *Folklore and Nationalism in Europe During the Long Nineteenth Century* (Leiden, 2012) 193–206

The Observer, February 7, 1847

Ockenden, William. *Letters Describing the Lakes of Killarney and Muckross Gardens* (*c.* 1760)

O'Donnell , Ruán. 'The Liberator', *Irish Arts Review*, Autumn 2006, 92–97

Ó Gráda, Cormac. *Black '47 and Beyond: The Great Irish Famine in History, Economy, and Memory* (Princeton, NJ, 1999)

Oliphant, Margaret. *Annals of a Publishing House: William Blackwood and His Sons, Their Magazine and Friends: Volume 1* (Edinburgh, 1897)

One in Babylon. *A Modern Visit from the Devil, Second edition with a postscript, and ten illustrations from D. Macdonald* (London, 1849)

O'Sullivan, Niamh. *The Tombs of a Departed Race: Illustrations of Ireland's Great Hunger* (Hamden, CT, 2014)

———. 'Lines of Sorrow: Representing Ireland's Great Hunger', *Ireland's Great Hunger Museum Inaugural Catalogue* (Hamden, CT, 2012)

Otway, Caesar. *A Tour in Connaught* (Dublin, 1839)

Owens, Gary. 'Constructing the Image of Daniel O'Connell', *History Ireland*, 1 (1999) 32–36

Plowden, Francis. *The History of Ireland, From its Union with Great Britain in January 1801 to October 1810*, vol. 1 (Dublin, 1811)

Rackard, Anna and Liam O'Callaghan. *Fish Stone Water: Holy Wells of Ireland* (Cork, 2001) (introduction, Angela Bourke)

Rattler, Morgan. 'Some Passages in a Visit to the Royal Academy', *Fraser's Magazine* (July 1834) 106–19

Roberts, Paul E. W. 'Caravats and the Shanavests: Whiteboyism and Faction Fighting in East Munster, 1802–11', in Samuel Clarke and James S. Donnelly, Jr., eds. *Irish Peasants, Violence and Political Unrest 1780–1914* (Dublin, 1983) 64–101

Rooney, Brendan. in *A Time and a Place: Two Centuries of Irish Social Life* (Dublin, 2006)

Smart, Robert. *Black Roads* (Hamden, CT, 2015)

Sontag, Susan. *Regarding the Pain of Others* (New York, 2003)

Sturgeon, Sinéad. 'The Politics of Poitín: Maria Edgeworth, William Carleton and the Battle for the Spirit of Ireland', *Irish Studies Review*, 14, 4 (2006) 431–45

———. '"Seven Devils": Gerald Griffin's "The Brown Man" and the Making of Irish Gothic', *The Irish Journal of Gothic and Horror Stories*, 11 (2012)

Sydney, Lady Morgan (née Owenson). *The Life and Times of Salvator Rosa* (London, 1824)

Townsend, Paul A. *Father Mathew and Irish Identity* (Dublin, 2002)

Townshend, Charles. 'The Making of Modern Irish Public Culture', *The Journal of Modern History*, 61, 3 (1989) 535–54

'The State of Ireland', *Blackwood's Magazine*, 9, 367 (1846)

Tromans, Nicholas. *David Wilkie: The People's Painter* (Oxford, 2007)

Uí Ógáin, Ríonach. *Immortal Dan: Daniel O'Connell in Irish Folk Tradition* (Dublin, 1995)

Weld, Isaac. *Statistical Survey of the County of Roscommon* (Dublin, 1832)

Westminster Review, April 1, 1824

Whelan, Kevin. 'The Cultural Effects of the Famine' in Joe Cleary and Clare Connolly, eds. *The Cambridge Companion to Modern Irish Culture* (Cambridge, 2005) 137–54

———. 'Brian Friel's *Translations*: Hinterlands' in *Field Day Review 6*, Seamus Deane and Ciarán Deane, eds. (Dublin, 2010)

Wilde, Sir William. 'Irish Popular Superstitions', in *Ireland: Her Wit, Peculiarities, and Popular Superstitions, with anecdotes, legendary and characteristic, by Distinguished Irish Writers* (Dublin, 1850)

Wilkes, John. *Encyclopedia Londinensis, or, University Dictionary of Arts, Sciences and Literature, Vol. XI* (London, 1812)

Williams, William. *Creating Irish Tourism: The First Century, 1750–1850* (London, 2011)

Woodham-Smith, Cecil. *The Great Hunger* (London, 1962)

Young, Arthur. *A Tour in Ireland, 1776–1779*, 2 vols. (London, 1892)

Cover
Daniel Macdonald
1820–53
The Fighter
1844
Oil on canvas
50 × 40 in (128.3 × 102.2 cm)
Collection of Sir Michael Smurfit

Frontispiece
Daniel Macdonald
1820–53
An Irish Peasant Family Discovering the Blight of their Store
1847
Oil on canvas
33 × 41 in (84 × 104 cm)
National Folklore Collection, University College Dublin

Figure 1 [DETAIL]
Daniel Macdonald
1820–53
An Irish Peasant Family Discovering the Blight of their Store
1847

Figure 2
Daniel Macdonald
Sídhe Gaoithe / The Fairy Blast
1842
Oil on canvas
35 × 45.3 in (89 × 115 cm)
National Folklore Collection, University College Dublin

Figure 3
Daniel Macdonald
1820–53
Public Characters
1843
Ink on paper
13.5 × 44 in (34 × 10 cm)
Collection of Clayton Love Jnr.

Figure 4
Daniel Maclise
1806–70
The Fraserians
From "The Maclise portrait gallery of illustrious literary characters with memoirs" By William Bates, London: Chatto and Windus, Piccadilly, 1883

Figure 5 a-b
Letter from James McDaniel to Thomas Crofton Croker
September 9, 1835
Cork City Council Libraries

Figure 6 a–c
Daniel Macdonald
Images from
A Modern Visit from the Devil
By One in Babylon
London, 1849

Figure 7
Daniel Maclise
1806–1870
Portrait of Thomas Crofton Croker
From "The Maclise portrait gallery of illustrious literary characters with memoirs" By William Bates, London: Chatto and Windus, Piccadilly, 1883
ESB Centre for the Study of Irish Art
3.8 × 6.1 in (9.7 × 15.4 cm)
Photo © National Gallery of Ireland

Figure 8
Daniel Macdonald
Sídhe Gaoithe / The Fairy Blast
1842

Figure 9 [DETAIL]
Daniel Macdonald
Sídhe Gaoithe / The Fairy Blast
1842

Figure 10
Daniel Macdonald
The Shower
1844
Pen and black ink on blue-grey paper
10.2 × 14.4 in (25.9 × 36.6 cm)
© The Trustees of the British Museum

Figure 11 [DETAIL]
Daniel Macdonald
Sídhe Gaoithe / The Fairy Blast
1842

Figure 12 [CROPPED]
Daniel Macdonald
Figures by a Coffin — a Scene from 'The Collegians'
1840
Oil on canvas
34 × 41 in (86.6 × 105.3 cm)
Photo © National Gallery of Ireland

Figure 13
Daniel Macdonald
The Fighter
1844
Oil on canvas
50 × 40 in (128.3 × 102.2 cm)
Collection of Sir Michael Smurfit

Figure 14
Daniel Macdonald
Kerry Peasantry
1844
Pen and ink on paper
20 × 15 in (53.34 × 40.64 cm)
Collection of Kevin Coughlan

Figure 15
Daniel Macdonald
Dan At Cork
1850
Pen and ink on paper
20 × 17 in (53.34 × 43.18 cm)
Collection of Kevin Coughlan

Figure 16
O'Connell's Caps

Figure 17
Daniel Maclise
1806–70
The Installation of Captain Rock
1834
Oil on canvas
67.7 × 96.1 in (172 × 244 cm)
Private collection

Figure 18 [DETAIL]
Daniel Maclise
1806–70
The Installation of Captain Rock
1834

Figure 19 [DETAIL]
Daniel Macdonald
The Fighter
1844

Figure 20
Italian School
The Fighting Gladiator
c. 1816
Plaster cast from the Roman copy in the Vatican Museum
63.8 × 38.6 × 26 in (162 × 98 × 66 cm)
Crawford Art Gallery, Cork

Figure 21
Daniel Macdonald
Portrait of General
Sir Rowland Smyth KCB
c. 1845
Oil on canvas
29.9 × 24 in (76 × 61 cm)
Crawford Art Gallery, Cork

Figure 22
Daniel Macdonald
After the Duel
1847
Ink on paper
7.5 × 10.5 in (19 × 27 cm)
Crawford Art Gallery, Cork

Figure 23
Daniel Macdonald
Returning from an Irish Funeral
1842
Pen and ink on paper
22.5 × 27.3 in (57.2 × 69.3 cm)
© Ireland's Great Hunger Museum,
Quinnipiac University

Figure 24
Daniel Macdonald
Going Home After a Funeral
1842
Pen and ink on buff paper
7.52 × 10.7 in (19.1 × 27.1 cm)
Royal Collection Trust / © *Her Majesty*
Queen Elizabeth II 2015

Figure 25
Daniel Macdonald
1820–53
An Irish Peasant Family Discovering
the Blight of their Store
1847

Figure 26
The *Illustrated London News*
January 5, 1850
Image courtesy of Ireland's Great Hunger
Museum, Quinnipiac University

Figure 27
Frederick Goodall
1822–1904
Irish Courtship / Irish Cottage Interior
c. 1844
Image courtesy of Richard Goodall

Figure 28
George Frederic Watts
1817–1904
The Irish Famine
1850
Oil on canvas
Watts Gallery, Compton, Surrey, UK
©Trustees of Watts Gallery
Bridgeman Images

Figure 29
Robert George Kelly
An Ejectment in Ireland
(A Tear and a Prayer for Erin)
1848–51
Collection of Anthony John Mourek
Image courtesy of Irish Arts Review

Figure 30 [CROPPED]
Daniel Macdonald
Eviction
c. 1850
Oil on canvas
25 × 29 in (63 × 75 cm)
Crawford Art Gallery, Cork

Figure 31
Edmund Fitzpatrick
"The Ejectment"
The *Illustrated London News*
December 16, 1848
Image courtesy of Ireland's Great Hunger
Museum, Quinnipiac University

Figure 32
Daniel Macdonald
Eagle's Nest, Killarney
1841
Oil on canvas
26.4 × 24.6 in (67.1 × 62.5 cm)
Image courtesy of James Adam's
Auctioneers

Figure 33
Daniel Macdonald
Irish Peasant Children
1846
Oil on canvas
20 × 24 in (50.8 × 61 cm)
© Ireland's Great Hunger Museum,
Quinnipiac University

Figure 34
Daniel Macdonald
Bowl Playing
1842
Oil on canvas
40 × 51.5 in (102.8 × 130.8 cm)
Crawford Art Gallery, Cork

Figure 35
Daniel Macdonald
A Country Dance /
A Wedding Dance
1848
Oil on canvas
29 × 35 in (75.5 × 90 cm)
Crawford Art Gallery, Cork

Figure 36
Daniel Macdonald
The Courtship
1847
Ink on buff colored paper
7.5 × 10.5 in (19 × 27 cm)
Crawford Art Gallery, Cork

Figure 37
Daniel Macdonald
An Irish Parish Priest
and His Coadjutor
1847
Ink on paper
7.5 × 10.5 in (19 × 27 cm)
Crawford Art Gallery, Cork

Figure 38
Daniel Macdonald
Preparing for Mass
1847
Ink on paper
7.5 × 10.5 in (19 × 27 cm)
Crawford Art Gallery, Cork

Figure 39
Daniel Macdonald
Preparing for Bed:
Scene in an Irish Cabin
1847
Ink on paper
7.5 × 10.5 in (19 × 27 cm)
Crawford Art Gallery, Cork

Figure 40
Daniel Macdonald
Soul Beggars
1847
Ink on paper
7.5 × 10.5 in (19 × 27 cm)
Crawford Art Gallery, Cork

Figure 41
Daniel Macdonald
Mr. Mike Scanlon's School —
Ballyshandrahan
1851
Image courtesy of
Auction House Peter Kiefer

Figure 42
Daniel Macdonald
The Hedge Schoolmaster
1847
Ink on paper
7.5 × 10.5 in (19 × 27 cm)
Crawford Art Gallery, Cork

Figure 43
Sir David Wilkie
1785–1841
The Irish Whiskey Still
1840
Oil on canvas
Scottish National Gallery

Figure 44 [CROPPED]
Daniel Macdonald
Tasting the Poitin in Ireland
c. 1844
Oil on canvas
13 × 17 in (35.56 × 45.72 cm)
Collection of Ms. Heide Roche

Figure 45
Daniel Macdonald
*Peace was Made for Coward Souls:
War, My Boys, For You & Me*
1847
Ink on paper
7.5 × 10.5 in (19 × 27 cm)
Crawford Art Gallery, Cork

Figure 46
Daniel Macdonald
*Rev. Theobald Mathew
(1790–1856), founder of the
Temperance League in Ireland*
Publisher: Colnaghi
Mezzotint
14.8 × 11.6 in (37.6 × 29.5 cm)
NGI.10916
Photo © National Gallery of Ireland

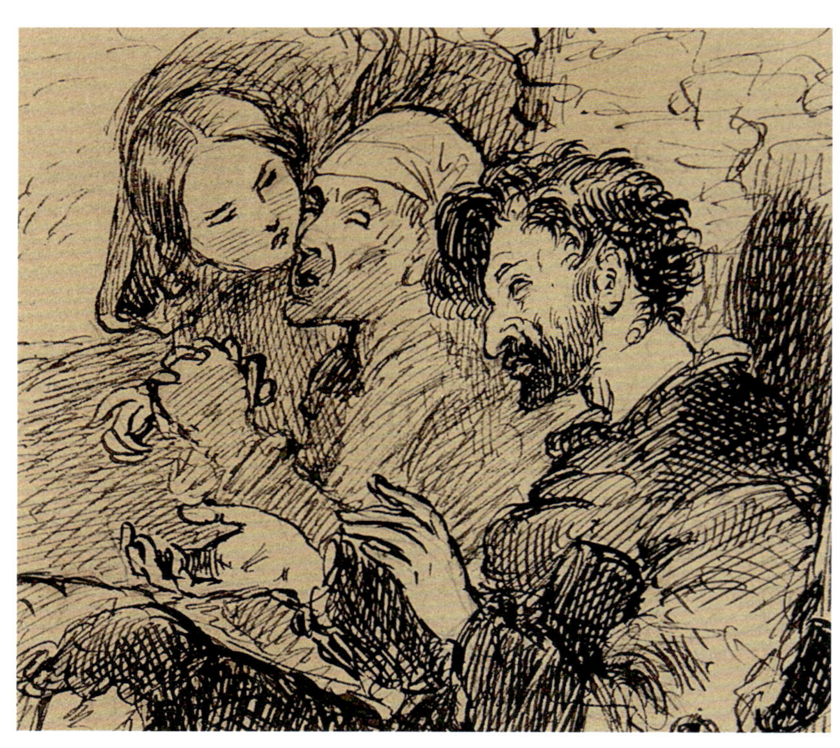

INDEX

ACKNOWLEDGEMENTS

Writing a book on a largely unknown artist who died without issue gives rise to myriad difficulties, without the help of colleagues and friends, collectors and dealers, archivists and genealogists, this reclamation would have been impossible.

A number of people have read and/or advised on this project, I value this opportunity to express my gratitude. Luke Gibbons's generosity as a great scholar is legendary, and as a friend I have benefitted enormously from his huge knowledge across the cultural and historical spectrums. I convey my deep gratitude to Angela Bourke for guiding me through the intricacies of the antiquaries and folklorists of nineteenth-century Ireland. I also express my debt to Tadhg Foley for his close reading and valued encouragement of the text at a formative stage. And to Deirdre O'Sullivan for assistance in compiling the catalogue, my best thanks.

James and Thérèse Gorry, friends of Irish art historical scholarship, have been, as ever, exceptionally supportive. And I greatly appreciate the generous assistance of David Britton at Adam's, and Ian Whyte, at Whyte's auctioneers.

For the imaginative decision to mount the exhibition at Ireland's Great Hunger Museum (January to April 2016), and publish *In the Lion's Den: Daniel Macdonald, Ireland and Empire*, I am enormously grateful to Grace Brady, Executive Director. In addition, I thank Claire Puzarne, Museum Manager, for her meticulous picture research. Without their unwavering commitment and management of both the curatorial and publishing aspects of In the Lion's Den, Macdonald's life and work would not have seen the light of the twenty-first century. And of course, the support of the Board of the Museum, President John Lahey, and Vice-Presidents, Jean Husted, Lynn Bushnell and Mark Varholak, have been invaluable in bringing this project to fruition.

I am very grateful to the designers Brad Collins and Lynne Talbot, Group C Inc., for bringing their highly creative energies to the design and production of this book, and I thank Ciarán Deane for his sensitive, skillful and professional editing. And to Mike Collins and Maria O'Donovan for the unstinting support of Cork University Press, I express my gratitude.

Peter Murray and his colleagues at the Crawford Art Gallery have been especially supportive, and I am very appreciative. In exploring the Cork connections, Peter, Jean O'Donovan, Terri Kearney, Brian McGee, John Mullins, Paul Devane, Tom Dunne, Clare O'Halloran, Rose Martin and Des O'Sullivan have been enormously helpful at various stages, and I thank them warmly. Many other curators, archivists and academics have also been very helpful, I thank Brendan Rooney, Donal Maguire, Anne Hodge, Niamh McNally, Mary Broderick, Eileen Lee, Kathleen James Chakraborty, Nicola Figgis, Ríonach uí Ógáin, Críostóir MacCárthaigh and Catherine Marshall.

For genealogical research, I owe a huge debt of gratitude to Ed O'Riordan and Karol Defalco who guided and supported the breakthrough into Macdonald's intractable but, as it transpires, fascinating genealogy. I am also grateful to Chris Ward and Jonathan Macdonald for support in contacting distant descendants.

Without the willingness of the public and private owners of Macdonald works to share them with us, neither the exhibition nor book would have been possible. The generosity of Sir Michael Smurfit, Clayton Love Jr., Heide Roche and Kevin Coughlan is much appreciated.

Mick Foley has been at my side from start to finish; his insights are deeply embedded in this book. In so many ways, research becomes a family project, to Rachel and Paul, Luke and Meg, Deirdre, Fiona, Kevin, Eavan and Derval, for their encouragement and support, my loving thanks.

IRELAND'S GREAT HUNGER MUSEUM | QUINNIPIAC UNIVERSITY PRESS ©2016

EDITOR

Ciarán Deane

IMAGE RESEARCH

Claire Puzarne

DESIGN / PRODUCTION MANAGEMENT

Group C Inc, New Haven
Brad Collins
Lynne Talbot

PUBLISHER

Quinnipiac University Press

PRINTING

GHP Media

ISBN: 978-0-9904686-8-4

Ireland's Great Hunger Museum
Quinnipiac University

3011 Whitney Avenue
Hamden, CT 06518-1908
203-582-6500

www.ighm.org